DR. BOWDLER'S
LEGACY

OTHER BOOKS BY NOEL PERRIN

A Passport Secretly Green

Amateur Sugar Maker

Vermont in All Weathers

The Adventures of Jonathan Corncob
Loyal American Refugee
Written by Himself (Editor)

First Person Rural:
Essays of a Sometime Farmer

Second Person Rural:
More Essays of a Sometime Farmer

Third Person Rural:
Further Essays of a Sometime Farmer

Last Person Rural

Giving Up the Gun:
Japan's Reversion to the Sword, 1543-1879

NOEL PERRIN

✳✳✳✳✳✳✳✳✳✳✳✳✳✳✳✳✳✳✳✳✳✳✳✳✳✳✳✳✳✳✳✳✳✳✳✳✳✳✳

DR. BOWDLER'S
LEGACY

✳✳✳✳✳✳✳✳✳✳✳✳✳✳✳✳✳✳✳✳✳✳✳✳✳✳✳✳✳✳✳✳✳✳✳✳✳✳✳

*A History of Expurgated Books in
England and America*

ILLUSTRATED BY
MARJORY WUNSCH

A NONPAREIL BOOK

David R. Godine, Publisher

BOSTON

This is a Nonpareil Book
first published in 1992 by
David R. Godine, Publisher, Inc.
Horticultural Hall
300 Massachusetts Avenue
Boston, Massachusetts 02115

Library of Congress Catalogue Card Number: 90-55280
ISBN: 0-87923-861-5

FIRST PRINTING

Manufactured in the United States of America

For Anne,
last and best

PSYCHE

If you'd climb the Helicon,
You should read Anacreon,
Ovid's *Metamorphoses*,
Likewise Aristophanes,
And the works of Juvenal:
These are worth attention, all;
But, if you will be advised,
You will get them Bowdlerized!

CHORUS OF GIRL GRADUATES
Ah! we will get them Bowdlerized!
Princess Ida, 1884

Damn the expurgated books! I say damn
'em. The dirtiest book in all the world is an
expurgated book.
Walt Whitman, 1888

PREFACE

IN 1780 A SMALL BOOK appeared in London called *The Delicate Jester; or, Wit and Humour Divested of Ribaldry*. The author was (and is) unknown. But he nevertheless has made a bold claim to be remembered as the inventor of a new literary genre. On the title page he says that his book has been edited "with such particular Care as not to offend the Ears of Chastity, or infringe on the Rules of Morality, Decency, and good Manners, yet at the same Time [the contents] lose nothing of their Force and Brilliancy; which indisputably renders this the only Book of the Kind yet published."

The claim is not, as it happens, correct. Even among joke books there had been one like it a couple of years earlier, and among English books in general there had been fifteen or twenty aimed at delicate ears. There had been at least as many in Scotland. The unknown author was making a reasonable statement, however. In 1780, leaving things out of books to make them decent was still a new and very obscure practice in England. It seemed touch and go whether the custom would catch on at all. For example, the first collection of "beauties" from the novels of Laurence Sterne came out in 1782, and it included only those highlights which would appeal to "chaste lovers of literature." It went through nine editions in the next five years, and then in 1787 a new editor took over for the tenth edition. His first action was to restore most of the dirty lines which "from dread of the ear of Chastity" had been kept out of the first nine. The book then went through another four editions.

About 1805 expurgation did begin to catch on, for reasons which I will discuss in the opening chapter, and for the next hundred and ten years it had an exceedingly prosperous career. Dr. Bowdler appeared in 1818 to give the practice a new name. He was followed by a host of distinguished text-cutters—Noah Webster, William Cullen Bryant, W. M. Rossetti, John Masefield, Palgrave of the *Golden Treasury* (though not in that book), Bulfinch of the *Mythology*, Lewis Carroll, Justice Brewer of the Supreme Court, Neilson of Harvard, Quiller-Couch of Oxford, and so on. Three or four generations in England and America grew up with a moderately inaccurate idea of their own literature as a result. Then, about 1915, the assumptions that supported bowdlerism ceased to seem true, and since then the practice has been slowly diminishing, though it is not dead yet, and probably never will be. (Not only is bowdlerism as Dr. Bowdler understood it still fairly common, but a new racial form is even now emerging.)

In the book that follows, I shall trace some of the history of English bowdlerism, from its obscure eighteenth-century beginnings up to the present. A good many things I have left out. I have nothing to say about it except in English-speaking countries, though it has flourished nearly everywhere at one time or another.

Even within the English-speaking world, this history is
far from complete. Only a little appears about bowdlerized translations, though they were and are common.
Even less appears about expurgations of classical texts,
though these have been around so long that John Donne
wrote an epigram on a "gelded" edition of Martial in
1633. Almost nothing appears about expurgation in
Australia or South Africa or Canada, though it has had
long careers in all these places. The reason, of course,
is that the bowdlerism of British and American literature
by British and American bowdlerizers is a vast subject
by itself—many times vaster than I realized when I
began this book. Furthermore, its history is only loosely
connected with that of expurgation in other languages.
In France, for example, the golden age of *livres châtrés*
or castrated books was in the seventeenth and eighteenth
centuries—in 1655 Pierre Costar is already joking that
to speak of a *livre châtré* is itself an indecency, and that
bowdlerizers ought to root the phrase out of dictionaries
"and have the following modest phrase substituted in
its place, *incommoder les livres & les faire Eunuques.*"

Since this is a history, I am not out to prove anything,
though I do, of course, hope to show a good deal about
changing taste in England and America, and especially
about changing standards of what constitutes decency.
The standards shift a little every few years. *The Delicate
Jester*, for example, was delicate only to the minds of
1780. A typical joke in it has a beggar with two wooden
legs following a gouty old gentleman down a London
street for about a mile, repeatedly trying for a handout,
and finally losing his temper and shouting, "You miserly

hopping son of a -----, *I would not change legs with you for all you're worth.*" There is a bona fide expurgation in that story, but a Victorian would not have been impressed.

The earlier joke book was even less prim, though no one realized it at the time. The woman who edited it was not sure that her jokes *would* keep all their force and brilliancy despite being expurgated. "Those who think that true Wit consists in profane Oaths, coarse Expressions, or indecent Allusions, not finding any Thing of that Sort, will probably deem this but a dull Collection," she wrote in the preface to the *Female Jester.* But a few pages later she is telling a story which I shall quote entire:

> A buck, walking down the street, met with an old decayed lady, with a gown that was by age worn thread-bare; the buck thinking to crack a jest with her, took up the hem of the gown and kiss'd it; which she looking back and taking notice of, asked him what he meant by that. "Only," says he, "to honour old age."
>
> "Alas! Sir," replied she, "you might have kissed my backside then, for that is forty years older."

One could make a little calendar of how that story would be told. In 1740 the old lady would probably have been represented as plainly telling the buck to kiss her arse. In 1778 refinement is on the march, and she says backside; this constitutes a bowdlerized version. From early in the nineteenth century to the First World War a lady would not have made the remark at all. In the 1920s and thirties she would probably have said "behind." (One of the most daring printers of unexpurgated literature in the twenties was a little New York press calling itself "At the Sign of the Blue-Behinded Ape.") Now we are just returning to arse and ass again. For those who think that progress is some kind of universal, the history of bowdlerism should be a good corrective.

It remains to say formally what bowdlerism is. This is a harder job than at first might appear. It can be separated from its ally, censorship, fairly easily. Censorship is imposed by authority; bowdlerism is a voluntary act. Censorship is usually something done by governments for political reasons; bowdlerism is something done by private individuals, usually for moral reasons. Censorship usually precedes first publication; bowdlerism always comes after. But bowdlerism is also just one more mode of editing, and to distinguish it from the other modes is the hard thing. The best way to begin is operationally.

Bowdlerism arises in a special set of circumstances. In order for it to exist, there need to be two conflicting desires on the part of an editor. He must want to preserve as much as possible of the text he is editing— ideally, all of it—and at the same time he must feel that there are words (or ideas) in the text so embarrassing or so pernicious that they can't be kept. His desire to keep the whole text, were that possible, separates the bowdlerizer from the abridger, the digest editor, and the extract maker, whose first principle is that any piece of writing is better shorter. His willingness to tamper at all separates him from the scholar, whose first principle is that the text is sacred, and that one therefore adds footnotes rather than altering the words.

In actual fact, of course, these boundaries are messy on both sides. Lots of expurgated books are also abridged, and it is by no means possible to say which act was dominant in any given cut. On the opposite boundary, there are many scholarly expurgations—ninety-nine per cent of the text or more reprinted with elaborate notes and comment, and thus treated as sacred, and the other fraction of a per cent reluctantly cut out, and thus treated as disposable. The Bible is the extreme example of a sacred text in Anglo-American culture, and here the stresses inherent in bowdlerism may be seen more clearly than almost anywhere else.

Bowdlerism not only has messy boundaries, it comes in a huge variety of forms. Dr. Bowdler himself used a fairly simple technique. He cut out of Shakespeare's plays everything "which may not with propriety be read aloud in a family," meaning most overt sexual and religious allusions. True to his medical training, he then neatly stitched the loose ends across each cut, so as to avoid scars. He substituted very few of his own words for Shakespeare's, and he neither abridged nor (with rare exceptions) added commentary. That is, he treated Shakespeare rather as an unusually scrupulous television producer might now. His sister, who started expurgating Shakespeare ten years before he did, used a similar approach, but also often cut "an uninteresting or an absurd scene," even though she considered it decent. That is, she treated Shakespeare rather as a normal television producer would.

This is the basic technique for prose or blank verse; it

has a score of modifications. One can be more scrupulous than the Bowdlers and leave all the cut places marked, usually with asterisks or dots. One can italicize or capitalize or footnote all new words. (This brings up problems of reader curiosity, of course.) One can be less scrupulous and, instead of making occasional cuts, freely rewrite. One can lie and pretend the book is not an expurgation at all.

Beyond all this, there are a number of special techniques for lyric poetry—a bowdlerist's stitchwork in a sonnet nearly always shows, which is one reason expurgated sonnets are so rare, though expurgated sonnet cycles are common. Even in comparatively loose poetic forms, bowdlerism is much harder than in prose. Hence the special techniques.

In the crudest one, you chop only in units of whole lines or stanzas, perhaps renumbering the survivors in the hope of concealment, perhaps not. In cases where one word is the whole problem, you may be able to find an innocent substitute which scans. There is also a more arduous and quite rare method in which you replace an improper passage with poetry of your own composition.

Finally, and perhaps commonest, you leave out not lines but whole poems. Here what constitutes bowdlerism becomes very much a matter of judgment. Palgrave's edition of Shakespeare's sonnets plainly is, if only because he himself has inserted a note saying that it is— four or five sonnets have "a warmth of coloring unsuited for the larger audience." If he had not put in the note, it would still pretty clearly constitute a bowdlerized edition, since normal practice with Shakespeare's sonnets is to print them all or else to print a selection of the best ones, but not to print a hundred and fifty, while omitting four.

But there are hundreds of other collections of poetry which are hopelessly borderline cases. For example, Robert Herrick's *Hesperides* consists of slightly over a thousand poems and epigrams assembled by Herrick himself in 1648. (So many are either two lines or four that the whole series fits comfortably into a medium-sized volume.) Herrick enjoyed a boom in England and America between about 1880 and 1920. Among the scores of editions of *Hesperides* then published, a few are complete, but the great majority include between two hundred and five hundred of the poems. Some of these are plainly selections by ordinary standards of good poetry, and a few, such as the volume John Masefield edited in 1906, are clear-cut expurgations. Most, however, are what Professor Richard Altick has called winnowed editions. That is, they select from only one-half of *Hesperides*—the flower poems, the pretty poems, the ones Watteau could have illustrated—and take nothing at all from the other half—the funny poems, the racy poems, the ones Hogarth could have illustrated. Is this bowdlerism? In some cases I have thought it was, and in some I have been almost certain that it was not. Either way, I am passing judgment on the editor's motives. He may—of his own will or at the demand of his publisher—been consciously bowdlerizing. Or he may not have intended any such thing, and every bawdy poem simply happened to strike him as aesthetically bad. In a prudish age such a response is common, just as in our own the reverse is common. Dr. Bowdler himself was very clear that in expurgating Shakespeare he was conferring a benefit not only on the reader but on Shakespeare as well. By a happy coincidence, he said, whenever you take an improper passage out of one of the plays, you do so "not only without injury, but with manifest advantage . . . to the sense of the passage and to the spirit of the author." Taste and morals are closely intertwined.

In any event, for the purposes of this book I have not often treated volumes of selected whole poems as expurgations unless the editor specifically says he had that intention.

One final note. I shall make no attempt to discuss or even to list every single expurgation that has appeared in Great Britain or America. There are too many. Shakespeare's plays have been bowdlerized at least a hundred separate times, and *Gulliver's Travels* almost as often. At the end of the nineteenth century, even a poet as austere as Milton sometimes appeared in school texts "with necessary omissions," designed to shield excitable teenagers from the knowledge that Satan committed incest, or from the realization that Eve had a good figure, or just from the knowledge that she and Adam did not, in their garden years, wear anything to bed. Even if I wanted to give a list of all the expurgations there have been, I would be prevented by lack of information. I know of perhaps three thousand British and American expurgations, but there are undoubtedly thousands more that I don't know about.

And while I am confessing ignorance, I should add

that I don't pretend to be an expert on the work of all the writers I shall be discussing. Bowdlerism took nearly all literature for its province, and I have tried to track it much of the way around that vast domain; but I am acutely aware that my own proper ground amounts to one or two townships in the county of American literature. If I have made mistakes, I shall be embarrassed but not surprised.

Noel Perrin
HANOVER, N.H.

FOREWORD

to the Nonpareil Edition

TWENTY YEARS IS a long time to go between editions of a book. It is no record, to be sure. There's an eighteenth-century novel I am fond of that went 189 years between editions. *The Adventures of Jonathan Corncob, Loyal American Refugee* was published in London in 1787. The second edition came along in 1976. Still, twenty years is long enough for the world to change quite a lot.

Dr. Bowdler's Legacy was first published in 1969, and got a second edition in 1971. I made a few minor changes that year. At the time, bowdlerism seemed to be—not a dying practice, but a steadily diminishing one. I thought the book would have mainly historical interest.

Events have proved me wrong. Bowdlerism has not diminished since 1971; it has increased. It continues to increase very rapidly right now. It is also changing targets. Traditional bowdlerism aimed to get sexual terminology out of books, and, as a secondary goal, profanity. Modern bowdlerism exists to get references to race and ethnicity out of books. There were early traces of racial expurgation back in 1971, but there was nothing like the present major force in children's literature.

The original bowdlerists, who began work a little over two centuries ago, were a high-minded lot. Their primary aim was to keep innocent children from being corrupted or hurt. The new bowdlerists are also a high-minded lot— and their aim, too, is to keep children from being corrupted or hurt.

The only difference I would confidently make between the two groups is one of perspective. It is easy now to judge the older bowdlerists. Easy and safe. Anyone who cares to look can see both their good intentions and their necessary absurdities. Anyone can smile, perhaps even gasp, at the intense Victorian prudery that lay behind their efforts. Anyone who looks will discover the deception and outright lies that most of them were led into.

But the new bowdlerists are too close to see or judge accurately. Their good intentions are obvious. So are the mutilations they make, often in classic texts. Are the cuts justified? The rewriting? To me, at this moment, the changes they are making in children's literature seem mostly, though not entirely, ones that should be made— to avoid giving pain to some children, to avoid perpetuating prejudice in others. How their actions will look a century from now I can't possibly know, any more than Dr. Bowdler could know in 1818 how his edition of Shakespeare would look in 1918.

What I can do is chronicle the events of the last nineteen years. There is a new last chapter in this edition, which both traces the rise of racial/ethnic expurgation, and reports the continuing decline of the older sexual/religious form. The rest of the book has stayed as it was.

Noel Perrin
THETFORD CENTER, VERMONT
December, 1991

ACKNOWLEDGMENTS

IN THE ENGLISH PHRASE, I have to thank—and in the American phrase, I also want to—the following: Dartmouth College, for giving me a year's leave with pay to work on this book; Elizabeth Ames and Polly Hanson for allowing me to write a good part of it at Yaddo; my cousin Janet Chenery for advice and help on the new last chapter; Cambridge University Library and Longmans, Green & Co. for permission to print unpublished letters; Professor Robert G. Hunter for a fine-toothed reading of the manuscript; many scholars and librarians, and especially Professors Peter Bien, David Daiches, Walter Houghton, Martin Meisel, and Thomas Vance, for information and advice at various stages; and finally my young daughters Elisabeth and Margaret for showing me what I hadn't known when I started the book, that some bowdlerism of the parental, reading-aloud sort is almost inevitable.

CONTENTS

DR. BOWDLER'S
LEGACY

****

CHAPTER ONE

The Causes of Bowdlerism

****

Can it call, whore? cry, bastard? O, then kiss it.
A witty child! Can it swear? The father's dearling!
Give it two plums.

BEN JONSON, 1616

A vulgar scribbler, certes, stands disgraced
In this nice age, when all aspire to taste;
The dirty language and the noisome jest,
Which pleased in Swift of yore, we now detest;
Proscribed not only in the world polite,
But even too nasty for a City Knight!

BYRON, 1811

In 1797 a young Welshman named Jenkin Jones wrote a long poem called *Hobby Horses*, in the course of which he discusses the reading suitable for teenage girls. "At gay fifteen," he says, "the lively Romp disclaims/ Frocks, schools, tasks, rods, wax dolls, and skittish games," and begins to read the novels of Samuel Richardson. From him she moves on to Fielding, and then to Laurence Sterne, first reading *A Sentimental Journey* and then climbing "Shandy's bolder height." If he omitted Smollett from the list, it seems not to have been because Smollett was the bawdiest of the great eight-

3

eenth-century novelists, but just an oversight. Smollett was for lively romps, too. When a leading bookseller gave examples in 1791 of the sort of book that girls were reading aloud to their parents on winter evenings, two of the four he named were novels by Smollett. The other two were a novel each by Richardson and Fielding.

The same year that Jenkin Jones made his list, Jane Austen began to write *Sense and Sensibility*, a novel in which the characters themselves read aloud. The three Dashwood girls and their suitors are especially prone to it. "O mamma! how spiritless, how tame was Edward's manner in reading to us last night!" Marianne Dashwood, who is sixteen, complains in the second chapter. (He was reading Cowper, and she feels he should stick to prose.) A few chapters later another beau has just been called away. Mrs. Dashwood picks up a book. "We have never finished *Hamlet*, Marianne," she says; "our dear Willoughby went away before we could get through it. We will put it by, that when he comes again. . . ." It was, of course, an unexpurgated edition that Mrs. Dashwood saved for Willoughby to finish reading with her teenage daughter.

In real life, three years earlier, a clergyman named William Bagshaw Stevens noted in his diary·a remark made by the twenty-one-year-old girl he was in love with. This was Fanny Coutts, a girl of breeding and a great heiress, who eventually married the Marquis of Bute. The two of them had been reading *Romeo and Juliet* together on summer afternoons in 1794. They had just got to a passage where the Nurse is giving down-to-earth advice to Romeo. The girl "paused, lifted her eyes

4

up to me and said, 'A very natural Observation, is it not, for a Nurse?' " She does not say, "William, this Play demands Purging."

A decade or two later, she might have. With the turn of the nineteenth century, a new literary morality appeared in England. The old calm acceptance of most literature as suitable general reading rapidly faded, and an intense prudishness replaced it. One result was bowdlerism. Books had been expurgated during most of the eighteenth century, to be sure, and with increasing frequency near the end of it, but it had been the obscure action of a minority. Now the majority got involved, beginning with the Bowdler family. *Hamlet* and *Romeo and Juliet* suffered at once. In 1807 Bowdler's *Family Shakespeare* appeared, the first book that can technically be described as bowdlerized. Large sections of *Hamlet* were missing, and *Romeo and Juliet* was gone altogether. (It came along in the second edition in 1818, with the Nurse playing an exceedingly diminished role.) Soon a rival expurgation came out, the editor explaining that in the hands of Bowdler few of the plays had been "sufficiently purified from coarse and profane expressions." By 1850 there were seven expurgated editions of Shakespeare on the market; by 1900, nearly fifty.

The novels suitable for gay romps came into question, too, though more slowly. A critic announced in 1814 that "complete" copies of Sterne's novels are "inadmissible into any society where good breeding and innocence are cultivated." He was, of course, talking about Regency society, not Victorian—Queen Victoria wasn't even born yet. Nor was he so much advocating expurgation as the use of the kind of book then called "beauties" or "elegant extracts." But the next generation went further. One critic in 1831 lumped a group of eighteenth-century novelists (Sterne, Fielding, Smollett, and Swift) together, much as Jenkin Jones had done, but no longer as part of a reading list for teenagers. He said all four were so out of harmony with "the refined notions of the present generation" that they really shouldn't be read by anybody. "They might have a partial sale," he admitted, "if it were possible to emasculate the productions of these witty writers, as Mr. Bowdler has done for Shakespeare: but this is out of the question." (It wasn't, of course, at all. It just seemed that way in 1831. Each of the four was duly expurgated before the century ended, Fielding once by his own great-granddaughter.* Nor did late-Victorian editors, long used to expurgation, find it particularly difficult. One of them said comfortably in the preface to his bowdlerized edition of Swift, "It is quite possible to purge his text of every trace of indelicacy without injuring either his sense or his style.")

Succeeding generations went further still, and eventually some people began to *want* to do injury to the sense and style of eighteenth-century novelists. When the poet Sidney Lanier once again lumped them all together in 1883, it was to speak an anathema. "If I had my way with these classic books," he wrote, "I would blot them from the face of the earth."

---

* Miss J. E. M. Fielding expurgated *Tom Jones* in 1896. She may have felt challenged by a second claim that it couldn't be done. The critic Frederic Harrison had announced in 1886 that *Tom Jones* was so indecent "that a Bowdlerized version of it would scarcely be intelligible."

6

In fact, by that time even eighteenth-century clergymen like William Bagshaw Stevens had come to seem
harmful. Stevens died young and unmarried, and his
diaries eventually came into the possession of a nineteenth-century clergyman, the Rev. Robert Dalby. In
1877 Dalby was trying to raise money to build a new
church in a coal-mining village. Hoping for a contribution, he wrote offering to present them to Baroness Burdett-Coutts, the richest woman in England and a niece of
the young Fanny Coutts who read *Romeo and Juliet* so
placidly in the summer of 1794. The baroness was sixty-
three, old enough to cope with almost any clerical journals. She told Dalby to send these along. He did, but it
made him nervous. In his accompanying letter he wrote,
"If I had aforetime noticed one or two offensive passages
on which I cast my eye only this morning, I should
certainly have hesitated about proposing to send them to
your Ladyship."

It is not easy to explain what caused this tremendous
awareness of offensive passages, and the resulting wave
of bowdlerism. Why should the eighteenth century have
been so slow to take offense, and the nineteenth century
so hasty? The Victorians themselves had an explanation
which seems correct as far as it goes, but which doesn't
go far. They said it was simply a reflection of moral
progress in the real world. People in the eighteenth century, and earlier, didn't take offense at coarse passages,
because they were coarse themselves. They all talked
like characters in Sterne and Fielding anyway, so how
could they find it wrong in a book? A certain Lady
Townshend was typical of the real eighteenth century

when, cross at the creation of a large new group of peers, she said "she durst not spit out of her carriage window, lest she should be guilty of a sort of *Scandalum Magnatum*, by spitting on a peer." A hundred years later, Baroness Burdett-Coutts would not have spat out of *her* carriage, even on a passing dog, nor used the word "spit" at all. And if people become more refined themselves, they want their environment more refined, too. We in the twentieth century remodel old buildings to make them answer modern needs (light, air, hygiene); why not remodel old books for the same purpose? A Victorian, looking at urban renewal, could easily describe bowdlerism as literary renewal. Sidney Lanier was just going a step further and advocating literary slum clearance.

There is no doubt that a vast change in manners really did take place just before the Victorian age. It was perfectly obvious to people as it happened. A few writers on etiquette begin to comment on it in the 1770s; these swell to a chorus over the next thirty years; and by the 1830s the process seems to be complete. (England is "a country where all are educated, accomplished, and refined.")

There is a famous story in the life of Leigh Hunt which shows the new refinement in the very act of taking over, shows a moment when it was swirling through the mainstream of English life but had not yet flowed into the backwaters. The year was 1805. Hunt, who was then a youth of twenty-one but already a successful poet, went on his rounds one day with a friend who was a country doctor. "I was startled in a

8

respectable farmhouse," he says in his autobiography, "to hear language openly talked in a party of males and females, of a kind that seldom courts publicity, and that would have struck with astonishment a eulogizer of pastoral innocence." Hunt was especially surprised that "a very nice modest-looking girl," the sort he felt should have blushed and fled the room, stayed right there, smiling serenely. He eventually concluded that what he heard was how everybody used to talk ("the language which was spoken in the first circles in times of old") still surviving among the yeomanry.

There is another story, involving Sir Walter Scott, which shows a slightly earlier phase. When *he* was about twenty-one, in the 1790s, one of his great-aunts wrote him saying that she was short of reading matter, and asking if he could get hold of the novels of Aphra Behn for her. Scott said yes, he could, if she insisted, but he warned her that she wouldn't like them, as they were improper. The old lady did insist, and Scott mailed them off to her as people sometimes mail sex manuals now ("curiously sealed up, with 'private and confidential' on the packet"). Very soon she mailed them back, having quit early in the first novel. It is "a very odd thing," she wrote Scott, "that I, an old woman of eighty and upwards, sitting alone, feel myself ashamed to read a book which, sixty years ago, I have heard read aloud for the amusement of large circles, consisting of the best and most creditable circles in London."

And there were odder effects than this, most especially the one Muriel Jaeger studies in *Before Victoria*, of the first new generation of the nineteenth century growing

9

up more strait-laced, inhibited, and conventional than its parents, so that sons discussed their fathers' wild oats, and daughters worried about their mothers' loose sexual behavior.

But granting that bowdlerism is a child of this new propriety, what caused the new propriety itself? There are undoubtedly hundreds and even thousands of causes. I shall discuss only four, and chief among them the rising vogue, during the eighteenth century, of sentiment and sensibility. Under these broad terms I mean to include the whole cult of feeling, whether stemming from Rousseau's *Nouvelle Héloise* and his noble savages (noble by instinct—no one had to teach them), or whether from Lord Shaftesbury's formal philosophy of the emotions. In particular, I am concerned with the part of sensibility called delicacy.

At the beginning of the eighteenth century, before sensibility arrived, a delicate person was simply someone with subtle tastes. In the opening lines of Congreve's *Way of the World* (1700), for example, Fainall has just refused to go on gambling with Mirabel, on the grounds that Mirabel is taking his losses too calmly.

> FAIN. I'd no more play with a man that slighted his ill fortune than I'd make love to a woman who undervalued the loss of her reputation.
> MIR. You have a taste extremely delicate, and are for refining your pleasures.

Fainall can have a delicate taste without being the least interested in chaste behavior, still less moved to refine the language of *Hamlet*.

Addison, defining the term in 1712, is pro-chastity, but equally unconcerned with language refinement. He wants to distinguish between false and true delicacy, false being squeamishness and true a love of virtue. Truly delicate people, Addison argues, call a spade a spade. ("Generally, people now call [it] an agricultural implement," William Dean Howells, the American novelist, wrote in 1891, explaining why there are some things a novelist can't say.) "Fornication and adultery are modest words," Addison goes on, because they are accurate words. "An innocent creature who would start at the name of strumpet, may think it pretty to be called a mistress, especially if her seducer has taken care to inform her that a union of hearts is the principal matter." A delicate person in 1712 therefore ought to call her a strumpet.

By the middle of the century, however, delicacy was something else again. The cult of feeling had crossed over from France. Richardson's Pamela had a good deal of delicacy, and in her case it caused her to faint whenever anyone spoke of being a strumpet—or, at least, whenever Mr. B—— made improper sexual advances. To have remained conscious (as Fainall's ladies invariably did) would have been proof of coarse fiber.

After 1750, delicacy came more and more to mean something shrinking, sensitive, easily wounded—but the "something" was an inner core of awareness, proof that one wasn't a clod. Delicate people cry easily (Fainall inclined more to sneers), which is one way they show they *are* delicate. One later editor of Henry Mackenzie's *The Man of Feeling* (1771) worked out a special "Index to the tears shed (chokings, etc., not counted)," in which the entries run like this:

Tears, face bathed with   page 130
Dropped one tear, no more   "   131
Tears, press-gang could not refrain from   "   136

They also blush easily, their feelings being so tender. Even a sixty-five-year-old monk does in *A Sentimental Journey* when Yorick speaks sharply to him. And again, when Yorick apologizes, "the poor monk blush'd red as scarlet," at which, says Yorick, "I blush'd in my turn."

Behind these outward manifestations of blushing, crying, and fainting lay something very impressive indeed. The delicate were supposed to have a wonderful power of intuition, which enabled them to spot the one good painting in a group of bad ones, with no formal training in art, and, more important, good and bad actions with no formal training in morality. Hannah More described this ability rather dramatically in a poem she wrote in 1781:

> Sweet Sensibility! thou keen delight!
> Thou hasty moral! sudden sense of right!
> Thou untaught goodness! Virtue's precious seed!

Or as Madame de Staël once said, if you were lucky enough to have a delicate sensibility, you could throw away your etiquette book and your code of ethics, too, because for you virtue is "a spontaneous impulsion, a motive which passes into the blood, and which carries you along irresistibly, like the most imperious passions." These are the light voices of the blood, well before

D. H. Lawrence wrote of the dark ones. And even this is only the positive side of delicacy. There is also a negative side. The sensitive heroine of an English novel of the 1760s is kept out of harm not by convention or by chaperones, both of which she scorns, but by her "sweet impulsive modesty," which keeps her safer than fifty commandments. Having the right impulses, she doesn't need rules.

Delicacy is thus a rare and wonderful quality, and in the later eighteenth century it was one that people increasingly desired to possess. In real life, of course, as opposed to fiction, it imposed quite a burden. When Lady Louisa Stuart read *Pamela* as a girl of fourteen (this was in the 1770s), she was worried lest she "should not cry enough to gain the credit of proper sensibility." Readers of Sterne worried lest they not blush enough. One solution was mockingly suggested by a magazine in 1793. You could take lessons. "GROWN LADIES AND GENTLEMEN TAUGHT SENSIBILITY ON MATHEMATICAL PRINCIPLES," the mock advertisement begins, and it goes on to promise "in the course of only twenty lessons, to teach a delicate embarrassment and gentle suffusion to the most unbending set of features." That is, graduates would be able to blush at will, just as in our own day, when happiness has replaced sensibility as a desideratum, graduates of Dale Carnegie courses have learned to smile at will.

But blushing, crying, and fainting are the least of the obligations that a reputation for delicacy imposes. "Delicacy is a very general and *comprehensive* quality," the Rev. John Bennett wrote in 1789. "It extends to every-

13

thing where woman is concerned. Conversation, books, pictures, attitude, gesture, pronunciation should all come under its salutary restraints." It sounds like, and is, a full-time job. You must have a spontaneous reaction to every situation you encounter, and it must be the right reaction, too. What if you don't? You prove yourself a clod after all.

Hardest of all, it extends to evil. If you instinctively recognize good and evil, are naturally good yourself, and also very sensitive, it follows that an encounter with evil is a shocking experience. *Every* encounter with evil is a shocking experience. You have to keep right on weeping and blushing and fainting every time. If you don't, you cease to be delicate and have become hardened.

Since there was at least as much evil around in the eighteenth century as there is now, and since it is a familiar fact that people do get hardened by repeated shocks, admirers of delicacy had a problem. They found two solutions. The minority, cynical solution was to abandon the idea of delicacy as a spontaneous response, and to make it a convention like any other, as in the mock-ad of 1793. The trained sensibilist could seem to be shocked by evil whether she was or not, to cry readily while reading *Pamela* even if she actually longed to yawn. She would be an accomplished hypocrite. Once delicacy became a prestige quality, such hypocrites abounded. They were duly denounced, as in Vicemus Knox's essay on "Delicacy of Sentiment" in 1778. "The appearance of a toad, or the jolting of a carriage will cause a paroxysm of fear," he wrote about the sensitive girls of his time. "But it is remarkable," he continues,

14

"that this delicacy and tenderness often disappear in solitude, and the pretender to uncommon sensibility is frequently found, in the absence of witnesses, to be uncommonly unfeeling." The twentieth-century jokes about women and mice are a relic of this attitude, surviving into the age of smiles.

The majority solution, however, was to try to think of ways to keep delicate minds from too frequent a contact with evil, and thus to keep their energy undischarged. Expurgating books presented itself as one such way. If there is nothing on the page to gasp at, the capacity for gasping can be preserved at full strength for future occasions. It might be supposed that a girl of sweet impulsive modesty wouldn't gasp anyway, since she wouldn't know the bad words—but, according to the theory of sensibility, she would recognize them by instinct. The Rev. John Bennett put this particularly well, describing the virtues of the perfect girl of 1789. This paragon, he says, "vibrates to the most distant touch of what is proper and becoming, and would tremble like the sensitive plant, where any thing that could stain the delicacy of her *mind* was conveyed in the most *distant* allusion." The ability to tremble thus is her most important possession. "If a girl ever loses it, farewell, a long farewell to all her greatness! . . . A girl should *hear*, she should *see*, nothing that can call forth a blush, or even stain the purity of her mind."

Such language implies that delicacy is, like virginity, something that you can lose only once, and that you can never recover. You are hardened, and there is no softening now. This view was beginning to be common even in

Bennett's time. In the nineteenth century, the idea of the virgin female mind—not just in the young girl, but in all women, even sixty-three-year-old baronesses—became standard. (There were sporadic attempts to extend it to the male mind—Francis Newman made one *—but they never really caught on, if only because men need to remain conscious to deal with the toad and the carriage.) By late Victorian times delicacy was an actual obligation, the concept now including both prudishness and helplessness. "Woman is a synonym for weakness," a man named Sydney Yorke wrote in a book called *The Ways of Women* in 1885. That's why career girls are impossible. Man, being strong, is able "to become a machine" when he needs to, Yorke says, but not woman. "She carries her sympathies and prejudices, in all their virgin sensitiveness, into whatever occupation or pursuit she takes up; and, consequently, she is most eminently unbusinesslike."

You did not have to be a male Victorian to feel this way. In 1889 a group of about a hundred high-minded women signed a public petition asking that they not be given the vote. The group included Lady Randolph Churchill, Mrs. T. H. Huxley, Mrs. Matthew Arnold, Mrs. Humphry Ward, Mrs. Arnold Toynbee, and so forth. Their argument was that they could "contribute more precious elements to the national life without the

* In *The Cure of the Great Social Evil*, London: 1869. ("No one imagines that a girl will be made purer by plunging her through impure reading or any thing that excites voluptuous thought: how then can any person of common sense think that this method is desirable for boys, who are so much more inflammable? . . . the first point is, not to break down that modesty and sensitiveness which they naturally have, in common with girls." Pp. 28, 27.)

vote than with it"—because if you get involved in politics you're likely to lose your virgin sensitiveness. Or as
the petition put it, having the suffrage "would tend to
blunt the special moral qualities of women." If you're
ready to give up the vote to retain your delicacy, you are
hardly going to hesitate to read expurgated Shakespeare
for that purpose.

There are three other possible causes of the new prudery and hence of bowdlerism that deserve to be mentioned, two of them very briefly. One is simply the rise
of evangelical religion in eighteenth-century England,
and of Methodism in particular. There is unquestionably
a connection. John Wesley himself was a pioneer expurgator, as will emerge in the next chapter. Dr. Bowdler
and the other three Bowdlers who bowdlerized, though
not actual Methodists, were notoriously evangelical; all
four specifically said they expurgated to help the cause
of Christianity. Scores of other nineteenth-century expurgators cited religious motives for their acts.

But it would be a mistake to see religion as a primary
cause of bowdlerism. Christianity has had a quarrel with
profane literature right along,* and there has not been

* There is an eighteenth-century story about a fourth-century
bishop which suggests how old the quarrel is. The bishop was named
Heliodorus, and he had written a novel. "It is related," said Clara
Reeve in 1785, "that a Synod, considering the danger that might
happen to youth, from reading a Romance (though there is nothing
in it, in the least degree offensive to morals or modesty) authorized
by the dignity of its author, proposed to him either to burn his work,
or resign his Bishopric, and that he chose the latter."

It is worth noting that as recently as 1929 the Encyclopaedia
Britannica disputed this view of the bishop's novel. "As a whole it
offends less good taste and moral decency than other romances of its
class," the 1929 Britannica said grudgingly. By 1964 we had regained
the view of 1785, and that year's Britannica said, "The work is free
from licentiousness."

bowdlerism right along. In an age of profound faith like the fourteenth century, there was not only no bowdlerism, there was a proliferation of Christian literature of a kind which to nineteenth-century minds, religious and agnostic alike, seemed flawed by indecency—*Piers Plowman*, Mandeville's *Travels* (to the Holy Land), Dunbar's poetry, and so on. Eighth-century Anglo-Saxon monks amused themselves by asking riddles of a kind which would have caused most Victorian libertines to recoil blushing *—and which have caused modern editors, up to and including a couple of professors at Columbia in 1936, to pretend not to know the answers. Tatwine, Archbishop of Canterbury in 730, wrote such riddles. Porteus, Bishop of London in 1800, ran the Society for Enforcing the King's Proclamation against Immorality and Profaneness. Robinson, Bishop of Woolwich in 1960, stood up in court to defend *Lady Chatterley's Lover*. The quarrel with profane literature is endemic to Christianity, but its intensity varies, and more according to conditions outside than inside the church.

Another cause may be the industrial revolution itself.

---

* For example, Riddle 44 of the Exeter Book:
> Splendidly it hangs by a man's thigh,
> under the master's cloak. In front is a hole.
> It is stiff and hard; it has a goodly place.
> When the man lifts his own garment
> up above the knee, he wishes to visit
> with the head of this hanging instrument the familiar hole
> he had often filled with its equal length.

All editors of the Exeter Book before Professor Paull Franklin Baum in 1963 pretended that the only answer they could think of to this riddle was "key." (For Anglo-Saxon monks, the whole point was tricking another monk into giving the penis answer, and then confounding him with the key.)

Among its innumerable effects were the commuting husband and the stay-at-home wife who never actually sees what her husband does down at the millyard or the foundry. This was new. Farmers' wives do see what their husbands do, just like the wives of eighteenth-century shopkeepers living over their shops. If the farmer cuts animals' throats or the shopkeeper cheats his customers, the wife not only knows, she's probably there helping. But the stay-at-home wife of the cut-throat industrialist gets her husband's edited account in the evenings, and is likelier to preserve a kind of innocence. At any rate, many Victorian writers—Ruskin, Carlyle, and Dickens, for example—contrast the fierce world of nineteenth-century industrialism with the chaste sanctuary of the home. Man has to go out and be corrupted, but, as Ruskin put it, "he guards the woman from all this; within his house, as ruled by her, unless she herself has sought it, need enter no danger, no temptation, no cause of error or offence." And even a complete edition of *Tristram Shandy* can be viewed as a danger.

That's pretty speculative, but there is one other cause which is much less so. This is the rise, in the early nineteenth century, of the general reading public, the same one that exists now. (It is, of course, more nearly a general viewing public now.) Coleridge, something of a conservative, said in 1816 that he was writing for "men of clerkly acquirements"—but adds that he knows others with less learning will see his books. "We have now a Reading Public . . . a strange phrase." As late as 1831, *Blackwood's Magazine* was still using quotation marks for the phenomenon. "The 'reading public' then [in the eighteenth century], had little to do with the lower orders," it said, plainly wishing this were still the case, but recognizing that it wasn't.

As to who comprised this new reading public, Jeffrey of the *Edinburgh Review* guessed in 1812 that there were 20,000 upper-class readers in Great Britain, and 200,000 of the common sort. Reprinting the essay in 1844, he changed the figures to 30,000 and 300,000. Other guesses ran even higher. "It was considered by Edmund Burke, about forty years ago," wrote the editors of the *Penny Magazine* in 1832, "that there were eighty thousand readers in this country. In the present year it has been shown . . . that there are two hundred thousand *purchasers* of one periodical work. It may be fairly calculated that the number of readers of that single work amounts to a million."

In short, for the first time there was a mass market for books to reach; and even people who did not see the need of expurgation for themselves began to think they had better protect all those new readers. This puts it on a class basis. The gentleman (Dr. Bowdler was a gentleman: on title pages he signs himself not as M.D., but Esq.)—the gentleman, moved by *noblesse oblige*, kindly sets out to save his inferiors from temptation. *He* can be trusted to read *Hamlet*, but a newly educated grocer will pick up bad ideas.

The phenomenon can also be put quite differently, on a commercial basis. From about 1820 on, the growth of the mass reading public—and the simultaneous development of cheap paper—made possible large editions of books at low prices, really for the first time. (As late as

1800, most books came out in editions of 250 or 500 copies; and a common price was one guinea—a week's income even for many curates and beginning lawyers. By 1850, with incomes no lower, one-shilling books and first editions of 5,000 were common.) It is probably a general truth that the larger the audience, whether for television, books, or cheese spreads, the blander the fare. There are more prejudices to avoid offending. At any rate, Victorian publishers tended to expurgate large editions, even while continuing to print small unexpurgated editions of the same authors at higher prices for the old upper-class audience.

The first expurgations directly in response to the new reading public were those inspired by the Society for the Promotion of Christian Knowledge. From its founding in 1698, the Society had been in the publishing business. Naturally, its speciality was religious books and pamphlets. But in 1817, "in view of the increased appetite for reading," the Society issued its first Supplemental Catalogue—secular books down to and including virtuous novels and poetry. Unlike the religious books, the works listed in the Supplemental Catalogue were not actually published by the Society. In secular literature it acted like an ur-Book-of-the-Month Club, recommending what it liked best from the whole range of publications, and sometimes offering a special price. Publishers then as now were eager to have their books taken by clubs, and sometimes even ready to adapt them to suit a club's policy. For the SPCK this meant protecting innocence. In 1823 an expurgation of Gay's *Fables* and in 1826 an expurgation of *Robinson Crusoe* were published, specially aimed at the Supplemental Catalogue. Others followed.

Strictly commercial responses to the mass reading public also followed. In 1829, John Murray, Byron's publisher, launched a series called the Family Library—a kind of ur-Everyman or Modern Library. A typical entry is "The Plays of Philip Massinger adapted for Family Reading and the Use of Young Persons, by the Omission of Objectionable Passages," which came out in 1830. Murray put out forty-seven such volumes in all, and other publishers put out hundreds and eventually thousands. By mid-century, in fact, expurgation for the sake of the reading public seemed so normal and necessary that editors of complete texts were often apologetic. The funniest case is probably that of the Rev. Alexander Grosart, a man of clerkly acquirements who put out a whole series of non-expurgations in the seventies and eighties. His edition of Donne, for example, printed in 1872–73, was limited to 156 copies, "Printed for Private Circulation." Despite these precautions, Grosart felt extremely nervous. "I do not hide from myself," he wrote in his preface, "that it needs courage to edit and print the poetry of Dr. John Donne in our day. Nor would I call it literary prudery that shrinks from giving publicity to such sensuous things. . . ." And then he goes on to justify himself on the grounds that his editions will reach only scholars—men, that is, " 'strong' enough to use them for literary purposes unhurt." "Respect is due to the 'strong,' " he explains, "equally with the 'weak.' "

It would be misleading to pretend that all Victorians who failed to protect the general reading public were as nervous as Grosart. James Russell Lowell edited a complete Donne in Boston in 1855, and he sounded no note of apology whatsoever. (He did choose to remain anonymous.) Charles Eliot Norton, who re-edited the volume in 1895, didn't even hide, but signed his own name and Lowell's both—but now the book was a limited edition of 383 copies for the Grolier Club. It remains true to say that throughout the nineteenth century and well into the twentieth, there were commonly expensive complete texts for the few, and inexpensive incomplete ones for the many. As recently as 1955, T. E. Lawrence's *The Mint* came out this way. In Canada, for example, the unexpurgated edition sold for $17.50 and the expurgated for $3.50; in England, three and a half guineas, complete, and seventeen shillings, sixpence, bowdlerized. (How the book was sold in America will appear in the final chapter.) There is some analogy to the simultaneous practice of putting very frank passages of a book in Greek or Latin, and the rest in English.* The "strong" know the classics; most of the "weak" do not. For that matter, the custom still survives in a small

* A minor but funny example of this occurs in Thomas Tyler's edition of Shakespeare's sonnets (London: 1890). Tyler did not expurgate. But he was wonderfully careful in his notes, of which there are a great many, this being a full-dress scholarly edition. In Sonnet 151 Shakespeare amuses himself, like an Anglo-Saxon monk, by punning back and forth between the rise of love and of the penis. Tyler says, "It has been thought that some lines in this Sonnet were so expressed that they might be taken *sense male pudico*; but whether this be so or not it is scarcely necessary to determine. . . ."

"Justice Holmes spotted a similar response to the same organ in 1907. Criticizing Jane Harrison's *Prolegomena to the Study of Greek Religion* in a private letter, Holmes wrote, 'Also she does not handle the phallus with the humpy indifference of a man bent on science. She puts on the gloves of a dead language, and blushingly shrinks.' "

23

way. Most anthologies for use in schools still shrink from giving publicity to such sensuous things as Donne's Elegy XIX—that "famous and much 'fie-fied' " poem, as George Saintsbury said, boldly helping to print it in 1896—or the complete text of *Macbeth*. High-school students are generally felt to be "weak." Strong students at the best schools, however, have been getting Shakespeare and Donne entire for years. But this, too, I will come to in the final chapter.

If I have convinced readers that the principal cause of bowdlerism was the cult of sensibility, which made the state of being easily shocked a social asset, and the chief secondary cause the rise of the general reading public, I have done all I can hope for. There are many other secondary causes, or possible ones, that might have been discussed, such as Vicemus Knox's theory that togetherness had something to do with it.* But now it is time to turn from speculations about causes to facts about beginnings.

---

* Knox wondered in that same 1778 essay why refined speech should be a growing thing in England, when the Greeks and Romans, "the most civilized people on earth," talked so coarsely. His answer, or part of it, was that Greek and Roman men didn't spend enough of their leisure at mixed parties. "It is no wonder," he said, "that the antients, who admitted not women to their social conversations, should acquire a roughness of manners." If women had been invited to more symposia in Athens, there might have been less trouble with Aristophanes. Or there might not have, too. Men spend more time than ever with women now, but instead of keeping pace, delicacy and expurgation have been in decline for fifty years.

CHAPTER TWO

Bowdlerism Before Bowdler

****

> *To rescue from oblivion the sterling ore of antiquity, to purge it of gross alloy, is an undertaking worthy of praise. It is like recovering a picture highly finished from obscuring filth. When this is done without impairing the master's beauties, it shews judgment; and if any retouching is necessary, to blend the addition with an able hand manifests genius.*
> The Dramatic Censor, 1770

> EUPHRASIA. *I have often wished that the first two volumes of Rousseau's* Eloise *could be abridged and altered. . . . I thought it might be possible to give a different turn to the story, and to make the two Lovers stop short of the* act. . . .

> HORTENSIUS. *I like your plan, and advise you to make this alteration yourself.*

> EUPHRASIA. *You must excuse me, Sir—I have not yet the presumption to attempt it, or to think myself able to do justice to* Rousseau *in such an alteration. It must remain as it is.*
> The Progress of Romance, 1785

THE EXPURGATION of British literature began in Scotland, some eighty years before Bowdler's time. Allan Ramsay, the leading Scottish poet of his day, initiated the practice in Edinburgh in 1724. Ramsay was much interested in his predecessors, and that year he published an anthology called *The Ever Green*, which is subtitled "A Collection of Scots Poems Wrote by the Ingenious Before 1600." About a dozen of the poems he expurgated.

Ramsay is not a likely person to have pioneered a moral movement. He was a moderately bawdy poet himself—no more than most of his contemporaries, but then, his contemporaries were Prior, Pope, and Swift. In fact, his poems are frank enough so that the Victorians considered them unfit to be read as written, and Ramsay was himself frequently expurgated during the nineteenth century—just like Prior, Pope, and Swift.

Furthermore, he not only wrote bawdy poems of his own, he encouraged the reading of other people's. Much of his life he ran a bookstore in Edinburgh; and a year or two after the publication of *The Ever Green*, he pioneered in another way by becoming the first person in Great Britain to open a lending library. His was utterly unlike the fortresses of propriety which went under that name during the next century. In 1728 a fellow citizen of Edinburgh made this entry in his journal:

> All the villainous profane and obscene bookes and playes printed at London by Curle and others, are gote doune from London by Allan Ramsey, and lent out, for an easy price, to young boyes, servant weemen of the better sort, and gentlemen; and vice and obscenity dreadfully propagated.

The question arises, of course, what led so unpuritanical a man to think expurgation desirable. The need for it

26

was not yet apparent in England. Out of many, I shall offer two pieces of evidence for this. One is a book somewhat similar to Ramsay's, edited by the English poet Ambrose Phillips. *A Collection of Old Ballads* . . . *With Introductions Historical and Critical* appeared in London the year before *The Ever Green* came out in Edinburgh. Some of the ballads in it are almost as improper as anything written by ingenious Scots before 1600. For example, there is one called "King Edward and Jane Shore," which sounds something like an ancestor of Robert Service telling dirty jokes. It manages to denigrate the (supposed) sexual behavior of almost everyone in history. A typical couplet reads like this:

And Joan of Arc play'd in the dark with the Knights
    of Languedock,
But Jane Shore met King Edward, and gave him
    Knock for Knock.

Another, which uses one of Shakespeare's pet metaphors —one that people in the nineteenth century took endless trouble to remove from him—goes:

Brave Carpit-Knights in Cupid's fights, their milk-
    white Rapiers drew,
But Jane Shore, Jane Shore, King Edward did
    subdue.

The ending is grosser still, as well as less metrical.

But brave King Edward, who before had gain'd
    nine Victories,

Was like a Bond-slave fetter'd within Jane Shore's
    All-conquering Thighs.

In his headnote to the ballad, Ambrose Phillips is very
cool.

> There are some little Expressions in it which had
> almost induced me to lay the Song aside, [he says]
> but I consider'd that it was really old, and therefore
> ought to be preserv'd, and that I might have readers
> of several Humours, so that this Ballad might hit the
> Taste of those who would probably not relish one
> more grave and solid. This little Introduction I have
> thrown in for the Service of the Ladies, that they
> may not unwarily go to read or sing this Song,
> unless by themselves.

Cool, and perfectly open. Obviously Phillips was not
worried about shocking his readers with "King Edward
and Jane Shore," only about creating a possible awkward
scene at the spinet; and obviously expurgation never
entered his mind.

My other example is an anthology published by a
master at St. Paul's School, London, in 1722. James
Greenwood called his book *The Virgin Muse*, obviously
to suggest an unusually careful selection of poems, and
he offered it "for the Use of Young Gentlemen and
Ladies at School." There are no milk-white rapiers in
the book, but there are no expurgations, either. Not even
in such a poem as Prior's "To the Hon. Charles Montague," which ends a long way from virgins. How little
life would be worth, the poet says, speaking directly to
his friend,

If you thought Fame but empty Breath;
I, Phillis, but a perjur'd Whore.

The same un-Victorian note is struck by the "Alphabetical Index, explaining all the hard Words," which Greenwood, like a good teacher, put at the back. "Cholick," for example, he defines as "Belly-ach, Pain of the Guts," which is clear, to the point, and on the whole minces words less than notes in high-school texts do now. Society itself minced words less in 1722.

Why, then, in such a milieu, did Allan Ramsay expurgate? And where did he get the idea? I think there are several answers to these questions. One sounds paradoxical. Unlike most earlier editors of old poems, he had a certain reverence for his text. Editors of classical texts had had this reverence right along, but it was a new thing to worry about keeping some old work in the vernacular in its original form, instead of just rewriting it, as Dryden rewrote one of Shakespeare's comedies in 1670 or Tate rewrote one of his tragedies in 1681. Ramsay didn't have very much reverence for his text, and he did a good deal of rewriting in addition to the expurgation, but he had enough to make him drop a few words from an otherwise unaltered line, sometimes, rather than cut the line altogether, or rewrite it.

Why not be even more reverent and print the whole line? Here prudence comes in. The passages in *The Ever Green* that he expurgated are in general much bawdier than anything that was being expurgated from his own poetry a century later, and certainly bawdier than anything a large and influential group in Edinburgh was prepared to tolerate. From the Reformation on, Scotland has had a higher proportion of men who object to villainous obscene plays and books than has England or America; and expurgation in Scotland has tended at any time to be more intense than that elsewhere in the English-speaking world, with the possible exception of Boston.

But the most important reason lies in Ramsay's own temperament. Expurgation is normally a high-minded practice, done in deadly earnest by serious men. They want to protect the innocence of their readers. Ramsay did it half as a joke, to protect himself. In his hands, expurgation was a device for eating his cake and having it—or, more precisely, for keeping the full bawdy flavor of an old poem without using words that might get him into trouble.

One of the earliest excisions is a fine example of his joking attitude. Ramsay has just cut half a line in the third stanza of a poem called "The Defens of Grissell Sandylands." (Grissell has been accused of going to bed "With every ane list gife hir half a Crown.") At the bottom of the page he explains his action thus. "In such Places as are so sullied or torn in our old Copies, that they cannot be read, we chuse rather to leave a Blank than to fill them up, tho' they might be supplied with small Difficulty."

This particular place might have been supplied with very small difficulty indeed. Ramsay was working chiefly from a single old copy, the Bannatyne Manuscript, which was then in private hands but is now in the National Library of Scotland. There is nothing either

sullied or torn about the third stanza of "Grissell Sandylands." The editor is covering his prudence with a joke.

The third bowdlerized poem also has a note attached.
This is "In Derision of Wanton Women," and it is a
piece of notable plain-speaking. Ramsay expurgated it
heavily. Stanza Seven, as he printed it, appears thus.
"Chestetie" is, of course, "chastity," and "gar" means
"make." To "guck" is to act foolishly, and "tigging"
means "stroking."

> Fareweil with Chestetie,
> Frae wenchis fall a Chucking,
> Thair follows things thre,
> To gar them gae a Gucking,
> Imbracing, Tigging, Plucking;
> Thir foure, the Suth to sane,
> Enforsis them * * *
> I shall not sayt again.

Here the footnote is practically all grin.* " 'Tis not

---

* Teasing footnotes were a passion with Ramsay, much as they are
with Nabokov. He put one in the 1721 edition of his own poems
which is exactly like the ones in *The Ever Green*. It's to a poem
called "The Dying Words of Lucky Spence." Lucky, the madam of a
Scottish brothel, is giving final instructions to a group of young
prostitutes. The fifth stanza reads:

> Whan he's asleep, then dive and catch
> His ready Cash, his Rings or Watch;
> And gin he likes to light his Match
>   At your Spunk-box,
> Ne'er stand to let the fumbling Wretch
> E'en take the Pox.

Ramsay has a note: "*Light his Match &*. I could give a large
Annotation on this Sentence, but do not incline to explain every
thing, lest I disoblige future Criticks, by leaving nothing for them to
do." For about a century, critics hung back from this invitation, and
for another century they responded by vigorously expurgating the
whole stanza.

impossible," Ramsay writes, "but a complete Copy of this old Ballad may be found to supply these few Blanks." The Bannatyne Manuscript is perfectly complete here; and it wouldn't matter if it weren't. The rhyme and the context bring the missing word to mind with no trouble at all, which is plainly what is amusing the bowdlerizer.

By no means all the expurgations that Ramsay made in *The Ever Green* can be restored by the reader from the context; often he took out all the rhyme words, and in some cases he cut so much as to leave a stanza almost meaningless. Here he was expurgating as later and more earnest men understood the term; and, in fact, in one or two cases Victorian editors followed his exact cuts when dealing with the same poem.

But there is one other example that shows just how gamesome Ramsay felt. He included another old poem attacking women, this one called "A Bytand Ballat on Warlo Wives." In the fourth stanza he did something which nineteenth-century expurgators were also addicted to. Instead of omitting an offensive word, he neatly changed it into a harmless one. Dr. Bowdler did the same in *Romeo and Juliet*, when he altered old Capulet's reference to his daughter and her friends as "fresh female buds" to "fresh female birds." Austin Dobson, the Victorian editor and minor poet, did the same thing in his 1889 edition of Prior. There is a line in "Answer to Cloe," in which Prior is imagining the personified sun hurrying home to a double bed. "At night he reclines on his Thetis's breast." Dobson switched the verb to "declines," thus bringing in an astronomical term and remov-

ing the suggestiveness at a single stroke.* It was this sort
of thing that Ramsay did in "A Bytand Ballat." The
poem has been talking about the classes of men who have
reason to wish their wives dead. One such class, as
Ramsay printed the poem, includes

> a Cuckald or his Bruther;
> Sunt Lairds and Cuckalds altogither.

Just as neatly as Bowdler or Dobson, he has in the second
line gotten rid of a problem word. But, unlike them, he
draws attention to his feat in a triumphant footnote. It
reads as follows: "*Sunt Lairds.* Here is spelled with an S,
as it ought, and not with a C, as many of the English do."
In the Bannatyne Manuscript the word is spelled just as
Englishmen did and do. The expurgator is playing it
both ways.†

There is still the question of where Ramsay got the
idea of expurgation. The answer is that it stared him in
the face from a poets' and journalists' practice then current. This was the use of dashes to replace words or parts
of words in one's own writing. It was done chiefly as a
safety device when writing about real people, to avoid

---

* "Of excision and suppression I have been sparing," Dobson told
his readers; "and I trust I shall be acquitted of the impertinence of
improving Prior, if I admit that in a couple of instances, I have
ventured to make slight alterations (in one case involving only the
addition of a letter) which enabled me to print two pieces that must
otherwise have been withheld."

† He was also maddening his critics. There was a pamphlet published in Edinburgh in 1736 entitled *The Flight of Religious Piety
From Scotland, upon the Account of Ramsay's lewd books . . . and
the Hell-bred Play-House Comedians.* In 1737 the city authorities
closed down the playhouse.

33

the dangers of formal identification while still making one's meaning clear. In 1711, for example, Swift wrote an extremely sharp satire on the Earl of Nottingham, called "The Speech." The earl is supposedly making a speech in the House of Lords, explaining to his fellow peers the means by which the Duke and Duchess of Marlborough have just bought his vote. (The poem naturally appeared anonymously.) Lines 5–8 read:

The D—— shew'd me all his fine House; and the D——s
From her closet brought out a full purse in her Clutches.
I talked of a *Peace*, and they both gave a start,
His G—— swore by ——, and her G—— let a F——t:

"The Speech" is, to be sure, an extreme case, in quantity of dashes and every other way. Indeed, publication of the poem led to a formal investigation by the House of Lords in search of the author. A more typical example would be a poem Pope wrote in 1717, laughing at the large number of people—himself included—then engaged in translating passages of Ovid for two rival editions of the *Metamorphoses*. He suggests they ought to work in committees.

> Let W—rw—k's Muse with Ash——t join,
>   And Ozel's with Lord Hervey's:
> Tickell and Addison combine,
>   And P—pe translate with Jervis.

Moreover, despite Swift's example in 1711, the process was not in general used to mitigate strong language, since most people didn't see any need to mitigate it. The second stanza of Pope's well-known "A Farewell to London in the Year 1715" makes a perfect example (even though it wasn't actually published until 1785). That runs:

> Soft B—— and rough C——s, adieu!
> Earl Warwick make your Moan,
> The lively H——k and you
> May knock up Whores alone.

You can't call that bowdlerism, or even self-bowdlerism, at least by the definition I am using in this book. A true bowdlerizer would have been likely to leave out the whole stanza, as some twenty editors of Pope did during the nineteenth century. But all the dashing and omitting of names going on in Ramsay's time certainly gave him a precedent. (Just as it gave a precedent to all those towns of O—— and "I was born in the year 184—" in nineteenth-century novels.) And, in addition, he could have found another precedent in the more or less systematic removal of oaths from old plays that went on for a while when the theater was reopened after the Restoration in 1660. That I shall go into in the chapter on Shakespeare.

Ramsay left no successors, though forty years later a new edition of *The Ever Green* inspired some ; and for a while the eighteenth century went on its normal bawdy way, Fielding writing novels, Lady Townshend spitting, and so on. Then in 1744 came John Wesley. He is the first serious bowdlerizer of English literature.

In 1744, Methodism was five years old. Wesley himself was a man of forty, still a fellow of Lincoln College, Oxford, and still a widely ranging reader of literature.*

---

* Shakespeare was a special favorite. After Wesley's death, one of his disciples, the Rev. John Pawson, burned his annotated quarto edition of the plays—"he judged they were not among the things that tended to edification."

He especially loved poetry. He loved decency even more, though, and some time back it had struck him that there was an essential conflict between his two loves. Only "an exceeding small Proportion" of the poems in existence, he had come to feel, could be read except "at the Hazard of Innocence or Virtue."

When the Countess of Huntingdon happened to say, around 1742, that she wished someone would edit an anthology of clean poetry, she thus struck a responsive chord. The result was Wesley's *Collection of Moral and Sacred Poems, From the Most Celebrated English Authors*, published in three handsome volumes in 1744. It contains about 250 poems, mostly seventeenth- and eighteenth-century, including twenty-five by the editor and his brother Charles.

The book has not generally been described as an expurgation; Wesley himself doesn't. In his dedication to the countess, he merely assures her that he has included "nothing that can any way offend the chastest Ear or give Pain to the tenderest Heart." The same could be said of hundreds of later collections of poetry which are in no sense expurgations but merely the products of extremely careful choice.

In actual fact, however, the book is bowdlerized heavily. Of the 250 poems, perhaps 150 are printed complete or are honest extracts. The other 100 have lines missing and words changed. Many of the missing lines are perfectly chaste, and simply struck Wesley as boring, or silly, or too metaphysical for an eighteenth-century taste. These I don't classify as bowdlerism but as normal editing in an age which almost always ranked taste higher than scholarship.* The other missing lines, however, could have been struck out by Dr. Bowdler himself. Taken together, they form a collection of all the threats to innocence to be found in the milder poems of Pope, Dryden, Cowley, and Prior—all oaths, references to King Solomon's concubines, and so on. What really establishes Wesley's intention to bowdlerize, though, is the substitution of words. He did this, for example, in Dryden's version of the tenth satire of Juvenal. As Dryden translated, lines 25–26 read,

> A troop of cut-throat guards were sent to seize
> The rich men's goods, and gut their palaces:

But as Wesley edited, the troopers act more delicately. They merely "spoil" the palaces. Later, in lines 404–5, Dryden is saying how lucky King Priam would have been to die before the fall of Troy, "when Hector, with the race/ Of royal bastards might his funeral grace." Not wanting to cut the lines, Wesley legitimized the race. In his version, it's royal children who would have graced the funeral.

Since no one seems to have noticed them among the welter of other changes, Wesley's bowdlerisms naturally did not attract much comment. Nor did he himself pursue the practice. When he abridged *Paradise Lost*

---

* Forty years after Wesley, a real scholar, a protégé of Gibbon, editing selections from an old manuscript, wrote in his preface: "Above all, it is to be hoped that the reader will allow, from the vast number of pieces rejected, that the editor has in no instance sacrificed the character of a man of taste to that of an antiquary; as of all characters he should the least chuse that of an hoarder of ancient dirt." "Dirt" here means trash, not obscenity.

twenty years later, his entire interest lay in making the poem comprehensible to working-class Methodists. He cut only "those lines which I despaired of explaining to the unlearned," and the passage in Book II describing the incest between Sin and Satan, for example (far more striking than a mere reference to bastardy), he left as Milton wrote it. It didn't, to be sure, get one of the stars he awarded to "peculiarly excellent passages," but not a word did he change. Wesley may have been more reluctant to tamper with the poem he regarded as the greatest ever written in any language than with a mere translation of Juvenal; and he had certainly ceased to regard literature as the "Elegant Amusement" he termed it in 1744, now thinking most of it something better avoided altogether, and hence not worth bothering to expurgate, any more than sepulchers are worth whitewashing.

In any event, the time was not yet ripe for a serious school of expurgation to arise, not in England and not quite yet in Scotland. The cases of three famous men will show how things stood in England. Two of the three, Oliver Goldsmith and Dr. Johnson, are famous still, though not for having expurgated; the third, Bishop Richard Hurd, was both famous and infamous in his own time, precisely because he did try to.

Goldsmith was the first and most light-hearted of the three. Like Wesley, though twenty years later, he had it suggested to him that what England needed was a good anthology of poetry. In his case, the nudge came from his publisher, who had in mind something suitable for schools to use and for parents to give their children. Goldsmith, always in need of money, responded by editing two anthologies. Both were published in 1767, one under his own name, and one anonymously. (He thriftily included a good many of the same poems in both of them.) The one he did for his regular publisher, and signed his name to, *Beauties of English Poesy*, is not expurgated, though it pretends to be winnowed. The anonymous volume, *Poems for Young Ladies*, is the second expurgated book in England.

Beauties, the "winnowed" anthology, though then aimed at the juvenile market, now seems strikingly adult. Goldsmith cut nothing. He can't have thought he needed to in "The Rape of the Lock," since that was *his* choice for the best poem, if not in the world, then in English literature. Like James Greenwood, he also saw no problems in Prior, two of whose bawdiest fables he included. And where Wesley wouldn't even allow Dryden to say "gut," Goldsmith cheerfully permits him to speak of "Pissing Alley," in "MacFlecknoe." It is true that when the book came out, one reviewer thought one of the two Prior fables a bit much for schoolchildren,* but even

---

* "Prior's Hans Carvel, notwithstanding its merit, ought to have been omitted in a selection of this kind," he said.

This very temperate criticism was the basis of a later myth about the book. When Bishop Percy wrote a memoir of Goldsmith in 1801, he reported that Goldsmith "carelessly, without reading it, marked for the printer one of the most indecent tales of Prior. This, as might be supposed, prevented the sale of the book." Actually, Goldsmith had not only read the poem, he wrote a headnote for it, explaining that it was the one "for which, by the bye, Mr. Prior has got his greatest reputation." But this was not an idea congenial to Victorians. By mid-century, *both* Prior fables were supposed to have caused a scandal. In the standard nineteenth-century biography of Goldsmith, John Forster says flatly, "He made that questionable choice of the 'Ladle' and 'Hans Carvel' which for once interdicted from general reading a book with his name on the title page." A mighty growth from a small criticism.

that solitary purist had no objection to the other one or to "MacFlecknoe."

The other anthology is quite different. *Poems for Young Ladies* has no fables by Prior, does not reprint Savage's "The Bastard," or even Browne's "A Pipe of Tobacco," with its hearty Townshendian command:

> Boy! bring an ounce of Freeman's best,
> And bid the vicar be my guest:
> Let all be plac'd in manner due;
> A pot wherein to spit, or spue.

Indeed, Goldsmith boasted in the preface that the poems he had selected "were not only such pieces as innocence may read without a blush, but such as will even tend to strengthen that innocence"—a statement that makes sense only if the second "innocence" is taken to mean something like "determination to remain chaste."

Two pages later he is claiming to be an expurgator. "I have here and there, indeed, when [a poem] of particular beauty offered with a few blemishes, lopt off all the defects, and thus, like the tyrant, who fitted all strangers to the bed he had prepared for them, I have inserted some, by first adapting them to my plan; we only differ in this, that he mutilated with a bad design, I from motives of a contrary nature." The naïveté and clumsiness of this account are what one would expect from a pioneer.

But, as usual, Goldsmith is claiming too much. He was not a true Procrustes. He included plenty of extracts in the book, like most anthologists then, and most now. But he bowdlerized exactly one poem, Gay's "The Fan," and even that he didn't do a very good job on. Gay was writing a long, humorous history of fans as devices for flirtation, with special reference to their use as camouflage. Goldsmith did cut the description of Leda making love to the swan (behind a fan of swan wings); he did silence a chorus of fan-bearing former virgins, who preach the doctrine that what you do in secret doesn't count. But no serious bowdlerist would agree that everything he left was such as tended to strengthen innocence. Venus remains in the poem as a sort of fashion consultant, comparing the tedious women's styles of the past, when "breasts within the stays repos'd," to the more effective new styles (of 1714) when "the bosom now its panting beauties shows." And after lowering her neckline, an innocent girl reading the book can go on from "The Fan" to Nathaniel Cotton's "Marriage, A Vision," which Goldsmith left untouched, and hear the sentence passed by the god Hymen on girls who marry old men for their money: "Be joyless ev'ry night, he said." * And so on. As an expurgator, Goldsmith plainly took himself about as seriously as Allan Ramsay. Such reviewers as noticed the book at all made no reference to the bowdlerism, but simply damned the anonymous editor for throwing the book together in such obvious haste.

The case of Bishop Hurd, five years later, is quite different and quite serious. In 1772 Dr. Hurd published the *Select Works of Mr. A. Cowley.* It was the first edition of Cowley in fifty years, it was a careful, precise, scholarly job, and it was expurgated. Besides half a dozen

---

* Fifty years later, Dr. Bowdler firmly cut the Nurse's command to Juliet, "Go, girl, seek happy nights to happy days."

cuts within poems, all carefully asterisked and footnoted, Dr. Hurd omitted entirely the series of Cowley's love poems known collectively as "The Mistress." In his preface he defends his having done so. "It would be using most writers of name very ill, to treat them with that freedom which I have presumed to take with Mr. Cowley," he said. "But everything he wrote is either so good or so bad, that, in all reason, a separation should be made." Dr. Hurd meant a permanent separation. "It is enough," he concluded his short preface, "if this small collection go down to posterity."

The edition instantly became notorious. A cheap anonymous anthology is one thing, and a would-be definitive edition is quite another. This was the first bowdlerism to come to general attention, and most literary men were shocked. The *Monthly Review* was more or less typical in demanding whether an editor may "merely on the strength of his own judgement, mutilate a poet at his pleasure, and make him undergo an arbitrary amputation of what he conceives to be the unsound parts, with the idea of preserving the rest." The reviewer was also typical in answering his own question with a firm no. "We have no doubt but that this mode of republication may be attended with some advantages," he conceded, admitting that Cowley wrote a good many "loose" poems. But mutilation is too dangerous to allow. What an age should do with loose poets like Cowley, he said, is to "suffer what *we* may esteem to be their less perfect productions to abide under the protection of their better and happier works." Here the eighteenth century speaks to the twentieth.

This disapproval didn't keep Hurd's edition from selling pretty well—it was an attractive and well-edited book—but it did cause his name to mean for the next thirty years what Bowdler's has now meant for a hundred and fifty.

Another eighteenth-century case, Dr. Johnson's, is more equivocal. On the one hand, Johnson is rightly famous as a defender of full publication. Long before Bowdler, he did an edition of Shakespeare (1765)—but in *his* preface he wrote, "The history of our language, and the true force of our words, can only be preserved by keeping the text of authors free from adulteration." When a friend of the poet James Thomson, thinking to do him a posthumous favor, cut one of his poems, Dr. Johnson said flatly that such action "cannot be justified by any supposed propriety of the alteration or kindness of the friend." As for Hurd's *Cowley*, Johnson thought as little of it as did the *Monthly Review*. He not only damned Hurd—Boswell records this on April 10, 1776 —but when he wrote his own preface to Cowley in *Works of the English Poets*, he made a point of saying that so far from being indecent, the poems in "The Mistress" are entirely cerebral. They might, he said, have been written "for hire by a philosophical rhymer who had only heard of another sex"—and he printed them complete. Prior, too. (Boswell once tried to make him say that Prior should be expurgated, and failed miserably.*)

* "I asked whether Prior's poems were to be printed entire: Johnson said they were. I mentioned Lord Hailes's censure of Prior, in his preface to a collection of 'Sacred Poems,' by various hands, published by him at Edinburgh a great many years ago, where he mentions

On the other hand, the very same day that he dismissed the need to clean up Prior, which was September 22, 1777, Johnson mentioned casually that he *was* arranging to have another poet's work bowdlerized. "Talking of Rochester's Poems," Boswell writes, "he said he had given them to Mr. Steevens to castrate for the edition of the Poets." ("Castrate," "geld," and "mutilate" were the customary English verbs for expurgation until around 1800, when the euphemisms "purge," "prune," and "chasten" begin to crop up alongside them. "Bowdlerize" was first used in 1836.)

Steevens duly performed the castration,* omitting a couple of dozen poems that had appeared in most previous editions of Rochester, plus one of the three stanzas of the poem "Upon His Leaving His Mistress." At first blush, so to speak, there appears to be an inconsistency here. Actually, there isn't, or only a slight one. Rochester is a special case. By most standards, including his own, he really did write indecent poetry—well beyond even the most ingenious Scot. He himself tried to keep it from surviving. He never published any. On the contrary, about a month before his death from venereal disease at thirty-three, he ordered the burning of all his "profane

---

'those impure tales which will be the eternal opprobrium of their ingenious author.' JOHNSON. 'Sir, Lord Hailes has forgot. There is nothing in Prior that will excite to lewdness. If Lord Hailes thinks there is, he must be more combustible than other people.' I instanced the tale of 'Paulo Purganti and His Wife.' JOHNSON. 'Sir, there is nothing there, but that his wife wanted to be kissed when poor Paulo was out of pocket. No, Sir, Prior is a lady's book. No lady is ashamed to have it standing in her library."

* The only one of his career. He was primarily a non-expurgating editor of Shakespeare; in fact, it was his edition that Dr. Bowdler later picked to bowdlerize.

and lewd writings" and his "obscene and filthy pictures." It was duly done, in the summer of 1680. One notebook got overlooked, but his mother burned that later.

Manuscript copies of most of his poems were in circulation, however; and an Olympia Press of the day succeeded in getting hold of some. Before he had been dead three months a book was out, containing about forty of Rochester's more lurid poems, and another twenty not by him but simply attached to his name by the publisher. "This book was obviously produced for readers interested in pornography," says the leading modern editor of Rochester. It was mostly sold under counters. The same editor believes that some of the forty genuine poems were doctored to make them dirtier than Rochester had already; if he is right, it makes the book one of the rare cases of anti-bowdlerism.

Rochester's friends eventually countered by bringing out a rival edition—which says firmly on its title page that it contains "only such pieces as may be receiv'd in a vertuous Court." An early winnowing, in short. And for the next two hundred and fifty years there were two canons of Rochester, one *sub rosa* which made him out worse than he was, and one public which made him better. Both were thriving in Johnson's time. Only about twenty years ago did it begin to be settled which poems Lord Rochester actually wrote and which were hung on him by seventeenth- and eighteenth-century purveyors of pornography. Nor has even settling that made Rochester an easy writer to handle. The present standard edition of his work, published in 1953, second edition

1964, omits two undoubtedly authentic poems: "The Imperfect Enjoyment" and "A Ramble in St. James's Park." Each is represented by a note saying, "This poem has been excluded from the present edition at the request of the publisher." The publisher was afraid of being prosecuted.* The only other non-scholarly edition now in print, either in England or America, is a tiny winnowing, containing twenty-four of Rochester's eighty or so poems. Johnson and Steevens, back in 1777, had some reason for giving Rochester special treatment. He is a poet liable to be bowdlerized in any century. And of what is now felt to be his actual work, Steevens omitted only six and one-third poems, changing no word in any of the rest. Bishop Hurd excepted, Englishmen still didn't normally bowdlerize.

Scotsmen, however, now frequently did, and had been for about ten years. Ramsay drew no followers in 1724, but when *The Ever Green* was reprinted in 1761, he attracted first one and then many. Some of them were serious, and some just being prudent, like Ramsay himself. The very first disciple was dead serious. This was Sir David Dalrymple, Lord Hailes, the man whom Boswell quoted against Prior.

Lord Hailes, equally prominent as a judge and as an antiquary, spent much of his life editing old Scottish texts, especially religious ones. Some of them it was no problem to edit complete. But in 1765 he came to one

---

* It seems a genuine fear. One of the milder passages in one of the omitted poems, first describing all men as the sons of mother earth, pictures filial activity in a London park:

> Poor pensive *Lover*, in this place
> Would Frigg upon his *Mother's* Face.

called *Ane Compendious Booke of Godly and Spiritual Sangs.* This was a curious work to begin with. The godly sangs are all in ballad form, like "Sir Patrick Spens" or "Jane Shore," only these ballads are Reformation propaganda. A typical one begins like this:

> With hunts up, with hunt is up,
> It now is perfite day:
> Jesus our King is gane in hunting,
> Quha likes to speed they may.

> Ane cursit fox lay hid in rox
> This lang and mony ane day,
> Devouring sheep, whilk he might creep,
> Nane might him shape away.

> The hunter is Christ, that hunts in haist,
> The hunds are Peter and Paul;
> The Paip is the fox, Rome is the rox
> That rubbis us on the gall.

Lord Hailes reprinted eighteen of these ballads, seventeen of them complete, and one, "The Paip That Pagane Full of Pryd," expurgated in the style of Ramsay. Of the eleven stanzas in it, three end in lines of asterisks. The eighth stanza, for example, appears like this:

> The Parson wald nocht have an hure [whore]
> But twa, and they were bony;
> The Viccar thoght he was pure,
> Behuifet to have as many;
> The parish Priest, that brutal beist
> *   *   *   *   *   *

47

Hay trix, trim goe trix, under the greene-wod-tree.

And the ninth:

> Of Scotland Well, the Friers of Faill,
> The limmery lang has lastit;
> The Monks of Melros made gude kaill
> On Friday when they fastit.
> The silly Nunis * *
> * * * * * *
>
> Hay trix, etc.

Again like Ramsay, Lord Hailes added a footnote. His is no joke, though, but a serious explanation. "Although this satyre be contained in a collection of *Gude and Godly Ballates,*" the note reads, "yet there are some expressions in it, resembling the style of *prophaine sangs.*" Plainly Hailes expected the reader to be satisfied with this laconic account. And here already, in the very dawn of bowdlerism, he has come up against one of the problems which in the end make the practice self-defeating. If, like Wesley, you keep your changes to yourself, and the reviewers don't notice, you may get away with them for a few years, or even for centuries, if the book remains sufficiently obscure. But if you are too honest for that, and you mark your omissions, you are in great danger of inflaming the reader's imagination far more than you would have by printing the full text. The missing lines above, for example, look extremely interesting. When you find out that the last line of Stanza Eight is actually only "He polit [tickled] them privilie," it comes as a severe anti-climax. The action of the nuns in Stanza Nine is livelier: They "cast up their bunnis

[bums]/ And heisit their hippies on hie." But even hip-
heisting is fairly proper compared to what happens in
many a poem of Gay's, much more to what the average
reader is capable of imagining, stimulated by a row of
asterisks.

Five years later, when Hailes published a second expurgated collection of poems, he had become aware of
the problem—but even here his solution has the innocence one generally associates with dawns. The new collection was to replace Ramsay. Lord Hailes had been
meaning for some time to put out a decently expurgated
edition of *The Ever Green*, but the more he studied the
book, the more he thought it would be better to go back
to the Bannatyne Manuscript and expurgate for himself.
Ancient Scottish Poems (Edinburgh, 1770) was the result. Primarily Hailes just winnowed. In the preface he
explains that he has "excluded the indecent, and omitted
the unintelligible poems." Ones like "In Derision of
Wanton Women" do not appear. But winnowing is easier with wheat than with poetry, because a poem is an
aggregate, and a grain of wheat is not. Twice Hailes
couldn't bring himself to exclude a poem by the great
medieval poet William Dunbar (an equal of Chaucer, Sir
Walter Scott said), even though he knew it contained
chaff. Again he resorted to lines of asterisks. But this
time his footnotes are less laconic and more urgent
("The 2 lines which follow . . . are so grossly indecent
that it was necessary to suppress them"); and for the
missing line in Stanza Thirteen of Dunbar's "The Sweirers and the Devill" he tried to slake curiosity by offering
an optional alternative. As printed by Lord Hailes, the
stanza reads:

Ane menstrall said, The Feind me ryfe [tear to pieces],
*   *   *   *   *   *
The devill said, hardly mot it be,
Exerce that craft in all thy lyfe,
Renunce thy God, and cum to me.

Those looking at the notes find the editor explaining that he has omitted the line because of its "blunt coarse style." (It reads, "Gif ocht I do but drink and swyfe"—*swyfe* being the same five-letter word for copulation that Chaucer generally uses. Rochester liked it, too.) "If anyone, however, inclines to fill up the blank," Lord Hailes continues, "he may do it in this manner:

> Ane menstrall said, The Fiend me gore,
> Gif ocht I do bot drynk and rore."

Lord Hailes's do-it-yourself euphemism does not, of course, work as a permanent change in the stanza, in the manner of the permanent changes so many Victorians hoped to make, since it leaves "lyfe" in the fourth line dangling without a rhyme. But it was an attempt, and the first attempt in English, to bowdlerize scrupulously without at the same time leaving gaps in the text. Succeeding Scottish editors, such as Sibbald, Morison, and Hailes's own brother, Alexander Dalrymple, were as expurgation-minded without always being as scrupulous.*

---

* Sibbald, for example, took Ramsay's laughing "sunt lairds" and changed it to "fondlars," with no hint to the reader that he was bowdlerizing. Alexander Dalrymple specifies in the preface to his *Collection of English Songs,* 1796, that he has expurgated "without scruple," and goes on to make the curious boast that his editing exhibits "*excessive delicacy.*"

South of the border, this sort of thing still looked pretty silly. It did, for example, to Bishop Percy, the Englishman who knew most about editing old ballads and who was the nearest Sassenach counterpart to Lord Hailes. Percy was not exactly a wild-eyed pornographer himself. His *Reliques of English Poetry* (1765) is not only a winnowed but a twice-winnowed collection. Percy, who had an old English manuscript to work from, much like Allan Ramsay's old Scottish one, decided at the very beginning to omit most of the really bawdy ballads. He was then intending to stay anonymous. At the last minute, when he was almost ready to publish, he decided to do it under his own name, and promptly dropped nine more. He has been accused of expurgating what he did print.*

* By W. J. Bate of Harvard twenty-five years ago, and more recently in a pseudo-pornographic reprint of *Loose and Humourous Songs from Bishop Percy's Manuscript* (Hatboro, Pa.: 1963). But the case rests chiefly on one stanza from a ballad called "The Boy and the Mantle." In the manuscript Percy was working from, the stanza reads,

> When she had tane the mantle
> And cast it her about;
> Then was shee bare
> All about the buttocks.

After passing through Percy's hands, the stanza says,

> Then was she bare
> 'Before all the rout.'

But this needn't be expurgation. Percy, a man of taste like everyone else then, habitually tried to restore missing rhymes, and this was almost certainly his motive here. He cheerfully printed lines 147-48 of the same ballad:

> She is a bitch and a witch
> And a whore bold.

The single quotation marks around the new line, incidentally, were put there by Percy; he marked all his emendations this way.

51

All the same, he thought Hailes's approach astonishing. The two men used to send each other their books, and Hailes duly sent Percy a copy of *Ancient Scottish Ballads* in 1770. That copy survives, full of Percy's marginal notes. One of the longest is opposite Hailes's account of why he left out the line in "The Sweirers and the Devill." "At this rate," Percy wrote, "half the book might have been expunged. By leaving out the Line in question, the whole Stanza has its meaning annihilated, and this remarkable testimony of the licentiousness of the Minstrels is withheld from the Reader." There spoke the scholar. What's more, Percy added, "The Line omitted might very safely have been inserted, as the only exceptionable word in it is sufficiently obsolete to prevent its giving offense to the most squeamish." (For some evidence that he was right, see p. 196.)

Later the bishop noted what he thought of his colleague's whole approach. "The Editor's squeamish prudery is truly ridiculous," he said. Ramsay being long dead, only an English resurrector of old poetry could have thought this. In Scotland, even the few editors who began by laughing at prudery tended to wind up adopting it. John Pinkerton, for example, was very superior in the preface to *Ancient Scotish Poems* (1786). He had seen and grasped Lord Hailes's problem. "As to castrating a book and putting asterisks," he wrote, "it tends solely to give a work an imperfect look, and to raise far worse ideas in the guessing reader than those omitted." As for him, his book admittedly contained some work "tinctured with immodesty." But, he boasted, "the reader has it as it stands in the Manuscript."

Two years later he was writing in quite a different vein. He wanted to dedicate his next book to the Earl of Buchan, who wasn't sure he liked the proposed contents. Pinkerton backed down at once. "I could not conceive, my lord," he wrote, "that Lindsay's piece should be so immodest. But it only forms *one* of *six* poems meant to be published together; and all the obscene parts shall be castrated, so I hope your lordship will have no cause to regret that the collection is inscribed to you." His lordship didn't. When *Scotish Poems, Reprinted From Scarce Editions* actually appeared in 1792, it was fairly riddled with asterisks, by no means all of them confined to Lindsay's "Eight Interludes." It is the very exceptional late-eighteenth-century Scottish editor, like David Herd, who didn't expurgate at all.*

England soon began to catch up with Scotland, however, as delicacy became more and more fashionable, the reading public began its long slow growth, and even as Methodism spread. The first (very slightly) purified Shakespeare and the first (very discreetly) purified Bible I shall treat elsewhere. An Oxford clergyman named William Lipscomb did the first expurgated edition of Chaucer in 1795. (Pinkerton the Scot had proposed one back in 1783, but couldn't find a publisher.) About the same time, a former New York lawyer named Lindley Murray published the first of his school readers, "purified of everything which might stain the delicacy of

---

* Even he leaned that way a little. *Ancient and Modern Scottish Songs,* 1776, includes an occasional passage like this:

> When she comes hame, she lays on the lads,
> The lasses she ca's them baith b——s and j——s,
> And ca's mysel' ay ane cuckold carlie.

their [adolescents'] minds." Murray, who was living in
England—he had been a Loyalist, like so many New
Yorkers, and had had to give up his law practice and
emigrate in 1784—ranks as the first American to promote bowdlerism. He gets this credit less for the readers,
which are careful selections rather than true expurgations, than for his never-realized plan to put out a rival
Works of the English Poets, in which Lord Rochester
would have been only one among scores of castrati.

In 1805, the Rev. James Plumptre of Cambridge (who
also gets separate attention later) came on the field with
the first of the collections of songs in which he not only
castrated but did a good deal of plastic surgery. The
same year an anonymous editor for the publisher Tabart
put out an edition of *Robinson Crusoe* "Revised for the
Use of Young Persons"—which principally means that
he cut it to a third of its length. But the spirit of the age
was working in the editor. In his foreword he says that
the abridgment is good, but that the really important
task has been to make the book "as unexceptionable as
possible." It's just the phrase a Victorian would have
used.

By then, the idea of expurgation had penetrated the
very center of the literary establishment, in England and
Scotland alike. For example, it had reached Joseph Warton, the great Oxford scholar, and it had reached Sir
Walter Scott. As a matter of fact, it reached them both
in the same context. Warton had edited the works of
Pope in 1797, and been a good deal criticized because his
edition was complete. "It was very bold and *very indecent* in the *Reverend* Dr. Warton" to print all of Pope,

wrote Thomas Mathias, who ran a sort of one-man, once-a-year *Times Literary Supplement* then, complete with anonymity. Mathias quoted four lines of Pope from Warton's edition:

> Or when a tight neat girl will serve the turn
> In errant pride continue * * * !
> I'm a plain man, whose maxim is profest,
> The thing at hand is of all things the best.

"I, though an anonymous layman," he went on, "refuse to print the passage *in full* which the *Reverend* Doctor Warton has printed and sanctioned *with his name* as Editor of Pope's Works. . . . I solemnly impeach him of a high crime and misdemeanor before his country." *
Perhaps because he found such attacks alarming, even from a minority of critics, Warton began to move with the times. His next major project was to be a definitive edition of Dryden, and he decided to make it "Dryden a la Hurd; that is to say, upon the same system as the castrated edition of Cowley."

Warton, who was seventy-five when his Pope came out, died in 1800, having castrated only two volumes of Dryden. (It's one of the mildest operations on record.)

---

* Thomas Mathias, *The Pursuits of Literature* (7th ed., 1798), pp. 324 f. The expurgated line reads, "In errant pride, continue stiff, and burn," the stiffness referring to an erection. To a modern eye this doesn't seem particularly worse than some of Mathias' own lines in the verse parts of *Pursuits*, such as I, 131–32:

> Some plain positions lay, as simply thus;
> Marriage *consists* in—*actu cöitus.*

Doubtless Latin makes the difference.

It took his younger son until 1811 to get two more volumes ready, and to bring out the four. During the long interval, Sir Walter Scott moved in. Like Goldsmith, but on a grander scale, Scott was always in need of money. When a publisher offered him £750 to get a rival edition of Dryden out first, he accepted on the spot. That was in 1805.

Scott began work by asking half a dozen friends what a definitive edition should be. One of the first to answer was George Ellis, the former editor of the *Anti-Jacobin Review*, who favored clean definitions. He suggested that Scott read Hurd's Cowley, and then go and do likewise. Scott sent back a now-famous letter, refusing. "I will not castrate John Dryden," he said.

> I would as soon castrate my own father, as I believe Jupiter did of yore. What would you say to any man who would castrate Shakspere, or Massinger, or Beaumont and Fletcher? I don't say but that it may be very proper to select correct passages for the use of boarding schools and colleges. . . . But in making an edition of a man of genius's work for libraries and collections, and such I conceive a complete edition of Dryden to be, I must give my author as I find him, and will not tear out the page, even to get rid of the blot, little as I like it. Are not the pages of Swift, and even of Pope, loaded with indecency, and often of the most disgusting kind? and do we not see them upon all shelves and dressing-tables, and in all boudoirs? Is not Prior the most indecent of tale-tellers, not even excepting La Fon-

taine? and how often do we see his work in female hands? *

Ellis wrote back to say that Scott must of course do what he thought right. But he couldn't resist adding that a few torn pages would have been nice.

Whatever is in point of expression vulgar—whatever disgusts the taste—whatever might have been written by any fool, and is therefore unworthy of Dryden—whatever might have been suppressed without exciting a moment's regret in the mind of any of his admirers—*ought*, in my opinion, to be suppressed . . . but it is foolish to say so much, after promising to say nothing. Indeed I own *myself* guilty of possessing all his works in a very indifferent edition, and I shall certainly purchase a better one whenever you put it in my power.

About the same time, another friend of Scott was giving him very different advice. He had also consulted Wordsworth about the edition. Wordsworth said he didn't really care for Dryden—"there is not a single image from nature in the whole body of his works," and there is far too much sensuality. All the same, he concluded firmly, there is only one way to proceed. "A correct text is the first object of any editor—then such notes as explain difficult or obscure passages."

* Scott was not the simple prig the second half of this letter suggests. The very month before, he was quoting with delight to a young cousin who was going abroad the following advice from an old clergyman to *his* traveling son: "There is a thing called Religion, think of it in the morning; there is something called honour, do not forget that in the transactions of the day; and for the rest, drink and whore—as little as you can."

Thus fortified, Scott set about giving the correct text. This mood lasted about three months. Then he wrote Ellis again. "After all," he said, "there are some passages . . . that will hardly bear reprinting, unless I would have the Bishop of London and the whole corps of Methodists about my ears." He sent Ellis two such passages to look at: "not only double entendres, but good plain single-entendres." One was from Dryden's translation of Lucretius, Book IV ("Concerning the Nature of Love") and the other from Ovid's "Instructions to His Mistress." Exactly which passages they were, I don't know, but there were plenty in both works capable of distressing Bishop Porteus. There is the section of Lucretius, for example, beginning "Of like importance is the posture, too/ In which the genial feat of Love we do." It goes on to advise women who wish to get pregnant not to "frisk and heave" while performing the feat, and so on.

Scott was obviously confident that Ellis would support his tentative decision not to print such passages, and just writing for a formal blessing. "I fear," he said, "that without absolutely gelding the bard, it will be indispensable to circumcise him a little, by leaving out some of the most obnoxious lines."

Whether Ellis was put off by the metaphor, or whether he had been converted by Scott's previous declaration of high principle it is impossible to tell. At any rate, he now did an about-face, and saved Scott from being a bowdlerizer in fact as well as in intention. "Having undertaken a complete edition of Dryden, you are not at liberty to leave out the obnoxious passages to

which you have directed me," he now answered; and
Scott obediently left them in.

Two years later, when the whole eighteen volumes of
Dryden had been published, Ellis went further still. "I
ought to have considered," he wrote, "that whatever
Dryden wrote must, for some reason or other, be interesting; that his bombast and indelicacy, however disgusting, were not without their use to anyone who took an
interest in our literary history." Though the year was
1808, once again the eighteenth century was speaking to
the twentieth, almost the last words it spoke. The year
before Ellis wrote that sentence, bowdlerism had burst
into bloom. Leigh Hunt, then a youth of twenty-three,
had completed his first expurgated text, Charles Lamb
had sat down to castrate Beaumont and Fletcher, and the
first edition of Bowdler's *Family Shakespeare* had appeared.

CHAPTER THREE

Dr. Bowdler and His Sister

****

> *The unbounded licentiousness of this and many other ages has made it almost impossible for men to come any thing towards years of discretion, without such a knowledge of vice, in theory at least, as must render them incapable of a proper command over their imaginations.*
>
> ELIZABETH S. BOWDLER, 1775

> *So much superior are the qualities of the Heart to those of the Understanding, that could unsullied Innocence be purchased by the sacrifice of every other consideration, the price would be cheap.*
>
> JOHN BOWDLER, JR., 1801

> *If any word or expression is of such a nature, that the first impression which it excites is an impression of obscenity, that word ought not to be spoken, or written, or printed; and if printed, it ought to be erased.*
>
> DR. THOMAS BOWDLER, 1823

THE YEAR 1807 contains three events of some importance in the history of Shakespeare. One represents a gain: he jumped the Atlantic. That is, a Boston publisher brought out the first successful edition of his plays to be printed

in the New World. It was aimed at college students, and it hit the mark squarely. Ninety-nine of the 175 undergraduates at Harvard bought copies, 28 of the 100 at Brown, and so on. These youths—the typical boy then entered college at fourteen and took his B.A. at eighteen —bought the book for their own pleasure, incidentally, not to use in class. Shakespeare wasn't taught in colleges for another fifty years.

The second event was also a gain, though a less clear-cut one. *Tales from Shakespear* came out in London, attributed on the title page to Charles Lamb. The attribution was not wholly false. Of the twenty tales, Lamb had done six, and his sister Mary fourteen. The book was intended as a child's introduction to Shakespeare, though it turned out to be chiefly "young ladies" who read it—that is, English girls the same age as Harvard and Brown students.

Lamb's Tales, too, was an immediate success. It went through five editions in ten years; and even before the first one had sold out, a leading magazine was saying that as a book for the young "it claims the very first place, and stands unique, and without rival or competitor, unless perhaps we except *Robinson Crusoe*."

The third Shakespearean event of 1807 was a sharp loss. The *Family Shakespeare* appeared, published obscurely in the little city of Bath. (It was the first Shakespeare ever printed there.) This was to become the most famous of all expurgated books, and thirty years later its editor's name turned into a standard verb. But in 1807 it was a minor provincial edition, and no one knew the editor's name. There was just an unsigned preface, saying that the time had come to remove from Shakespeare "everything that can raise a blush on the cheek of modesty"—which turned out to be about ten per cent of all he wrote. Only after a couple of years did it begin to leak out that the editor was Dr. Thomas Bowdler, a retired physician turned country gentleman. (He had quit practice at thirty-one, when his father died, leaving him wealthy.)

It is illuminating to compare these three books of a year. The American entry is a holdover. America was still remote in 1807, and new fashions took a long time to reach us. To bring out a complete edition of Shakespeare, and then to sell it principally to teenage boys, marks the Boston publisher as a trifle old-fashioned. He would have known better in London. (We were still behind the times in 1823, when a Philadelphia publisher brought out the first works-of-the-English-poets to be published in America. Those fifty small volumes *are* expurgated, but in a quaint, ineffective, eighteenth-century way. Their story appears in Chapter Seven.)

The two English books, however, were completely modern—one was even a little ahead of its time. The *Tales* had been suggested to Mary Lamb as something certain to please the market, and the person who made the suggestion—Shelley's future mother-in-law, as it happens—was right. Mrs. Godwin's only mistake was in supposing that simplified and purified versions of Shakespeare would appeal more to pre-teens than to teenagers themselves. To this extent she was less forward-looking than the editor of the *Family Shakespeare*, who from the beginning had seen the purity market as including just about everyone under twenty, and many adults as well. In 1807 this was still visionary, but half a generation later the vision was triumphantly vindicated.

Modernity is not all the two English books had in common. Lamb's *Tales* and Bowdler's *Shakespeare*, one still so reputable and the other now so disreputable, can be made to sound and to some extent really are remarkably similar books. Both take twenty of Shakespeare's thirty-six plays and revise them into innocence. Both omit not only everything that might start a blush, but everything that might provoke a yawn, which is to say that both operate on aesthetic as well as moral grounds. And both were the work of women who chose not to take public credit, but to hide behind their brothers' names. In the case of Henrietta Maria Bowdler, known to her family as Harriet, the hiding was so successful that only after a hundred and sixty years has she emerged as the true author of bowdlerism.

There are equally vast differences, to be sure. Mary Lamb did not try to weed Shakespeare like a garden, but spaded up the old plots and planted fresh. Or to drop this metaphor (a favorite with Shakespeare himself and with several generations of expurgators *), she rewrote the plays in such charming prose that Lamb's tales became new objects in their own right. She did it in a fairly light-hearted way, moved at least as much by the sixty

---

* "Fie on't! ah fie! 'Tis an unweeded garden," says Hamlet of life itself. Francis Gentleman said the same of *Romeo and Juliet* in 1770—"many weeds in its original state to choak up some beautiful flowers of genius." The culmination was probably Leigh Hunt's 1855 description of a typical Beaumont and Fletcher play as "a torrent of feculence beside a chosen garden." That's what made the weeds grow.

guineas her publisher had offered as by the opportunity to protect young people from Shakespeare's indelicacy. Harriet Bowdler, on the other hand, did weed the plays, keeping what she regarded as the flowers, and pulling the nettles with unsparing hand and with the very highest motives.

Mary Lamb stayed off her title page partly because of her Lizzie Bordenish past, and partly through obedience to the same prejudice against women writers that led Jane Austen and the Brontës to hide their names for a while. In any case, it was no more than a dozen years before her role became publicly known and she began to be listed in reference books as co-author of the *Tales.* Harriet Bowdler's long concealment is a much more complicated story, and one which even now is hard to explain. This is true of most things about her and about the *Family Shakespeare.* The Bowdlers were a passionately private family.

One of the few clear facts about the *Family Shakespeare* is that it's an absolutely typical work for the family that produced it. Most Bowdlers over a span of three generations were inclined to expurgate. If one were to write a detective story, a kind of "Who Castrated William Shakespeare?" at least six Bowdlers would be under suspicion, and another three would be exempt only because they weren't alive at the right moment. Besides Dr. Bowdler himself, the candidates would include his mother, his father, his sister Jane, his brother John, his sister Harriet, and his nephews Thomas, Charles, and John. All had the combination of prudery and zeal which leads to expurgation.

The mother and father, in fact, *were* expurgators, two of the earliest and most aristocratic in England. Squire Thomas Bowdler (1720?–1785) did not publish any bowdlerized books, but almost every night of his life he bowdlerized orally, reading aloud to his family. The rise and fall of paternal voices was as characteristic of living rooms in the 1760s as the glow of television screens is now.

Shakespeare was the squire's favorite victim. "In the perfection of reading few men were equal to my father," Dr. Bowdler once wrote, "and such were his good taste, his delicacy, and his prompt discretion, that his family listened with delight to Lear, Hamlet, and Othello, without knowing that those matchless tragedies contained words and expressions improper to be pronounced; and without having any reason to suspect that any parts of the plays had been omitted by the circumspect and judicious reader." These childhood evenings, Dr. Bowdler added, were what inspired the *Family Shakespeare*.

The circumspect and judicious reader's wife went further. She did publish an expurgation, or at least a proposal for one. Mrs. Bowdler, a daughter of Sir John Cotton, fifth baronet of the great book-collecting family, was a learned woman, and learned most of all in Bible scholarship. In 1775 she published a small book—anonymous, like fourteen other books published by Bowdlers over the next eighty years—called *A Commentary on the Song of Solomon Paraphrased*. The paraphrase was one Bishop Percy had done in 1764, and Mrs. Bowdler didn't like it. In particular, she complained that Percy, "intending to clear this beautiful Poem from the false charge of indecency . . . himself gives fresh occasion for the charge." Her commentary includes a series of proposed expurgations. For example, Percy has the Bride say amorously of the Bridegroom, "He shall lie all night between my breasts." Mrs. Bowdler suggested changing that "he" to "it," meaning a bundle of myrrh. She had two reasons. "That he should lye between her breasts would be impossible," she pointed out, revealing a literal-mindedness which few expurgators have failed to share. "Besides," she went on, "the indelicacy of the expression would suit ill with this poem."

Mrs. Bowdler had other objections, too. The Bride several times uses the word "bed." This seemed as disgusting to her as it later did to her son for Juliet Capulet, when *she* was a bride, to wish openly that night would come. And every time Percy let the Bride say "bed," Mrs. Bowdler would add a note wishing that he had made her say something harmless, like "bridal chariot."

It is fair to add that she did not advocate the kind of unlimited tampering that John Wesley went in for. When she came to the famous line, "Thy belly is as an heap of wheat," which Percy left unchanged from the King James Version, she actually defended it. "Some would understand this verse and Ch. V. 14. of garments embroidered," she wrote, "as thinking it more modest. If it can be so rendered, without force to the sense of the original, I am well pleased to take it so. But perhaps, had these writers considered the daughters of Jerusalem as alone present, and the circumstances of coming from the bath, they would not have looked upon the passage as any way indecent." Already in 1775 it was a Bowdler editorial trait to be firm but scrupulous.

Of this couple's six children, at least four shared the parental interest in pure books. One died in childhood, and of one I know only that her name was Frances and that she was alive in 1825. The other four, however, demonstrably inherited the true family temperament, as well as a good deal of money and an assured social position. (Dr. Bowdler made regular rounds of visits to various barons and earls he knew, and even delayed an expurgation once, to avoid hurting the feelings of one.*)

Jane, the eldest, did no actual expurgating, but she could have. She was a clever, tormented spinster who died at forty, leaving behind the usual anonymous book: *Poems and Essays by a Lady Lately Deceased,* 1786. In it Jane said nothing about expurgation. She said a great deal, however, about the need for delicacy and about how "continued watchfulness must restrain the freedom of conversation." The book was well written, and had a considerable success; Queen Charlotte once read it for comfort three times in a single winter.

John, the second child, was a country squire like his father, but one even more concerned with purity. He had, for example, a standard letter he used to send to the daughters of his friends when they were about to get married. It told, in ten numbered paragraphs, how to be

* "I see by my Swansea Papers that my Old Friend Lord Sheffield is at last departed. While he lived, I would not have given him pain by what follows.

"What would you say to an attempt at publishing an Edition of Gibbon from which all Indecent, Immoral, and Irreligious Expressions should be excluded?" Dr. Bowdler to the Earl of Hardwicke, June 6, 1821.

a good wife. Paragraph Seven covered social discourse. "Above all," John urged the girls of the late eighteenth century, "avoid everything which has the *least tendency* to indelicacy or indecorum. Few women have *any idea* how much men are disgusted by the slightest approach to these in any female. . . . By attending the nursery or sick bed, women are too apt to acquire a habit of conversing on such subjects in language which men of delicacy are shocked at."

Apart from form letters, John wrote very little. But his anonymous pamphlet *Reform or Ruin* (1797) went through even more editions than Jane's essays. And his poetry anthology (*Poems Divine and Moral*, 1821) is an old man's jump onto the family bandwagon. As he explains with some dignity in the preface, "My object was not to produce a collection of elegant poetry, but to *do good*. . . . I therefore . . . extracted and abridged freely, and even ventured, in a few instances, to alter a word or phrase when not suited to my purpose." * Presumably this is what bowdlerism feels like to any bowdlerist.

Harriet and Thomas, the two youngest children, carried the family traits most strongly of all. Both were high-minded intellectuals. A glimpse of Harriet as a

---

* Some of the cuts necessary in order to do good go far beyond ordinary bowdlerism. For example, Dryden's "Character of a Good Parson," otherwise complete, is missing the two lines in which Dryden says the good old man never goes to St. Paul's Cathedral

To chaffer for Preferment with his Gold,
Where Bishopricks and *sine Cures* are sold.

Presumably John Bowdler felt it better for people not to know that such traffic ever took place, at least in the Church of England.

young woman survives in a letter written by Sir Gilbert
Elliot, Earl of Minto, in 1787:

> On Thursday, I dined at Mundy's with Mrs.
> Gally, etc., and a Miss Bowdler. She is, I believe, a
> blue-stocking, but what the colour of that part of
> her dress is must be mere conjecture, as you will
> easily believe when I tell you that . . . she said she
> never looked at [the dancers in operas] but always
> kept her eyes shut the whole time, and when I asked
> her why, she said it was so *indelicate* she could not
> bear to look.

By the time the *Family Shakespeare* appeared, Sir Gilbert would have said *the* Miss Bowdler. Despite the
anonymity of her best-selling *Sermons on the Doctrines
and Duties of Christianity*, which went through fifty
printings in fifty-two years, she had become a prominent
woman. Everyone in evangelical circles knew the story
of how the Bishop of London, completely taken in, had
written care of the publisher to beg her to accept a
parish in his diocese. Half the leaders of high-minded
thought in England were in correspondence with her,
and many had visited the salon she kept in Bath.

Dr. Bowdler had a lesser reputation but an equally
high mind. Having freed himself from medicine in
1785—he had a physical aversion to sick people—he
spent fifteen years in London, busy in prison reform
work with Sir Charles Bunbury, busy attending meetings
of the Royal Society, busy playing chess. He still had
plenty of time to haunt London blue-stocking circles
and talk books. He became a special friend of Mrs.

Montagu, "Queen of the Blues," by then an old woman, and particularly admired her famous essay on Shakespeare. This proved him, against the sneers of Voltaire, to be the greatest dramatic writer in the world—except for his vulgarity. ("Every scene in which Doll Tearsheet appears is indecent, and therefore not only indefensible but inexcusable.") It is probable he knew her private expurgation of Gibbon.* He also began to write books himself, and to sign his name to them, the only member of the family so far who did.

In 1800 he left London, partly in disgust at the repeated failure of prison reform—it was just beginning to succeed when the economic advantages of transporting convicts to Australia for forced labor caused Parliament to forget the whole thing—and partly to get away from the smog. He leased a country estate on the Isle of Wight, and there in 1806 at the age of fifty-two he got married, the second and last Bowdler of his generation who did. Whether his wife, being the widow of a naval officer, was addicted to coarse language, or whether the trouble lay elsewhere, the marriage was not a happy one, and after a few years he and the ex-Mrs. Trevennen seem to have lived apart. So great was the family passion for privacy that when one of his nephews wrote a forty-page obituary of him in 1825, he never even mentioned this marriage, with the result that Dr. Bowdler is

---

* "I remember Mrs. Montagu's telling Mr. Gibbon or his Friends, that she had order'd her Bookseller to leave out his 2 last Chapters in her Copy: She would have been much better pleased to have this excellent Refutation [the one Lord Hailes had just written] to bind up at the End of them, & I hope 8vo Impressions will be prepared for the smaller Editions." Bishop Percy to Lord Hailes, May 30, 1789. The octavo refutation never did appear.

still usually assumed to be a bachelor. There were no children.

John Bowdler had many, though, including three sons. All were old enough in 1807 to have expurgated Shakespeare, and each of the three young men had it in his character to have done so. The eldest, another Thomas, did in fact help his uncle with the expurgation of Gibbon a dozen years later. Charles, the youngest, though he was literate and high-minded and once wrote a book called *The Religion of the Heart*, did none. But the middle brother, John, Jr., is the really interesting candidate.

John, Jr., was in many ways the ablest and most appealing member of the whole family—though all the Bowdlers seem to have been nice if rather earnest people. John, Jr., was earnest even beyond the rest. As a young law student in 1802, he had already decided that his public school should have expurgated its textbooks. A friend protested that no dirty line was ever assigned for reading or discussed in class.

> You fight hard, I see [John, Jr., wrote back], for the use of the classics as conducted at Westminster, but I cannot allow your defence. The object is to hinder the mind of youth being corrupted, which can never be effected by the mere omission of every offensive passage in the public lessons . . . and perhaps no boy ever omitted an indecent line in reading, merely because he knew he should not be allowed to construe it."

This may be true of most boys, but it was not true of John, Jr., himself. That same spring, when he was nineteen, he read Juvenal's *Satires* twice through, omitting, however, the sixth and ninth, which he had been told were indecent. He was, of course, reading alone for pleasure, with construing for class quite out of the question.

Alone of the three boys, John, Jr., also has a traceable connection with the *Family Shakespeare*. When it appeared, and was promptly attacked in a magazine that might have been expected to approve, it was he who rushed to the defense. Even his early death makes him suspect. All the Bowdlers I have discussed except his grandparents and his Aunt Jane were alive and healthy when the second and revised edition of the *Family Shakespeare* came out in 1818. Why shouldn't any of them have done his own revision, if he had been the original editor? But the death of John, Jr., in 1815, aged thirty-one, would explain why Dr. Bowdler took over, as he undoubtedly did.

Hindsight makes things easy, though. At the time, few of these facts were known to anyone except the Bowdlers themselves and a narrow circle of Harriet's friends. To all but them, the four little volumes that appeared anonymously at Bath in 1807 could have been edited not only by any Bowdler but by almost anyone at all—Coleridge (he *said* in his Shakespeare lectures that there was a lot of obscenity in the plays that had probably been inserted by early actors, and implied it should come out), Mrs. Inchbald, Jane Austen, anyone. The only certainties were that here was Shakespeare mutilated as no English author had been mutilated before, and that the person who had done it wished to remain anonymous.

A close reader might have figured out a little more from internal evidence, notably that the hidden expurgator must be a Protestant. A Catholic, a Jew, or an atheist would have made different cuts in the profanity. Shakespeare is richly profane in many modes, and the expurgator duly slashed away—as, indeed, an occasional government censor had done as early as 1606, when Parliament passed an act "for the preventing and avoiding of the great abuse of the Holy Name of God in Stage playes, Interludes, Maygames, Shows, and such like." But whereas the government censor had frowned more or less impartially, in this new edition only some profanity counted.

What counted most was irreverence toward God or Jesus. No character in the *Family Shakespeare* takes God's name in vain. This is plainly not some atheist's distaste for the word altogether. The characters are allowed to invoke it to make a solemn occasion more solemn. When the Queen hears, in *Richard II*, that Bolingbroke has landed, she is perfectly free to say solemnly, "Now God in heaven forbid." But Lancelot Gobbo, the comic servant in *The Merchant of Venice*, is not free, when he is joking about his proposed departure from Shylock's service, to say, "I will run as far as God has any ground." The context of a servant quitting his job is too trivial, and he has to curb his tongue, spoil the alliteration, and say, "I will run as far as there is any ground."

The characters are even more sparing in their references to Jesus. They not only don't use His name to swear with, they prefer not to say it at all, except in formal prayers. The robbed travelers in *Henry IV*, for

73

example, were made by Shakespeare to exclaim, "Jesu bless us!" when Falstaff and the others held them up, and they certainly intended no impiety. They were just scared. But now they have grown braver; they clench their teeth and say nothing.

On the other hand, it is perfectly all right for Falstaff himself to say "By'r lady" as much as he likes, since this is only a reference to the Virgin Mary. He can also say " 'Sblood." This only means "God's blood," and that mostly refers to transubstantiated communion wine, and a reference to a cup of Catholic wine is no oath at all. It had been to the government censor, licensing a new play (not Shakespeare's) in 1611. The Catholic past was much closer then. For that matter, whether Harriet Bowdler would have permitted the phrase in its full form is an open question—perhaps she wouldn't have. Yet she did sometimes change the exclamation "Marry" back to its original form of "Mary," just to make clear who was being sworn by, so one can't be sure. One *can* be sure that "by the mess" was an acceptable oath, since this allusion to mass is always retained. (The government censor cut it in 1611.) Captain Jamy in *Henry V* says it, though in the same scene Captain Macmorris is firmly restrained from saying "by Chrish" in his Irish accent, and Captain Fluellen from saying "by Cheshu" in his Welsh one. Plainly a Protestant hand.

This is about as far as an 1807 detective could have gone. For any further identification of the editor he would have had to wait for external evidence. The first hint came in 1808, and it was misleading. It came in response to one of the three reviews the *Family Shake-*

speare got. Two were ordinary short notices. The *Monthly Review* said briefly, "All admirers of Shakespeare must be aware that such a *castrated* version of his plays has long been desirable." The *British Critic* said almost as briefly, "There are doubtless squeamish people to whom these mutilations would be acceptable. In printing from Beaumont and Fletcher, such a process would have been necessary [Charles Lamb thought so, too, and was at that very time engaged in it]; Shakespeare, we should think, might have escaped."

The third review, a long one, was in a magazine specially edited for squeamish people. This was the *Christian Observer*, and its reviewer was appalled. He felt the expurgation wasn't nearly thorough enough. An adequate job, he indicated, would practically consist of a volume of blank pages. He also felt that expurgating Shakespeare was a poor idea to begin with, since it might tempt people to read him. The reviewer didn't put it this way, but the gist of his complaint is that expurgating plays is rather like setting up clinics to treat prostitutes. The girls may emerge free of disease, but they're still prostitutes, and decent men should keep away.*

---

* The view that a fallen work of literature, like a fallen woman, cannot be redeemed was fairly widespread. It is most funnily expressed by the Scottish poet Allan Cunningham in the introduction to his *Songs of Scotland* (1825). Discussing the "unusually licentious and indelicate" songs of pre-Reformation Scotland, Cunningham says, "It has been my good or bad fortune to retrieve several of these regretted worthies; and it has cost me a labour equal to original composition to recall them back to something like modesty and discretion. I am not sure that I shall act prudently in pointing them out; the antiquary will regret the change of what was old into what is new, and the nice and the inquisitive will regard them with a

This attack from a supposed friend drew an indignant and very well-written reply from someone who called himself "Philalethes," or "Obscurity Lover." It was really John, Jr., of course. He didn't defend the actual edition ("Let it live or perish as it deserves"), but he defended both drama and expurgation with great skill. And in the course of his article, he constantly refers to the editor, whom he evidently knows, as "he." Another piece of evidence, partly just of how the English language uses gender, but one that certainly doesn't point to his Aunt Harriet.

The next year a much bigger piece of evidence appeared, a seemingly conclusive one. In a note in one of his own books, a faculty member at Cambridge University guardedly praised the *Family Shakespeare*. (He was guarded because he, too, thought the expurgation didn't go far enough.) Still, he concluded, "The World is much indebted to the excellent Editor, to which appellation, I believe, may now be added the name of Thomas Bowdler, Esq."

Since this man knew perfectly well that the excellent editor was really Harriet, he was deliberately throwing people off the scent. Why should Harriet want him to? Like the color of her stockings, this must remain mere conjecture, but it seems safe to assume that she wanted to avoid the odium of admitting that she, an unmarried gentlewoman of fifty, understood Shakespeare's obscenity well enough systematically to remove it. Brothers

---

suspicious eye, and imagine that under the outward garb of decency and decorum the evil spirit still remains—that I have not wholly succeeded in evoking [*sic*] the fiend of licentiousness."

were the recognized recourse when sisters wished to stay concealed.*

At any rate, from 1809 on Dr. Bowdler has been concealing his. When the second edition of the *Family Shakespeare* appeared, his name was on the title page as sole editor. It remained there until the book finally went out of print well over a hundred years later. He usurped the credit in Harriet's very obituary, of which the second sentence reads, "This lady was sister to the late Thomas Bowdler, Esq., F.R.S. and S.A., the editor of the 'Family Shakespeare.' " As recently as the 1950s he was being tried by the BBC and mocked by Bertrand Russell as the author of bowdlerism. There have even been attempts to account for the practice (also his supposed bachelorhood) on the basis of a mysterious accident he had at the age of eight—just as attempts have been made to explain the novels of Henry James on the basis of *his* "obscure hurt."

All the time, however, a small circle knew that Harriet was the family innovator. She covered her tracks well, and written evidence is scarce, but there is some. One is a

---

* The recourse was so familiar that every now and then a brother had trouble getting credit for his legitimate work. This happened to the poet Henry Kirke White in 1804. He had just, at nineteen, brought out his first book, while still an undergraduate at Cambridge. His name appeared on the title page, but no one paid the slightest attention. Soon after the book appeared, he wrote angrily to his brother, "The Nottingham gentry, knowing me too poor to buy my poems [*i.e.*, have them ghost-written], thought they could do no better than to place it to the account of family affection, and lo! Mrs. Smith is become the sole author, who has made use of her brother's name as a feint! I heard of this report first covertly: it was said that Mrs. Smith was the principal writer: next it was said that I was the author of one of the inferior smaller pieces only; and lastly . . . that my 'sister was the sole quill-driver of the family.' "

letter from her young protégé the Rev. Robert Mayow
of Bath to the faculty member at Cambridge. This was
James Plumptre; and he was an old and close friend of
Harriet's. The letter was written in 1811, just after
Plumptre had finished his own ambitious expurgation,
The English Drama Purified. Mayow had a small suggestion to make. "I don't know whether it be your intention
to publish your 'English Drama' so that it may be uni-
form in point of size with Mrs. Bowdler's Shakespere. If
it were of that size, perhaps it might recommend it to
those who have her work."

"Mrs." was, of course, the common usage for spinsters
of good family in Harriet's time. Plumptre uses it for her
specifically in the next letter. This one is from him to
Thomas Burgess, Bishop of St. David's, and a longtime
friend of Harriet and Thomas Bowdler both. Plumptre
was trying to get his support for a reformed National
Theater. On September 4, 1821, he wrote a wheedling
letter which begins:

My Lord,
    Agreeably to your obliging permission, commu-
nicated to me by Mrs. H. Bowdler in a letter of the
31st ult., I enclose a copy of my printed Letter to
the Marquis of Hertford. . . .

On September 8th the Bishop replied:

Rev. Sir,
    I thank you for your obliging letter. . . . It
would be a most fortunate circumstance for the
country, if the theatre could be deprived of its im-

moral tendency. . . . Mrs. Bowdler and her Brother have done a good deal toward moralizing Shakespeare; but it will, I think, be more difficult to moralize the Playhouse and the Players.

By 1821, when this letter was written, the second edition of the *Family Shakespeare* had been out for three years, and Dr. Bowdler had indeed joined his sister as a bowdlerizer.

After Harriet's death in 1830, the nephew who settled her estate provided one more piece of evidence. This was the Rev. Thomas Bowdler, the same nephew who helped his uncle expurgate Gibbon. He was now in Bath disposing of his aunt's belongings. One parcel of about ten books he sent to a neighbor, Mrs. William Cowburn, with this note:

Dear Mrs. Cowburn,

Your Husband is so very scrupulous about accepting a few books from a friend, that I venture to address myself to you, because I am sure of a request being favorably treated. . . . The Shakspeare is my Aunt's edition, but may serve for young folks; and it is pleasant to have a copy for common use.

Mrs. Cowburn did overcome her husband's scruples, and Cowburn himself wrote on the flyleaf of one book: "The Gift of the Rev'd Thos. Bowdler, at Bath, in March, 1830, after the death of his Aunt Mrs. Harrietta Bowdler, whose book it was, and whose autograph above, gives additional value to it." Mayow, Plumptre,

Bishop Burgess, and the Cowburns all knew the true story, and all kept their mouths shut. *Delicatesse oblige.* The edition that Mr. Cowburn thus acquired is not especially interesting, as expurgations go. Harriet was far too levelheaded a woman to try to remake plays altogether, as her friend Mr. Plumptre did, or even to go out of her way to find offensive passages, as so many Victorians did. Expurgators can take offense at almost anything, but historically they have devoted themselves almost entirely to religion, sex, and politics. Harriet stuck to religion and sex. On Shakespeare's religious terminology, as I have indicated, she did a standard Protestant expurgation. On his sexual terminology she was equally conventional. She substituted very few words of her own, though the greatest single interest of bowdlerism lies in the substitutions that a bowdlerist makes—like De Quincey (here a self-bowdlerist) using the word "prostitute" in the 1822 edition of *Confessions of an Opium Eater* and substituting "the outcasts and pariahs of our female population" in 1856; like Dr. Bowdler changing Shakespeare's "Well, Susan is with God" to a theologically neutral "Well, Susan's dead"; like a later editor of Shakespeare systematically changing "cuckold" to "wronged man," which asks a very different emotional response. Harriet did virtually none of this. She just cut.

As to what she cut, it will make sense to wait a minute and compare her edition to her brother's, which came out in 1818.

What led Dr. Bowdler to take over as family expurgator is not known, at least not to me. He may have felt that having received public credit for the first edition, he had in honor actually to do the second. Harriet may have wanted to find something to keep him busy after the break-up of his marriage. Both may have felt that the book ought to be transferred from a Bath printer to a proper London publisher, and that this was a man's job. At any rate, Dr. Bowdler had become the new editor of the *Family Shakespeare* by June 1817, when negotiations began for the second edition. Thanks to the comparatively small size of the bombs used in World War II, some of the records of these negotiations survive. (See the appendix.) What they show is Dr. Bowdler approaching the London syndicate which owned the regular "trade" edition of Shakespeare, and being firmly brushed off. They then show one member of the syndicate risking the *Family Shakspeare* (Dr. Bowdler spelled the name differently from his sister) on his own, and after a few years finding he had published a best-seller.

Dr. Bowdler's best-seller and Harriet's obscure provincial book are quite different, even in size. He edited all thirty-six plays, sixteen from scratch and twenty by going back through her work. In some ways he was much more respectful. He restored all the boring passages that she had cut on aesthetic grounds, and sometimes he put back as much as he dared on the edges of improper passages she had cut, even at the price of making substitutions. For example, it apparently disturbed him that those travelers Falstaff held up couldn't so much as gasp when they felt the swords in their ribs. "Heaven bless us!" they are now allowed to exclaim. Eight lines of Touchstone's poetry (surrounding one problem couplet, which stays out) are restored in *As*

You Like It, and so on.

At the same time, he also cut hundreds of passages that Harriet had left alone, and he discovered many new improprieties in passages she had dealt with. The results of this are sometimes fascinating, as in their two treatments of the first encounter between Falstaff and Prince Hal. In all three versions, Shakespeare's, Harriet's, and Thomas', Falstaff comes on stage rubbing his eyes and asks, "Now, Hal, what time of day is it, lad?" In Shakespeare only, he gets this answer:

> PRINCE. Thou art so fat-witted, with drinking of old sack, and unbuttoning thee after supper, and sleeping upon benches after noon, that thou hast forgotten to demand that truly, which thou wouldst truly know. What a devil hast thou to do with the time of day? unless hours were cups of sack, and minutes capons, *and clocks the tongues of bawds, and dials the signs of leaping-houses,* and the blessed sun himself a fair *hot* wench in flame-color'd taffeta —I see no reason why you should be so superfluous as to demand the time of day.

The words in italics Harriet took out, and she also changed "what a devil" to "what the devil," presumably because she thought it sounded better. That is, she took out two direct references to whoring, and one suggestion of sexual desire on the part of women. But she was perfectly willing to let Falstaff unbutton himself after dinner, to let Prince Hal alter the sun's gender, and to allow a touch of very mild profanity. Her brother allowed none of these things. (He was apparently just being his mother's son in one case. The sun can't turn into a girl any more than a bridegroom can fit between his wife's breasts.) In the case of the buttons, however, the cut comes close to prurience. What Falstaff unbuttoned was his doublet, presumably to give his stomach more room after dinner. Inelegant, perhaps, but no worse than that. But in the nineteenth century, when trousers have come in, though not yet zippers, and what a man most frequently unbuttons is likely to be his fly, it is easy to read in a suggestiveness that isn't really there. Dr. Bowdler did, here and many times elsewhere.* In this he was perhaps a truer bowdlerist than Harriet.

At first his edition attracted no more notice than hers had. It came out, it got a few reviews, it sold a few hundred copies. But after three years of this obscurity, Bowdler's edition suddenly leaped up to become the best-selling Shakespeare in England. The steady advance in delicacy between 1807 and 1820 and the continued growth of the reading public are doubtless the main reasons; but the immediate cause of the leap was the enmity existing between the two great critical journals of the time: *Blackwood's Magazine* and the *Edinburgh Review*. It happened that in February 1821 *Blackwood's* came down hard on the new edition—"that piece of prudery in pasteboard"—and proceeded to savage the idea of expurgation altogether. What *Blackwood's*

* And got criticized for it. The *Monthly Review*, for example, which had praised the 1807 edition without reservation, felt one doubt about the 1818. "We cannot, however, avoid remarking that the editor has sometimes shewn the truth of the old saw, that the *nicest* person has the *nastiest* ideas, and has omitted many phrases as containing indelicacies which we cannot see, and of the guilt of which our bard, we think, is entirely innocent."

damned, the *Edinburgh* was apt to praise. In October it fired a double salvo on behalf of the *Family Shakspeare*. Lord Jeffrey himself wrote the review. "We have long intended to notice this very meritorious publication," he began, "and are of opinion, that it requires nothing more than a notice to bring it into general circulation." (A notice in the *Edinburgh*, he meant, of course.) He specified that there was nothing "precise or prudish" about the expurgation, no matter what other reviewers might claim. And finally he announced what no one else yet had, certainly not Harriet or Thomas Bowdler. He said all other editions of Shakespeare were now obsolete. "As what cannot be pronounced in decent company cannot well afford much pleasure in the closet, we think it is better, every way, that what cannot be spoken, and ought not to have been written, should cease to be printed."

This magisterial praise did indeed bring the *Family Shakspeare* into general circulation. It even as an accidental by-product produced a small wave of other expurgations. (One of them figures in the next chapter.) Dr. Bowdler in great excitement urged his publisher to print a long extract from the review at the front of future editions—it flew there like a banner for sixty years—and the firm itself quickly responded to the one tiny criticism Lord Jeffrey had made. He complained that the type was too small. "For we rather suspect, from some casual experiments of our own, that few *papas* will be able to read this, in a winter evening to their children, without the undramatic aid of spectacles." Four months after the review, Owen Rees of Longmans & Co. re-

84

ported to Dr. Bowdler that a new edition "in octavo with large type for *papas*" was in the works.

Henceforth things went swimmingly. By 1825, when Thomas the nephew wrote his uncle's obituary, he could indulge in so triumphant a peroration as this:

> Seven years have now passed since the Family Shakspeare was published in 1818; and a third edition [really the fourth, counting from 1807] is now on sale in octavo and a fourth in duodecimo. The merit of the work, therefore, may be considered to be acknowledged and established; the readers of Shakspeare will henceforth probably increase tenfold; the Family Shakspeare will be the edition which will lie on the table of every drawing-room; and the name of the editor will be remembered, as of one who has perhaps contributed more than any other individual to promote the innocent and rational enjoyment of well-educated families.

This, of course, is nonsense, but it need not have seemed so in 1825, or for many years thereafter. As late as 1860, when the *Family Shakspeare* emerged from copyright, demand for it was running high enough so that another publisher instantly brought out a rival edition. As late as 1894, when a man could choose from over forty different expurgations of Shakespeare, Swinburne, of all people, was still saying about Dr. Bowdler, "No man ever did better service to Shakespeare."

The later history of that service belongs in the next chapter and in the appendix, and of Dr. Bowdler's other expurgation, the *Family Gibbon*, there is no history. It duly appeared in 1826, the year after his death, in an edition of a thousand copies; and when it vanished from sight in the 1840s that edition still had not sold out. Sexual allusions were what roused the mass of Victorians, not jibes at early Christianity. Almost the only interesting thing about the *Family Gibbon* is the cocksureness of its editor, in contrast to his previous modesty toward Shakespeare. Dr. Bowdler is still in some ways modest; he still says that he is only trying to help a great author be greater, not to win glory for himself. But whereas he never even raised the question of how Shakespeare felt about being castrated, he now says that Gibbon is grateful for it. If Mr. Gibbon could only speak from heaven, that posthumous preface concludes, "he would say that he desired nothing more ardently than the laying aside of the former editions of his history, and trusting his name and reputation" to Mr. Bowdler. It is tempting to imagine what Mr. Gibbon actually did say to Mr. Bowdler on publication day.

****

CHAPTER FOUR

Shakespeare in Shreds

****

> *Emendations, curtailments, corrections* (all
> for his own good) *have been multiplied to in-
> finity.* . . . *They have purged and castrated
> him, and tattooed and beplaistered him, and
> cauterized and phlebotomized him.*
> The British Critic, 1822

> *I have no objection whatever to an intelligent
> cutting out of the dead & false bits of Shak-
> spere. But when you propose to cut me, I am
> paralysed at your sacrilegious audacity.*
> BERNARD SHAW TO ELLEN TERRY, 1896

SHAKESPEARE, prominent in so many other ways, also
leads English-speaking authors in the number of times he
has been expurgated. Only Chaucer even comes near.
The Bowdlers are merely one chapter in a long history.
He was lightly pruned three centuries ago, during the
reign (and by order of) Charles II; he continues to be
expurgated now, during the reign of, though not by
order of, Elizabeth II. Nor is it a hole-and-corner opera-
tion, even yet. Oxford University Press keeps a bowdlerized version of his plays in print; so does Cambridge

University Press; so does Ginn & Co. of Boston. Until recently nearly everybody did. In the early twentieth century there was a special "Australasian Shakespeare," decontaminated locally by a group of professors in Australia and New Zealand; there have been almost as many American bowdlerized versions as there are major American publishers. And so on practically forever.

The curtain rises on all this in October 1660, forty years after Shakespeare's death and a few months after the Restoration. The theater, banned under Cromwell, has also been restored, but it is to be kept chaste, so the Puritans won't mind it so much.

Act One: Sir Henry Herbert, Charles II's Master of the Revels, orders the managers of the two licensed playhouses to send him advance copies of all the old plays they intend to put on, "that they may be reformed of prophanes and ribaldry." Act Two: In December, Sir William D'Avenant, one of the managers, gets exclusive rights to eleven of the old plays, nine of which are by Shakespeare. He duly prunes several of them. In general he just takes out the stronger profanity, as managers as well as censors had occasionally done even before Cromwell, but now and then he makes a change that reflavors the text entirely. Macbeth's unkind words to a frightened servant, for example,

The devil damn thee black, thou cream-faced loon!
Where gott'st thou that goose look?

he smooths down to "Now Friend, what means thy change of Countenance?" He also puts a few euphemisms into lines otherwise left intact. Hamlet's phrase "To grunt and sweat under a weary life" he moderates

88

to "groan and sweat," a change followed by Shakespeare editors for the next hundred and twenty years.* The blunt word "lechery" in *Measure for Measure* he makes into mild "incontinence." Most blunt words he leaves as they are.

Act Three—but there was no Act Three. Or, rather, there was an intermission of about a hundred and ten years before it occurred. This was not a true dawn of bowdlerism in 1660, but a sop thrown to the Puritans. Sir William D'Avenant seems to have been sincere enough, but the King and most other people were just being prudent for a year or two. The Restoration was, after all, bloodless, and the Puritans were all still there when Charles returned, as much against levity as ever. They got progressively fewer sops thrown them as the years went by, though. And since the dominant literary taste of the time was not in the least puritan, Shakespeare not only soon ceased to be bowdlerized, he began to be pushed in the other direction. A play like *The Tempest* was not too bawdy for Restoration playgoers, it was too pure, and in 1670 no less a poet than Dryden juiced it up. "I never writ anything with more delight," Dryden remarked, after giving the innocent Miranda a sexy twin sister named Dorinda, and inventing scenes in which Prospero warns them both against men.

* Dr. Johnson, for example, printed "groan" in 1765. He knew better. "All the old copies have, to *grunt* and sweat," he explained in a footnote. "It is undoubtedly the true reading, but can scarcely be borne by modern ears." Edmund Malone finally restored "grunt" in 1790, with misgivings. "On the stage, without doubt," *his* footnote reads, "an actor is at liberty to substitute a less offensive word."

The offense, hard to perceive in a time when phrases like " 'Come in,' he grunted" occur in half the detective stories written, presumably lies in the word's animality. Whether via pigs or defecation, it is strongly there, more offensive to pre-Darwinians than to us.

MIRANDA. But you have told me, Sir, you are a Man;
And yet you are not Dreadful.

PROSPERO. I, child! But I am a tame Man; Old men are tame
By Nature, but all the Danger lies in a wild Young Man.

DORINDA. Do they run wild about the Woods?

PROSPERO. No, they are wild within Doors, in Chambers, And in Closets.

DORINDA. But Father, I would stroak 'em, and make 'em gentle,
Then sure they would not hurt me.

PROSPERO. You must not trust them, Child:
No woman can come near 'em but she feels A Pain full nine Months.

This is anti-bowdlerism, and Shakespeare suffered a good deal from it during the next thirty or forty years. John Dennis added some scenes to *The Merry Wives of Windsor* in 1702 which people have been nervous about quoting even in the twentieth century. Dennis was not, of course, merely touching up the play—or pulling it down—he was adapting it with a very free hand. He even changed the title, preferring to call his version *The Comical Gallant*, after Falstaff. In all this he was typical of his age. Early meddlers with Shakespeare can't really be called bowdlerists, or anti-bowdlerists either, since they don't stay sufficiently close to the text to fit those categories at all. They are predecessors of Mary Lamb more than of Harriet Bowdler.

Even when they seem to be bowdlerizing, they're

usually up to something quite different. David Garrick prepared an acting version of *Romeo and Juliet* in 1750, for example, which takes almost the identical lines away from Juliet that Dr. Bowdler did in 1818. He wasn't trying to spare the audience, though; he just thought it out of character for such a nice girl to speak of maidenheads, much less to wish openly that Romeo would hurry up and take hers. Other characters keep many of *their* bawdy lines. Nahum Tate's version of *Lear* (1681) drops the line "Rumble thy belly full," replacing it with "Rumble thy fill." This seems a true expurgation, and technically it is. But Tate wasn't thinking about the word "belly" bringing a blush to the cheek of modesty; he was thinking it brought inelegance to the mouth of a king. It is a change made strictly on artistic grounds, like the famous marriage he arranges at the end of the play between Cordelia (who doesn't die after all) and Edgar.

Everyone thought artistically then, even the serious scholars. George Steevens, for example, was one of the two leading Shakespeare scholars of his time. Except for that early lapse with Rochester, his own editing was austere and accurate. But in his heart he yearned after artistry. When Garrick took the grave-diggers out of *Hamlet*, Steevens shot him off a letter of congratulation. He had been wishing for years that someone would get the low comedy out of *Hamlet*, he said. And then he gave Garrick a mock-suggestion.

> You had better throw what remains of the piece into a farce, to appear immediately afterwards. No foreigner who should happen to be present at the

exhibition, would ever believe it was formed out of the loppings and excresences of the tragedy itself. You may entitle it "The Grave Diggers; with the pleasant Humours of Osric, the Danish Macaroni."

These loppings and excrescence removals for art's sake are the precursors of oncoming bowdlerism. Its true dawn, for Shakespeare, broke over the eastern hills in 1774, when a man named Francis Gentleman edited a complete plays for the publisher Bell. Gentleman was just as much an artist as Garrick, Steevens, and the rest. He, too, felt that Shakespeare, genius though he was, needed someone to teach him classical form and a sense of decorum. In fact, once in discussing *Macbeth* (he started as a drama critic), he brought up the very lines that D'Avenant smoothed a century earlier. He could hardly stand them. "The expressions [Macbeth] uses to the servant or officer who enters with intelligence of the English army are low and gross, far beneath even a private gentleman; and why Shakespeare should make a monarch run into such vulgarisms is not easy to guess." For a peasant to speak of goose looks is bad enough, but that the ruler of Scotland (and a born thane at that) should is awful. Gentleman feels similarly upset when Cleopatra says hotly to her maid Charmian,

> By Isis, I will give thee bloody teeth,
> If thou with Caesar paragon again
> My man of men.

Gentleman protests. "This is rather an objectionable exclamation, unworthy of a person in a middling station, much more so of a royal character."

But besides wanting to preserve the dignity of kings, Gentleman also wanted to protect the delicacy of readers. That is, he wanted to bowdlerize. In a feeble and completely unsystematic way, he did.

Bell's Shakespeare is a very curious edition. Gentleman worked from the scripts (including Garrick's) of the two royal theaters in London, and officially his edition is a prop for theater-goers. Read the very words you'll hear tonight at Drury Lane. You can't follow the play without a Bell's Edition. In actual fact, however, he aimed at a much wider audience. The main text does indeed follow the acting versions. But for the benefit of home readers he stuck all the good passages not spoken on stage down at the bottoms of the pages. And to make Shakespeare "more instructive and intelligible, especially to the ladies and to youth," he bowdlerized. That is, he omitted such "glaring indecencies" as had remained in the acting versions, while minor indecencies he printed in italics, as a signal for ladies and youths to skip them.

At least, this is what he says in his preface that he is going to do. Sometimes he did, and sometimes he didn't. There are lines gone, all right—many in *Romeo and Juliet*, some of Touchstone's surviving jokes in *As You Like It*, and so forth. Other lines merely get scolded in footnotes. Gentleman printed Touchstone's remark, "So come, sweet Audrey,/ We must be married, or we must live in bawdry" in his main text. But at the bottom of the page he says primly, "The sentence with which Touchstone makes his exit is very objectionable, and should be altered." By future editors, perhaps. (It was.) Again, in

Henry V he prints all the oaths, those that Harriet Bowdler took out and those that she left in. But by one of Captain Macmorris's "by Chrish's" he notes, "The oaths in this scene, and especially in this speech, are too forcible, and return too frequently. A careful pruner might remove the objectionable phrases, and still retain the spirit of the character."

As for the minor indecencies that he proposed to print in italics, he carried out his intention in one play only. In *Othello* there are just such italics. They make his version very curious reading indeed. A speech in the main text will run like this:

IAGO. Zounds, sir, y'are robbed! For shame, put on your
gown!
Your heart is burst; you have lost half your soul.
Even now, now, very now, an old black ram
Is tupping your white ewe. Arise, arise!

John Bowdler, Jr., himself would have had trouble skipping lines thus marked.

In other plays Gentleman tried all sorts of systems. In *Troilus and Cressida* (which he couldn't adapt from a theater script, because there wasn't one) he put parentheses around the lines he felt people should skip. These are boring lines as well as dirty ones. In *A Comedy of Errors* he used quotation marks. In *Henry IV* he used none of these things. The Prince calls Falstaff a "whoreson, obscene, greasy tallow catch," and Falstaff calls the Prince a "bull's pizzle," and there are no skip marks of any sort, or even a disapproving footnote. If a foolish consistency is the hobgoblin of little minds, Gentleman had one of the largest minds of his century.

His edition is still the first serious attempt to bowdler- ize Shakespeare, though. The second is equally odd. It consists only of *King Lear*, expurgated by the young forger William Henry Ireland in 1795, and published by his father the next year. This was not billed as an expur- gation, of course; it was billed as Shakespeare's original manuscript, miraculously recovered and now first printed. But it was an expurgation all the same.

It was for a reason that might have been designed for this book. William Henry thought his forgery would be more convincing if he cleaned the text up. As he ex- plained after he got caught, "It was generally deemed extraordinary that the productions of Shakespeare should be found so very unequal, and in particular that so much ribaldry should appear throughout his dramatic compositions." Perhaps it wasn't really Shakespeare's at all. (All the good critics were saying this.) So if you want to simulate real, original Shakespeare, expurgate. "I determined on the expedient of rewriting, in the old hand, one of his most conspicuous plays, and making such alterations as I conceived appropriate."

The plan worked beautifully. William Henry, who was a boy of eighteen at the time, simply took an early edition of *Lear* belonging to his father and copied the whole play out on old paper, adding archaic spellings and making expurgations and other improvements as he went. Then, having "discovered" the manuscript, he gave it to his father, who was an avid collector of Shakespeareana. His father was completely taken in, along with the Duke of Somerset, James Boswell, Bishop Burgess (then only a prebendary), and many others. They found the alterations especially convincing. One of the father's principal arguments, when he published the play, was that it *must* be a genuine manuscript because of the pure but elegant style.

As for the son, he maintained all his life that he had done Shakespeare a favor. As long as his *Lear* passed, "the world supposed that all the ribaldry [in Shakespeare's] other plays was not written by himself but foistered in by the players and printers; herein it cannot be said I injured the reputation of Shakspear, on the contrary, the world thought him a much more pure and even writer than before." By this formula it was the scholar Edmund Malone who injured the reputation of Shakespeare, by exposing the fraud.

Considering what a favor he thought it was, William Henry's expurgation is not very thorough. It's there, all right; he was especially attentive to the sexual allusions. When Lear cries,

> Behold yon simp'ring dame
> Whose face between her forks presages snow,

William Henry cuts him to "Look atte yonne Ladye," rather like D'Avenant smoothing Macbeth. The Fool's codpiece song is also cut; Goneril's complaint about brothel behavior among the knights vanishes, and so forth. But no expurgation can be called thorough that leaves words like "whoremaster" untouched, not to mention Edmund's long soliloquy on the problems of being a bastard. Thoroughness had to wait for the Bowdlers, and even more for their many successors. To the first of these I now turn.

The Rev. J. R. Pitman, was called forth by the *Edinburgh*'s praise of the *Family Shakspeare* as surely as the genie is summoned by the lamp. His *School-Shakspere* appeared in the spring of 1822, a little less than six months after the *Edinburgh*'s article, or about as long as it takes hastily to edit and publish a book. Pitman's idea was to undercut the Bowdlers by offering a smaller quantity of expurgated Shakespeare at a much lower price. Instead of thirty-six plays at a cost of three guineas, he offered twenty-six plays ("the more celebrated passages," actually, with "enough of the general plot" to link them) for eighteen shillings. He also claimed to offer a much more rigorous expurgation.

Since Pitman was printing only extracts, a direct comparison of rigor is difficult. The "more celebrated passages" in Shakespeare turn out to be mostly clean ones, anyway. In *As You Like It*, for example, nothing that Touchstone or Audrey said is celebrated, and these two characters vanish altogether. Lots of things that Silvius and Phebe (whoever they are) say are celebrated, and these two survive.

Where comparison is possible, though, it emerges clearly that Pitman was indeed a more thorough expurgator. The Porter's scene in *Macbeth* makes a good example. Shakespeare himself devotes about twenty lines to the Porter's drunken soliloquy. Dr. Bowdler cuts him to six, removing every trace of his speculation on what it would be like to serve as the porter of Hell, but still leaving a hint of his drunken incoherence. Pitman does the whole speech in three lines:

> PORTER. Here's a knocking indeed! [*Knock.*]
> Knock, knock, knock. [*Knock.*] Anon,
> anon; I pray you, remember the porter.

For what, one might ask. The same question would apply to Pitman. Nevertheless, this brief version of Shakespeare stayed around for forty years, going through five editions.

A second successor appeared that same spring, summoned less by the *Edinburgh* than by the continued success of Lamb's *Tales*, and less by either than by the new spirit of the age. Elizabeth Macauley published her *Tales of the Drama*, which, despite the title, are pretty much in the original words. They are plays for people who don't believe in plays. Or as her publisher put it, "The object of this Work is to convert the acted drama into the more popular form of narrative, for the purpose of rendering the real beauties of the British stage more familiar, and even of extending that knowledge to circles where the drama itself is forbidden." But the conversion is partial. "The colloquial and scenic effect is preserved, and the whole rendered obedient to the most refined ideas of delicacy."

Four of the plays Miss Macauley included are by Shakespeare, and all four are trimmed roughly to Bowdler standards, though not to Pitman. There were now three expurgations of Shakespeare on the market at once. His Victorian age had begun, fifteen years before Victoria's own.

This is not to say that the old age simply vanished

overnight. Regency bucks were still plentiful in 1822, along with unexpurgated editions of Shakespeare. In fact, a large section of the public hadn't even noticed the new age springing up around it, much less bought a bowdlerized Shakespeare. The painter Sir Martin Archer Shee, for example, plainly had not. In 1824 Shee stopped painting long enough to write a tragedy called *Alasco*, which was accepted for production at Covent Garden. To his surprise and fury, the Lord Chamberlain's office demanded extensive cuts first. Shee refused. He then counter-attacked by publishing the play with all the condemned passages printed in italics, *à la* Francis Gentleman. Each time he came to one, he would tell off the Lord Chamberlain in a footnote. One footnote shows just how little he had noticed of the new age. The drama censor in the Lord Chamberlain's office had demanded that the exclamation "Hell's hot blisters" come out. (A few years later the same man was forbidding "o lud" to be spoken on the stage, saying it really meant "Oh, Lord.") Shee wrote furiously: "The official critic here takes new ground—his delicacy rejects this expression as a matter of taste. . . . It is to be hoped that his zeal will induce him to [give] to the world an 'editio expurgata' of our principal dramatists: a 'Shakspere' reformed, according to the official standards of politics and politeness, would be a great acquisition to the stage." * Plainly Shee

* It made Shee even madder that the "official critic" whose delicacy rejected this was the playwright George Colman the younger, who had just taken over as censor that year. (The previous censor, an elderly Methodist named John Larpent, had confined himself to political changes.) Colman had made his own reputation at the turn of the century with plays called things like *Broad Grins*. Now he said he was sorry he had written so vulgarly, and as censor would demand changes of himself.

was not aware that three "editiones expurgatae" were competing for the market already.

A once-famous passage in Mrs. Trollope's *Domestic Manners of the Americans* suggests that she wasn't, either. Mrs. Trollope had gone from England to Ohio in 1827 to seek her fortune. In the summer of 1828 she was asked to a literary party in Cincinnati, at which she met a man "said to be a scholar and a man of reading; he was also what is called a *serious* gentleman." That is, he had the Victorian temperament. They fell into a discussion of Byron, whom the serious gentleman denounced, then Pope, whom he also denounced; then Mrs. Trollope asked, "And Shakspere, sir?"

"Shakspere, Madam, is obscene, and, thank God, WE are sufficiently advanced to have found it out! If we must have the abomination of stage plays, let them at least be marked by the refinement of the age in which we live."

In 1828 England was, of course, well ahead of Ohio in dealing with Shakespeare, but it is obvious that neither party in the discussion knew it. The American thought the English hadn't even grasped the problem yet, whereas actually they had already bought out five editions of the *Family Shakespeare* and were racing through the sixth. (Bowdler wasn't printed in America until the 1840s, and even then he was such a failure that in the second American edition the publisher put all the expurgations back in.) Mrs. Trollope may have known what was happening in London, but suppressed it, in order to further the impression she wished to give of the English as gentlemen who read what they please and of Ameri-

cans as a bunch of smut-hunting prudes. It seems unlikely, though, since in that same passage she herself pays
at least lip service to prudery.*

For roughly twenty years, ignorance like this remained possible. Expurgated books were thriving, but by
no means dominant. In fact, after Miss Macauley there
was a kind of lull, at least for Shakespeare, a quiet last
scene to the new act that began with Gentleman in 1772.
Only one expurgation appeared in the 1830s, a rather
feeble affair called *Select Plays From Shakespeare;
adapted chiefly for the use of Schools and Young Persons,* which contained only six plays. After that, nothing
until a man named H. L. Broenner published a similar
volume in Frankfurt, Germany (in English) in 1846.
But then Act Four begins with a rush. The curtain rings
up on a busy scene in England, and on a bright dawn in
America. Hereafter new expurgations come so fast that
it would be cumbersome even to list them all. I therefore
skip to 1849, when the *Shaksperian Reader* was published in New York, edited by Professor John W. S.
Hows of Columbia. It is the first expurgation of Shakespeare done in the United States.†

---

* When the American denounced Byron, she noted, "It was evident
that the noble passages which are graven on the hearts of the genuine
lovers of poetry had altogether escaped the serious gentleman's
attention; and it was equally evident that he knew by rote all those
which they wish the mighty master had never written. I told him so,
and I shall not soon forget the look he gave me."
† There is one possible exception. A series called *Modern Standard
Drama* began to be published in New York in 1846. Ten volumes, the
first seven edited by Epes Sargent and the other three by Hows
himself, were out by 1848. They contain many plays by Shakespeare
—acting versions, drawn more or less intact from *Cumberland's
British Theatre* (1827–28), which in turn got them from Covent

Perhaps because he was a college professor, Hows was fairly apologetic about what he was doing. "Of the liberties I have been compelled to take with my author," he wrote in his preface, "I scarcely know how to speak with becoming propriety. I profess to share the common veneration for the pure unmutilated text of Shakespeare; and can estimate at what it is worth that ultra fastidiousness, which denounces the great 'Poet of *Nature*' for having made his characters speak agreeably to the spirit of *his own age*." A graceful academic disclaimer. He then gets down to business, and makes it clear that veneration is no impediment to the expurgation of true poets. "I have not hesitated to exercise a severe revision of his language, beyond that adopted in any similar undertaking—'Bowdler's Family Shakspeare' not even excepted —and, simply because I know the impossibility of introducing Shakspeare as a Class Book, or as a satisfactory Reading Book for Families, without this precautionary revision." And forgetting his previous low estimate of fastidiousness, he adds that he has made it his goal to please "the most fastidious Teacher."

He surely must have succeeded. Considering that he was trying to present whole plays, and not just cele-

---

Garden and Drury Lane. That is, they are much curtailed and mildly purified to begin with.

Epes Sargent seems to have done a little extra purifying on his own. For example, Cumberland's *Romeo and Juliet* allows the Nurse to quote her joke-loving husband as having said to Juliet when she was two, and had just taken a tumble, "Yea, dost thou fall upon thy face? Thou wilt fall backward when thou hast more wit, wilt thou not, Jule?" Sargent changed this to read, "Thou wilt not fall so when thou hast more wit," thus concealing the dirty part of the joke. On the slim basis of a few changes like this, he can be said to have preceded Hows as an American bowdlerizer of Shakespeare.

brated passages, Hows cut with a truly extravagant hand. *Henry IV*, Part One, and *Othello*, the two plays he cut most, lay on the floor in heaps when he had finished. Falstaff dominates roughly a third of the scenes in Shakespeare's *Henry;* he doesn't figure as a character in Hows's at all. *Othello*, reduced but coherent up to that point, simply stops after Act III. "The catastrophe of this noble domestic tragedy, is foreshadowed in our extracts," Professor Hows wrote by way of summarizing the missing two acts, and went on to the next play.

In making cuts of this magnitude, Hows is indeed more severe than Bowdler. In the smaller changes which are a bowdlerist's usual work, however, the two men run about neck and neck. They are to the same degree opposed to sexual allusions, even to both keeping Iago from the little metaphor with which he prefaces a poem: "My muse labors, and thus she is delivered." Both are so set against profanity as to stop Henry IV from speaking soberly of "the great magician, damned Glendower"— Bowdler making him call the Welsh leader "vile Glendower" and Hows "curs'd Glendower." Hows may move an inch ahead when he adds four years to Juliet's age, while Bowdler lets her stay a nymphet of just under fourteen. (Hows was not being original: many of the artist-improvers in the eighteenth century aged her, too.) On the other hand, he loses ground in that he completely missed one of Romeo's plainest double entendres and left it glaring on the page, while Bowdler spotted it and cut it. This is when Romeo, before he meets Juliet, is describing the stubborn chastity of his previous girl:

She will not stay the siege of loving terms,
Nor bide th'incounter of assailing eyes,
Nor ope her lap to saint-seducing gold:

Hows seems to have thought that if you open your lap to saint-seducing gold, you are to be imagined holding up your apron while a stream of gold ducats pours in, and he was right. Bowdler knew, however, that you are also to be imagined opening your body for sexual intercourse. ("Lap" even had a seventeenth-century meaning which Allan Ramsay would have spelled "sunt"—Hamlet uses it so to Ophelia, and Hows missed that one, too.) Bowdler took the line out.

Only in the Yankee sweep of his religious cuts does Hows have a small but clear edge. He expurgates everything that Bowdler does, and more, too. " 'Sblood," for example, he will not tolerate, Catholic origin or not. And from the mouths of low characters he even strikes the word "Christendom," which is no oath at all, but a term in geography.

Whether because of this religious pluralism, or simply because they were proud of the fact that it was done over here, Americans took to the *Shaksperian Reader*. It kept having new editions up through 1881, after which new and better expurgations swamped it, and it even had a sequel, the *Historical Shaksperian Reader*. If he was still alive in 1857, Mrs. Trollope's serious gentleman must have been delighted to see a Hows edition come out in Cincinnati—the first Shakespeare ever printed there, and only the second printed west of the Appalachians.

Meanwhile, the expurgation industry was roaring

ahead in England. Kean did one, Kemble did one, and—to leap ahead for a moment—even Wordsworth's nephew, forgetting his uncle's dictum about correct texts, did one. The Secretary of the Working Men's College in London did one for working men. The novelist Charlotte Yonge did one for schools. A man named Henry Cundell did one to keep in boudoirs. Lewis Carroll began one for girls.*

In 1861 the first pair of scholars did one. (Hows was only a professor of elocution.) This was the *Household Edition of the Dramatic Works of William Shakespeare* in ten stout volumes, heavily annotated. William Chambers and Robert Carruthers, the editors, had a serious and respectful idea which in practice turns out to be extremely funny. All previous expurgators of Shakespeare, it struck them, had got in the awkward position of passing their own words off as his. Someone reading Bowdler had no way of knowing that "vile Glendower" or "fresh female birds" was spurious—needful, perhaps, added in all humility, but still not Shakespeare. In the interests of scholarship they decided to mark their own substitutions

---

* Carroll worked intermittently all through the 1880s on an expurgation he planned to call *The Girl's Own Shakespeare*. It was to be truly rigorous. "Neither Bowdler's, Chamber's, Brandram's, nor Cundell's 'Boudoir' Shakespeare seems to me to meet the want," he wrote; "they are not sufficiently 'expurgated.' Bowdler's is the most extraordinary of all: looking through it, I am filled with a deep sense of wonder, considering what he has left in, that he should have cut anything out!" Carroll completed *The Tempest* and perhaps other plays, but never got around to publishing.

It is fair to add that he intended all this only for girls from ten through seventeen. Girls under ten don't read Shakespeare at all, he said, "and those who have passed out of girlhood may be safely led to Shakespeare in any edition, 'expurgated' or not, that they may prefer." This was not a common view among expurgators in 1890.

with quotation marks. (Mere omissions they concealed, like everybody else.) The results easily surpass Francis Gentleman.

Iago, for example, comes out a pedant addicted to quoting the song "Frankie and Johnnie." Shakespeare's Iago says,

> I hate the Moor;
> And it is thought abroad that 'twixt my sheets
> He has done my office.

The household Iago says,

> I hate the Moor;
> And it is thought abroad that "with my wife"
> He has done "me wrong."

Falstaff and Prince Henry, on the other hand, seem primarily a pair of euphemists. Falstaff tells the Prince, "I'll be 'undone' [*damned*, he used to say] for never a king's son in Christendom." Later, in the mock-trial, he says, "But that he is, saving your reverence, a 'misleader' [*whoremaster*], that I utterly deny." Prince Henry says, "Falstaff, you carried your 'self' [*guts*] away as nimbly. . . ."

Another and more serious result is that one can see with unusual precision what words Victorians objected to, and what seemed good ways around them. For Chambers and Carruthers often replaced a single word in a line or passage that previous bowdlerists had invariably cut altogether. A striking example is Touchstone's rhyme

> He that sweetest rose will find
> Must find love's prick and Rosalinde.

Harriet Bowdler cut ten lines here, Thomas Bowdler two, Epes Sargent four. Carruthers and Chambers change one word. They thus pinpoint the objection:

> He that sweetest rose will find
> Must find love's "thorn" and Rosalinde.

Another example is one of Hotspur's speeches in *Henry IV*. He and his wife are in Wales. Their relations Lord and Lady Mortimer are showing a good deal of public affection, and Hotspur proceeds to tease his wife about copying them. "Come, Kate," he says, "thou art perfect in lying down. Come, quick, quick, that I may lay my head in thy lap." Dr. Bowdler simply omits the speech. Chambers and Carruthers have Hotspur say, "Come, Kate, thou art perfect in 'obedience.'" If nothing else were known about the nineteenth century, this single change would reveal a good deal about its sexual mores.

Another scholarly edition, three years later, carries the old distinction between Protestant and Catholic profanity to a new height. "God" is so uncomfortable a term to Charles and Mary Cowden Clarke that Juliet's nurse can't even swear by the Virgin Mary in the form "O God's lady dear," but has to say "O Heaven's lady dear." With priests it's different. When Friar Lawrence exclaims, "Jesu Maria!" the Clarkes not only permit it, but add an approving footnote. "With marked propriety has Shakespeare placed this remark in the mouth of an Italian friar. It is an exclamation exclusively belonging to Catholic countries; and is a contracted form of *Jesu Mariae,* 'Jesus the son of Mary.' "

A quite unscholarly edition published at the same time shows the concept of delicacy still advancing, too. Miss Rosa Baughan in 1863 expurgated lines that Harriet Bowdler in 1807 never even realized were problems. Among other things, Miss Baughan out-Garricked Garrick and lopped *all* the humor out of *all* the plays she included. "It is precisely in the humourous scenes that the greatest freedom of expression is to be found," she explained, "and . . . moreover, humour is the quality least appreciable by the class of readers [girls] for whom I have laboured." Miss Baughan was so little inclined to permit freedom that she even cut old Capulet's playful remarks at the beginning of the ball in *Romeo and Juliet:*

> Gentlemen, welcome! ladies that have their toes
> Unplagu'd with corns will have a bout with you—
> Ah ha, my mistresses! which of you all
> Will now deny to dance? she that makes dainty,
> She, I'll swear, hath corns.

Even references to sore feet have now become indelicate, and these five lines disappear. Did reviewers laugh such prudery to scorn? They did not. "We have seen many revised editions of Shakespeare, but none so fitted as this for the Girl's study," said the *Illustrated London News.* "We prefer this *thorough* weeding to the half measures to which we have been accustomed," wrote the *Critic.*

Miss Baughan was, admittedly, an extremist, but she was not the only extremist at work in the 1860s. Compared to the weeding done by Thomas Bulfinch of Boston, hers may actually be a trifle lax. Bulfinch, son of the great architect and himself the well-known author of Bulfinch's *Mythology*, published *Shakespeare Adapted for Reading Classes and the Family Circle* in 1865. In it he carried delicacy so far as to deny Lady Macbeth what is the most famous and least-mutilated blasphemy in all Shakespeare. In his version she looks at her hand and says, "Out, crimson spot." I have found no other case of this.

Bulfinch gave a powerful boost to the American side, but in 1865 England was still well ahead—in Shakespeare if not in expurgation generally. So far there had been no more than three or four bowdlerized versions in America, as compared to at least twenty in England. But now the United States moved up fast; and by 1870 new ones were coming out at about equal speed in both countries. With us the Gilded Age and the Age of Innocence are one. Every major American publisher had a house Shakespeare expurgator—for Harper's it was W. J. Rolfe, for Houghton Mifflin, Richard Grant White— just as every major English publisher had one.

The greatest of American expurgations came in 1872, perhaps naturally in Boston. The publisher was Ginn. In the beginning it consisted of three volumes containing twenty-one plays, "selected and prepared for use in Schools, Clubs, Classes, and Families." But it soon flowered into thirty-eight volumes, one for each play, including the doubtful ones. This version was to America what Bowdler was to England, and even more. In its heyday, between 1880 and 1930, about five million copies of individual plays were sold. Even since then (six of the plays are still in print), another three-quarters of a million have been sold.

The editor, Henry Norman Hudson, was a Shakespearean scholar, like the Cowden Clarkes, but a much better one. He is comparable to George Steevens in the eighteenth century. But where Steevens, longing to make Shakespeare classical, held himself in and merely wrote encouraging letters to Garrick, Hudson, longing to make him pure, was too good a Victorian not to go ahead and do it. (He also published two unexpurgated editions of Shakespeare, one before and one after his bowdlerism.)

Precisely because he was an important scholar, Hudson's expurgations led to greater harm than those of most of his predecessors. Not immediately. The editions during his lifetime are, for expurgations, models of care and wisdom. Once grant his assumption that "purity and rectitude of manners are worth more than any intellectual benefit to be derived from the poetry and wisdom even of a Shakespeare," and what he does compels admiration. Like Carruthers and Chambers, he identifies all his own substitutions for bawdy Shakespearean words, "it being a fixed principle with the Editor to abstain religiously from making unmarked changes." Unlike their quotation marks, his brackets don't come out foolish—partly because they occur about a twentieth as often. Like Francis Gentleman, he is inconsistent—but his inconsistencies are the product of much thought, and even make sense. He retains, for example, all the ribald remarks Ophelia makes after going mad. "Though quite unpronounceable in class," he explains, "they cannot be cut away without overthrowing the whole delineation." Almost his only weakness as an expurgator is a touch of high-minded naïveté. He either didn't know himself or assumed his readers wouldn't understand the colloquial meaning of the word "prick," for example, which he retains both in Touchstone's verses and in *Romeo and Juliet*, when Mercutio says, "The bawdy hand of the clock is now on the prick of noon." (He did omit the word "bawdy" from that line, which suggests that he knew, but hoped that without this clue his readers wouldn't.)

After his death, though, his edition was kept in print by other men, trading on his name, and it is here that the harm occurred. The "New Hudson Shakespeare" crept into print in 1909. There are two new editors, distinguished college professors. They do not admit that they are producing an expurgation at all. On the contrary, they say coolly that they are following the best scholarly editions, and that "every variation from the First Folio" is recorded in the notes. This is true, except for the bowdlerisms, which are not recorded anywhere. In the New Hudson *Hamlet*, not only is everything that Hudson himself omitted still missing, but Ophelia doesn't even get to sing her Saint Valentine song. Or, rather, she sings the four opening lines, which the new editors annotate learnedly from Sir Joshua Reynolds and Scott, and then she leaves out the twelve bawdy lines to which the four openers were a prelude, a fact which they do not mention at all. Presumably they were afraid that if the high-school and college students who read the New

Hudson Shakespeare knew what they were missing, some of them might go look in the attic for pre-Civil War editions. It seems a reasonable fear. But bowdlerism now involves not merely tampering with one's author but lying to one's readers.

Not that the later editors of Hudson were the first to do this. They are only among the first to lie in so many words. For many years the custom had been growing up of identifying an expurgation only by its title or subtitle —calling it a select edition, or a school edition, or a family edition, all three of which terms during the nineteenth century normally meant an expurgation.* But since nothing in the preface or any note *said* the book was bowdlerized, the publisher was able to convey this information to parents over the heads, so to speak, of their children.

Rolfe's 1884 edition for Harper's is a fair example of the new discretion. There are twenty volumes, each with one or two plays. In the preface to Volume One, Rolfe says plainly, "The 'expurgation' is limited to the very few words and passages which cannot be read aloud in the family." The other nineteen volumes say nothing about the matter in any way, however; and unless one happened to be reading *Titus Andronicus* or *Henry VI, Part One*, which are the plays in the first volume, one would have no way of knowing. (This must have pro-

---

* In the eighteenth century, the same terms usually meant a book without a lot of scholarly apparatus. For example, when Edmund Malone announced in 1783 his plan to produce "a useful *family* Shakespeare," expurgation was the last thing he had in mind. He merely meant that he planned "to reject all superfluous and controversial notes."

duced a certain ignorance at Harvard and Cornell, where the English departments were enthusiastic users of Rolfe.*) Houghton Mifflin's "Riverside Shakespeare" in 1883 is a still fairer example. It simply says nothing about its unusually savage cuts.

And even before 1909 and the New Hudson, a few editors had begun to lean toward positive deception. J. M. D. Meiklejohn, Professor of the Theory, History, and Practice of Education in the University of St. Andrews, Scotland, for one. The Scots have been pioneers in every stage of bowdlerism. If you look at the preface of the *Hamlet* that Meiklejohn edited in 1880, you see no mention of cuts. Instead you find the resounding claim that "The text has been as carefully and as thoroughly annotated as any Greek or Latin classic." This is true. You learn that the close study of Shakespeare will "have the effect of bringing back into the too pale and formal English of modern times a large number of pithy and vigourous phrases." Only if you happen to know *Hamlet* already will you discover that Professor Meiklejohn has quietly eliminated four or five hundred of the pithiest and most vigorous. The open approach of Dr. Bowdler has completely vanished. Castration is now preceded by anesthesia. On this somewhat darkening note, the curtain comes down on Act Four.

Act Five, modern times, follows at once. Its principal event is the unexpected happy ending, in which Shakespeare recovers from all this. At the darkest moment, which was about 1910, the revulsion had already begun

---

* Child of Harvard and Corson of Cornell each wrote a blurb for this very edition; they are to be found at the back of Vol. I.

which was to lead back to honest editing. The *Family Shakspeare* fell by the way in 1925. Meiklejohn had fallen already. Editions like Rolfe's and White's held on much longer—but by 1940 American college students had regained the position of their predecessors in 1807, and were nearly all reading editions with accurate texts. (They still weren't back to the freedom of 1780, when editions of Shakespeare were not only complete, but editors felt free to comment on any lines they chose.*) A certain number of high-school students were also free again. But Act Five is still in progress, and its history belongs in the last chapter, not here.

* T. J. Mathias in *Pursuits of Literature* complained bitterly about this. He proposed that instead of continuing to illustrate Shakespeare's bawdry with such a wealth of learning, editors should print the following standard note: "This or that passage contains an indecent allusion not uncommon in the novels or plays of the time."

****

CHAPTER FIVE

The Assault on the Bible

****

Both read the Bible day and night,
But thou read'st black where I read white.
WILLIAM BLAKE, 1818

The truth is, that when a Library expels a book
of mine and leaves an unexpurgated Bible
around where unprotected youth and age can
get hold of it, the deep unconscious irony of it
delights me and doesn't anger me.
MARK TWAIN, 1907

OF ALL THEIR customs, men are most reluctant to tamper
with their religious practices, which is why the world is
full of archaic languages, such as Sanskrit, used only in
religious texts, and of archaic clothing, such as chasubles,
worn only by priests. Where a religious text has been
taken, like the Bible, to be directly inspired by God, or
even dictated by Him word for word, change is particularly unlikely to occur.

Nevertheless, the English text of the Bible has been
seriously bowdlerized at least twice, and more or less
tidied up around the edges half a dozen times.

The first clean-up was done by a woman educator,

Mrs. Sarah Kirby Trimmer, whose *Sacred History* came out in 1782. This book is in some ways a freak, quite outside the general pattern of bowdlerism. For one thing, it began very modestly, as a bundle of manuscript designed to introduce her own twelve children to the more innocent parts of the Bible, and only gradually grew into its role as a public expurgation. More important, Mrs. Trimmer never admitted that she was producing a Bible at all.

The first edition, aimed solely at children between seven and fourteen (but nevertheless printed in six full-length volumes), consists of the Old and New Testaments treated as a group of *Reader's Digest* editors might. About half the text is cut, and the rest is arranged so as to give a more coherent and slightly rosier account of things than the actual Bible does. Naturally all references to things like onanism have vanished. Where necessary, Mrs. Trimmer uses her own words to bridge across the cuts, and occasionally she replaces a Bible chapter with a summary in juvenile language, rather in the fashion of Lamb's *Tales*. Otherwise the words remain those of the King James Version. After each section of Scripture she inserts a brief commentary, suitable for eight- and ten-year-olds.

In succeeding editions a series of changes took place which change the book radically. What happened was that she found the book would sell to adults, and little by little she altered it for their benefit, making it into a true expurgation in the process. The childish summaries disappear, and the chapters they replaced are restored—in a bowdlerized state, naturally. The commentaries expand

and take on an adult tone. Even the typography changes. "I had a view to the improvement of *young persons only*," Mrs. Trimmer says in the preface to the fourth edition (1801), but "the flattering attention which was bestowed on my labours by persons of a maturer age" changed all that, and in the end she was ready to improve everybody.

A typical example of Mrs. Trimmer at work would be her version of Genesis 19. This is the chapter in which the two angels come to spend the night in Lot's house in Sodom, and a large crowd of homosexuals gathers out front. She follows the King James Version until the moment when Lot is standing on his doorstep and the crowd is demanding that he hand over the two visitors, at which point she cuts the phrase "that we may know them." "Know" has, of course, its Biblical meaning here. The chapter then continues unchanged until Lot offers the crowd his daughters instead, and that verse she removes entirely. Again it proceeds unchanged while Sodom and Gomorrah are destroyed (the reasons for this action now being much less clear), and Lot and his daughters become refugees in the wilderness. Then Mrs. Trimmer eliminates the six verses which recount the plan the daughters evolve to have children even though they are now living in a region where the only surviving man is their father. At the very end of the chapter she retains the verses in which the two daughters each bear a son— one named Moab and the other Ben-ammi—but the fathers of these two little boys might as well be the two angels, for all the light *Sacred History* casts.

Mrs. Trimmer was able to get away with such lavish

changes chiefly because she was very careful not to claim that her book was a real Bible.* The title distinguishes it sharply from one; and in theory even the later editions were intended to be either a prelude, something a teenager read before venturing on the entire Bible, or an *aide-mémoire*, something an old man read afterward. She was very clear that her version was not for official use, as in pulpits. "No *human compositions*," she once wrote, "ought to be used as *substitutes* for the BIBLE itself."

Just how much she gained by pretending that *Sacred History* was not a Bible may be seen by an incident that occurred in the very middle of its success. In 1794, Matthew Lewis's novel *The Monk* was published, and in that novel there is a fifteen-year-old girl named Antonia who is both well-read in the Bible and stunningly naïve. Another of the characters wonders how this is possible. It turns out that, like Mrs. Trimmer, Antonia's mother has copied out the Bible by hand, leaving out all coarse passages. Unlike Mrs. Trimmer, she has been quite explicit about what she is doing. ("That prudent mother, while she admired the beauties of the sacred writings, was convinced that, unrestricted, no reading more improper could be permitted to a young woman. Many of the narratives can only tend to excite ideas the worse calculated for a female breast; everything is called plainly and roundly by its name; and the annals of a

---

* This doesn't mean that none of her contemporaries recognized it as one. James Plumptre certainly did. Lamenting in 1811 the many passages in the Bible "translated in terms not now generally made use of in polished society," he rejoices in a footnote that there is at least the Trimmer version, where "these passages are either omitted or the expressions altered."

brothel could scarcely furnish a greater choice of indecent expressions.")

This passage caused a tremendous outcry. The Bishop
of London, among others, said hotly that such slurs on
the Bible were intolerable, and demanded that Lewis
withdraw them from future editions of the book, which
he did. Part of the outcry, of course, was caused by
Lewis' rather smarty language—he was only twenty
when *The Monk* came out—but the message itself was
the principal offense.

There is also a secondary reason why Mrs. Trimmer
was able to get away with her changes. This is the
Reformation itself, with its emphasis in England on re-
forming sacred texts as well as doctrines. Before Mrs.
Trimmer, no one had ventured to bowdlerize the incidents in the Bible, but many had tried to improve the
English into which they were translated. In Shakespeare's time, for example, there were three Bibles going
at once. The Bishops Bible (1568) was the authorized
version used in church, but most laymen preferred either
the stately language of the Great Bible (1539) if they
were old-fashioned, or the crisper Geneva Bible (1560)
if they were modernists. In Mrs. Trimmer's own time
the King James Version ruled supreme, but people felt
free then as now to try bettering it. About the time she
was having the sixth of her twelve children, for example,
Dr. Edward Harwood was producing his *Liberal Translation of the New Testament* (1768), of which the
avowed purpose is to replace "the bald and barbarous
language of the old vulgar version" (the King James)
with up-to-date elegance. In his day that meant, of

course, a kind of super-formality. "You are convinced, Thomas, of the identity of my person, merely because of the testimony of your senses—be assured that those discover a better disposition, who tho they have not ocular demonstration, yet are persuaded," Harwood's Christ says to Doubting Thomas. Harwood was perfectly serious about this.*

And in addition to making new translations, people were also constantly putting out abridged Bibles, junior Bibles, and books of Bible selections. Such a work as *The Holy Bible Adapted to the Use of Schools and Private Families* (Birmingham: 1783) cuts many of the same passages that Mrs. Trimmer does, and could be classed as a similar work—if it didn't also omit most of St. Paul's epistles, the entire Book of Revelation, and, in short, turn out not to be a Bible with some pieces cut out, but some pieces left after the Bible has been cut away.

The Bible's semi-sacred companion, the Book of Common Prayer, has been tinkered with even more. Cromwell, of course, banned it in 1644, replacing it with a new Puritan prayer book which was in turn banned in 1660. Dissenters often rewrote it to suit their own theology, this habit being expecially popular among (and needful for) Unitarians. By Mrs. Trimmer's time there were something like twenty versions of it in existence, the one on which Benjamin Franklin and Sir Francis Dashwood—"Hell-Fire Francis"—collaborated being

---

* His hope was that "YOUTH could be allured by the innocent stratagem of a *modern style,* to read a book which is now, alas! too generally neglected by the young and gay." There is an obvious parallel to the jazz mass of our day.

clearly the most colorful.* None of these with the possible exception of the Franklin-Dashwood version could be called an expurgation, but they did all help to provide a climate in which using one's ingenuity to improve sacred texts could seem like a good idea.

Oddly enough, the first person after Mrs. Trimmer to use his ingenuity in this way was Beilby Porteus, Bishop of London, the same one who was so outraged by Matthew Lewis (and the same who offered Harriet Bowdler a parish). It was even about the same time. *The Monk* appeared in 1794, and the first Bible with a Porteusian Index came out in 1796. The difference is that where Mrs. Trimmer covertly and Antonia's mother openly proposed to expurgate the Bible as one might expurgate Shakespeare or Dryden, Bishop Porteus and his col-

---

* Franklin and Dashwood had made contact while each was a postmaster general, and found themselves agreeing that the great trouble with church services is that they are too long. They then put out their anonymous *Abridgement of the Book of Common Prayer* (1773), in which the communion service takes about ten minutes, and a funeral six. ("The Order for the Burial of the Dead is very solemn and moving; nevertheless, to preserve the health and lives of the living, it appeared to us that this service ought particularly to be shortened," Franklin wrote jauntily in the preface.) The book could be called expurgated only in the sense that Franklin and Dashwood both disapproved of Old Testament ideas of vengeance, and therefore omitted the service of Commination and all psalms which contain maledictions.

A Francis Gentleman variation on this was done in Boston in 1785, when the First Episcopal Chapel published its *Liturgy*. No psalms were omitted, but cries for vengeance were printed in italics, so that the congregation could skip them. (A few ordinary indelicacies were also italicized, like Psalms 38:5, "My wounds stink and are corrupt through my foolishness," so that the congregation could skip them, too. "Stink" seems to have been anathema to Americans, as the case of Noah Webster will soon show.)

More recently, the *Psalter* edited in 1966 by the Archbishop of York and a Church of England commission put the same cries in brackets, for the same reason.

leagues were determined to make it proper reading without removing a single word.

A Porteusian Index is a sort of navigation chart to the Bible, though one which marks only the safe channels, and which thus deals with rocks, shoals and bawdy passages only by implication. The index is actually a grading system—three kinds of marks which sort Scripture into four classes of reading. Every chapter in the Bible has at its head either a starred 1, an ordinary 1, a 2, or no mark at all. Starred firsts occur mainly in the New Testament (though there are some in Psalms and quite a lot in Isaiah) and are normally reserved for the words of Christ and for prophecies which foretell His coming. They are the best reading in the Bible. Ordinary firsts are those chapters "which are of a more *spiritual* or *practical* nature" [than seconds or unmarked chapters]. They include most of the chapters in the Gospels that are not starred, much of Job and Ecclesiastes, and occasional chapters throughout. Together with starred firsts, they form a select list of chapters which are worth meditating on. They are also the ones which should be turned to "by children and others, when called upon to read to their parents or sick friends."

Seconds are "the leading *historical* chapters," and are good safe reading, though not worth much meditation. Unmarked covers everything else—that is, just under half of the Old Testament and a dozen or so chapters in the New. The story of Lot is an unmarked chapter. The Song of Solomon is a book of unmarked chapters.

The compilers of the Porteusian Index showed a good deal of cleverness in writing their "key," the explanation of the whole system which appears in the front. If the key had warned readers away from unmarked chapters, as tending to excite ideas the worse calculated for a female breast or being full of improper expressions, human nature is such that most people would have leafed patiently from one to the next until they found the Song of Solomon and the story of Onan. The key does no such thing. On the contrary, it urges readers to look at the unmarked chapters—but it does so in a way that makes it unlikely that they actually will. What it says is this:

> Although a considerable number of the chapters, *not* distinguished as above, relate to the Jewish laws, genealogies, and other subjects not so generally interesting to the youthful reader, yet it is manifest, there is among them an extensive distribution of important portions of Holy Writ: which are earnestly recommended to the attention of the advancing reader; and indeed which cannot fail inviting and rewarding his more general and thorough research.

That statement is masterly. It has a friendly candor, as of one who won't attempt to deny that genealogies and Jewish law are pretty dull stuff. It neatly tells a half-truth—many unmarked chapters do indeed relate to these boring matters; it's just that even more of them don't. And then the last part, earnestly recommending one to have a look, so perfectly mimics the tone of a pompous teacher that even someone who knew his Bible already might find himself vowing never to look at an unmarked chapter again.

The Porteusian Bible had a considerable success—alone of English purified Bibles, it was "appointed to be read in churches"—and for a time there was a Porteusian Bible Society, with headquarters in Frith Street, London, which was entirely devoted to distributing copies of it. But it did not, of course, solve the problem of cleaning up Scripture. Not only was anyone who failed to be moved by the key perfectly free to turn to Ezekiel and read about people committing whoredoms in Egypt —and even free to say he was just doing the extensive research the key recommended—but in addition, plenty of chapters with firsts and seconds contain words that the early nineteenth century on the whole regretted. Between 1818 and 1828, four new attempts to purify the Bible without actually expurgating appeared. Each tries a different method; and each, as it happens, has its roots in a different branch of Christianity.

The first of them is the most ingenious. This is John Bellamy's *Holy Bible, Newly Translated*, the lead volume of which came out in 1818. Bellamy, a Swedenborgian, started with the assumption that an Old Testament patriarch such as Lot or Jacob couldn't really have done the things which the King James Version seems to say he did, and that therefore the trouble must lie in bad translation from the Hebrew. He spent ten years learning Hebrew, and proceeded to work out new meanings for most of the passages in the Bible which seemed to him improper. A fair example is his handling of the famous incident in Genesis 9 when Noah gets drunk in his tent. As preceding Bibles, including the Porteusian, tell the story (Mrs. Trimmer skips it), Ham goes into the tent and finds his father passed out naked on the floor, but does nothing about it. Shem and Japheth then go into the tent walking backward, and spread a garment over him without turning their heads, "and they saw not their father's nakedness."

Hebrew being a language without vowels, it is fairly easy to read alternative meanings into words, and Bellamy was able to change all this so that Noah is in his tent fully clothed, but with the door of a small tabernacle open. What Ham sees are "the symbols of his father" in the tabernacle (Bellamy doesn't say what they are), and these are what Shem and Japheth go in backward and cover. Noah also wasn't drunk. On this matter, Bellamy has a long and very learned note. It is the Hebrew phrase *va yishkaar* which has caused all the trouble, he says. It has always been translated "and he was drunken," but what it really means is "and he was satisfied." That is, Noah had admittedly been in his tent drinking a glass of wine, which he enjoyed, as well he might, it being the first vintage after the Flood, but he has not taken too much. Bellamy then tries to prove his point by citing all the other appearances of *va yishkaar* and its related forms. There is one in Isaiah, for example, in a phrase which has always been translated "drunk in my fury."

"This cannot mean drunkenness with strong drink," says Bellamy; on the contrary, "it signifies a disordered state of mind by trouble: *satiated in my fury*." Another example occurs in Deuteronomy, in a passage which the King James Version renders, "I will make mine arrows drunk with blood." "This is a striking figure," Bellamy grants, rather in the tone that Mrs. Bowdler would have —but how can an arrow be drunk? Those arrows were *sated* with blood. (How an arrow can be sated any more than it can be drunk, he doesn't, say.)

Again, in Ezekiel an army just before battle is given the command, "And drink blood until ye be drunken." A mere way of speaking, says Bellamy. Since the soldiers "were not assembled to eat flesh and drink blood, it means a state fully satisfied with shedding blood; and should be rendered, 'And drink (or shed) blood, till ye be SATISFIED.' "

And therefore Noah had simply had enough wine to slake his thirst, and wasn't drunk at all—just as Lot wasn't when his daughters played the trick on him in Genesis 19. (In fact, there wasn't any trick. He and his daughters have a farewell glass of wine, and then the girls emigrate to find husbands.) In the same way, it's a mistake to suppose that Onan practiced withdrawal. In Bellamy, Onan knows that "posterity is not for him," *i.e.*, he's a born bachelor, and when he goes in to his brother's wife they simply don't do anything. The original writer of the passage, says Bellamy, never meant "to convey such an indelicate sense as is given in the common version."

Bellamy's Bible was not a success. It started life with a bang, having the Prince Regent and ten other members of the royal family among the subscribers for the first volume. But when the scholars got hold of it, high patronage didn't even begin to help. The theologian George D'Oyly spent thirty pages demolishing the author in terms like these: "His knowledge of Hebrew consists in little more than a common acquaintance with the meanings of the roots . . . he is, besides, totally destitute of judgement." The Professor of Arabic at Cambridge concurred; all scholars did. Conscious of their ignorance of Hebrew, the eleven royal subscribers tiptoed rapidly away. Bellamy chose to ignore them, and the scholars, too. He went right on translating and publishing further sections until he ran out of money, at which point he appealed to Parliament—unsuccessfully —for a public grant to see the work through. But by that time—it was 1832—no one was reading Bellamy even to attack him.

Instead, the pure-minded were reading Dr. Benjamin Boothroyd's *New Family Bible and Improved Version*, which had come out in 1824. Dr. Boothroyd, a Congregational minister, had mixed motives. In part he merely wanted to bring the language of the Bible up to date, as Harwood had done before him, and as the translators of the Revised Standard Version and the New English Bible have done since. But he couldn't help noticing that there are "many offensive and indelicate expressions," and rather than bring *them* up to date, he decided, not exactly to expurgate them, but to find inoffensive ways around them which would nevertheless "convey the sense clearly."

This is a hard trick, and Dr. Boothroyd did not really manage it. When he conveyed the sense clearly, as with Noah's getting drunk and passing out, the passage remained offensive. Dr. Boothroyd could do no more for Noah than to add a footnote saying, "It is probable that

the venerable Patriarch was overcome with the fruit of
the vine from inexperience; and if this does not remove
his crime, it diminishes the guilt of it." *

Lot's seduction by his daughters also remains clear in
Boothroyd, and the note here only makes matters worse.
"The conduct of his daughters, from whatever motive it
arose," Dr. Boothroyd wrote, "was as unwarrantable as
it was singular. They were probably influenced by a
regard to their own family connexions, out of which
they thought it not right to marry." To get pregnant by
your father because there are no other men alive may be
understandable, but to do it rather than marry out of the
family seems a shocking snobbery, and one not suggested
in either the King James Version or the original Hebrew.

On the other hand, when Dr. Boothroyd found a way
to be inoffensive, he doesn't convey the sense. Onan's
story is a case in point. The Boothroyd version goes like
this: "And, as Onan knew the seed would not be ac-
counted his own; so, though he went in to his brother's
wife, yet did he avoid raising up seed to his brother. But
what he did was so wicked in the sight of Jehovah, that
he slew him also."

* Palliative footnotes were common in Bibles of the period. The
Reverend T. Priestley, who edited the *New Evangelical Family Bible*,
an unexpurgated King James Version which came out in 1793, wrote
one which excuses Noah in three different ways. The old patriarch
may have gotten drunk, Mr. Priestley theorizes, because of "not being
accustomed now of a long time to drink any wine." (Priestley
assumes there was none on the ark.) Or maybe he needed "to chear
his spirits, being almost alone in the earth." Or, most ingenious of all,
maybe Satan, "not having many now to tempt," was concentrating his
whole force on one person—and if sinless Eve fell under such
circumstances, what chance had Noah?

Though decent, the second sentence is strikingly unclear. It merely starts the reader wondering just what did
go on in the brother's wife's room. As usual, Boothroyd
adds a note, and, as usual, it doesn't help. "The sin of
Onan was double," he explains, "his refusing to raise up
seed to his brother, and the manner in which he did it."
Any who failed to be made curious by the text are given
a second chance. Some of the more depraved readers
must have been ready to rush out and borrow a Porteusian Bible or even a regular one, and learn what really
happened.

Such bowdlerisms are rare in Boothroyd, though.
Most of the time he chose to be clear rather than inoffensive—though he does regularly drop the word "belly,"
and he once mysteriously transmuted a girl's navel into
her "waist." Furthermore, he really was a Hebrew
scholar. Except in the notes, his version contains no
Bellamian fantasies. He corrected a number of un-
doubted errors that occur in the King James Version.
Perhaps for that reason most of all, his Bible was treated
with respect. Glasgow University gave him an honorary
D.D. on the strength of it. There was a second edition in
1835–37, and even a third edition in 1853, fifteen years
after his death. Histories of the Bible to this day deal
kindly with him.

They ignore another man whose expurgation was
published the same year. This is John Watson, "a layman
of the Church of England," editor of *The Holy Bible
Arranged and Adapted for Family Reading.*

Mr. Watson's chief innovation was not to number
chapters or verses, presumably to make it harder to tell

what he had left out. Instead he invents divisions of his own; for example, he divides Genesis into seven "sections" instead of the customary forty-nine chapters. What he prints in them is rather more than Mrs. Trimmer and rather less than Dr. Boothroyd. Noah's spree he omits altogether, but the story of Lot, on the other hand, he prints verbatim right through the destruction of Sodom, omitting only the final scene in the wilderness. Making even minor cuts in the Pentateuch must have been very hard for him, of course, since he believed that Moses personally wrote every word of it, and further that the "authenticity and sacred character" of each word was guaranteed by Christ himself.

Later in the Bible he felt freer. Of the Song of Solomon, to take the most striking case, he printed only the title, together with a note explaining that adolescents should not encounter this book at all, "lest in the fervor of youth they give too wide a scope to fancy, and interpret to a bad sense the spiritual ideas of Solomon." (Boothroyd in *his* general note on the book said frankly that, narrow the scope of his fancy as he would, he couldn't find any spiritual ideas in it, just a lot of sex. Not that he used so gross a phrase. The purpose of the book is "to exhibit the chaste passions of conjugal life, as they existed among the Jews, to whom polygamy was allowed," he said. "I cannot recommend the reading of it in families," he added.)

Mr. William Alexander, the final member of this quartet, was a Quaker who ran his own printing business. His *Holy Bible, Principally Designed to Facilitate the Audible or Social Reading of the Sacred Scriptures* (York:

1828) shows it. Even now, when so many people have been to college, studied the new math, read the toughest sort of detective stories, and so on, Alexander's Bible would be impossible for most people to make head or tail of, much less read audibly and socially.

Alexander intended to elaborate on the Porteusian system—but "elaborate" is not really an adequate word for what he intended. The general effect of his Bible is rather like that of a magazine unusually addicted to continuing its articles in the back, if such a magazine can be imagined using Gothic type, italic type, and three or four sizes of Roman type on almost every page. The basic Porteusian division into classes is there: Alexander's are called Devotional Series, General Series, and Private Perusal Series. But instead of just putting one's and two's and stars into an otherwise unchanged Bible, his idea was physically to segregate the good and bad parts of the Bible, like male and female authors on a Victorian bookshelf, at the same time keeping every chapter and nearly every verse in its normal order. This is an even harder trick than Dr. Boothroyd's. Furthermore, both the Devotional and the General Series were to form coherent and readable books in their own right, and there was to be ample room for notes.

If you open Alexander's Bible to the first page of Scripture, you find that you are simultaneously beginning Devotional Section 1 and Genesis 1. On that first page are three verses of Genesis, printed two different ways (English word order and Hebrew word order), and half a page of footnotes, plus more notes in the margin. This is one of the simpler pages. You then pick your way through Devotional Sections 2, 3, and 4, at which point there is a note saying "Dev. Series continued Ch. VI," and General Section 1 commences. The two series henceforth alternate, a single Bible chapter sometimes being jumped back and forth two or three times from one to the other, until the story of Lot looms up. Private Perusal Series now starts. This series is unnumbered, and printed in italics at the bottom of the page. (General Series page directions are in Gothic.) All three then take turns.

Unlike Devotional and General, the Private Perusal Series makes no sense if read as a continuous story, and Alexander never meant it to. It is his equivalent of the unmarked chapters in a Porteusian Bible, only he is somewhat franker about what he is doing. In his key, he identifies it as consisting of "genealogies, rites of the law, and some few important and faithful delineations of men and manners, not adapted to AUDIBLE reading in a circle consisting of DIFFERENT SEXES; but without which, the Holy Scripture, as a faithful record, would be incomplete." That is, it's all the things which, if God hadn't joined the Bible together, he would have put asunder.

As a Porteusian, Alexander should have stopped right now. The whole point of streaming is to render Scripture harmless without actually changing anything. But he couldn't bring himself not to change just a little. In all three of his classes he found—he won't call them improper words—expressions "not congenial to the views and genius of the present age of refinement." The least congenial of these he changed. "Belly" seems to have been his *bête noire*, as it was Boothroyd's, but he also turned many whores into harlots; and the passage in Leviticus which says no one can be a priest who "hath his stones broken" (King James) or "crushed testicles" (Revised Standard Version) he quietly altered to "who hath a rupture."

But after all that, and despite strong backing from the Quakers of York, his Bible was a failure. No one could follow the directions. Of the twenty parts in which he intended to publish the scriptures, only six were ever printed. It was left to an American, with strong backing from the Congregationalists of Connecticut, to make bowdlerism of the Bible a success.

This American was Noah Webster, who is one of the most dedicated expurgators in history. His Bible, though he regarded it as the crown of his life's work,* was only the crown, and it had been preceded by a long series of expurgated dictionaries, and before that by expurgated spelling books.

Webster was a man of sixty when he began to think of crowning his life's work. Isolated in far-off Connecticut, he knew nothing about the work being done in England. He only knew that what he called the Bible in the Common Version—"King James Version" was an unsuitable name for citizens of a republic to use, he felt— was not a nice book for American girls to have to read from in Sunday school, or even for the president of Yale to quote in chapel. And he knew from having asked them that the girls and President Day shared this view. There was a general readiness for a purified Bible, "al-

* "I consider this . . . the most important enterprise of my life, and as important as any benevolent design now on foot."

though no man appears to know how or by whom such revision is to be executed."

About 1821 Webster began to realize he had better do the job himself; and by way of a trial balloon (he was an infinitely more experienced editor than a Bellamy or a Boothroyd) he bowdlerized and generally scrubbed up one sample book of the Bible and sent it off to Professor Moses Stuart of Andover Theological Seminary for comment. In April 1822, Stuart reported that he and the rest of the faculty felt that Webster had carried the scrubbing much too far, and they were not prepared to back him. But they did agree that a Bible "free of words offensive to modesty" was a good idea.

The trial balloon having been so promptly shot down, Webster turned back for a while to a plan he had to expurgate the whole of English poetry, and then he spent some years finishing the first Webster's Unabridged. When he returned to the Bible, he was a man of seventy, Dr. Webster now (Yale had given him an LL.D. for the dictionary), and distinguished enough not to have to beg the support of the professors at Andover. Like Dr. Johnson, Dr. Webster could use his own name as an imprimatur. On his own authority, he again began to scrub the Bible around 1830, and his new version was published in New Haven, Connecticut, in 1833. It is the first and last avowed expurgation the Bible has ever had. Elizabeth Bowdler would have been delighted with it.

Webster's system was wholly unlike that of Mrs. Trimmer. She left the wording alone (in her later editions), but freely cut embarrassing incidents. Webster retained every incident in the Bible, but freely changed words. In the New Testament this meant a handful of refinements like changing the scarlet whore of Babylon into a scarlet harlot. In the Old Testament it meant endless hard work. There were thousands of changes to make. These included, of course, everything Mrs. Trimmer had cut, Bishop Porteus had put into an unmarked chapter (not the genealogies and Jewish laws), and Bellamy had figured out a new meaning for. Onan, for example, now "frustrates the purpose" of his visit to his sister-in-law. The rules for priests in Leviticus now specify that no one whose "peculiar members" are defective is eligible for ordination. The Israelites down in Egypt no longer go a-whoring, they have "carnal connections," and they commit "lewd deeds."

But Webster's changes went far beyond that. He hated the word "stink," for example, even more than Boothroyd hated "belly" (he hated that, too), and he showed extraordinary ingenuity in changing it. If the King James Version says that the Nile stank after all the fish in it were killed by Jehovah, Webster has it become "offensive in smell." Overripe manna stops stinking and begins putrifying. If the prophets Amos and Joel complain that the heathen make a stink in the nostrils of the Lord, Webster tones them down to an "ill savor" (Amos) and an "odious scent" (Joel). And Egyptians don't have buttocks in Webster, they have hind-parts. Israelites never lust after things, they just desire them.

Beyond all this for decency's sake, Webster changed a good deal of Biblical poetry into prose, apparently for his own sake. He was a born schoolmaster. Sometimes

135

decency could be invoked, as when he changed Ezekiel's splendid accusation, "Thou hast opened thy feet to every one that passed by, and multiplied thy whoredoms," to a prosy "Thou hast prostituted thyself to everyone that passed by, and multiplied thy lewd deeds." Sometimes it was sheer pedantry. There is nothing immodest about Ecclesiastes 11:5, "As thou knowest not what is the way of the spirit, nor how the bones do grow in her that is with child: even so thou knowest not the words of God." Webster nevertheless changed it to "As thou knowest not what is the way of the spirit, nor the structure of the parts of conception in her that is with child." Maybe there *is* a touch of grossness in Job's lament: "Why died I not from the womb? why did I not give up the ghost when I came out of the belly?" which Webster changed to "Why did I not expire at the time of my birth?" But there certainly isn't in the account all four Gospels give of the Crucifixion: "About the ninth hour our Lord yielded up the ghost," yet Christ, too, is made to expire.

It was Webster's pedantry, in fact, that ruined his version—even as an effective expurgation. He was just as determined as William Alexander not actually to leave anything out of the Bible, and he was too much of a teacher to be able to resist correcting the syntax of the King James Version whenever needed. Sometimes, as once in the Song of Solomon, the result was to underline a difficulty that had been less apparent before. "Stay me with flagons, comfort me with apples, for I am sick of love," wrote Solomon. The verse seems to suggest that those who commit lewd acts wind up in a state of acute boredom, their only remaining desire a craving for fresh fruit. Webster dispelled that illusion at once. You are sick *with* love, he firmly corrected Solomon, thus making it clear that the illness arose from a lack of carnal connections rather than from a surfeit.

All the same, Webster's reputation stood high in 1833, and this was the only cleaned-up Bible available in America. Those who were bothered by the indecency of the King James had to choose it or nothing. After a couple of years of hesitation ("I wish a few clergymen would summon courage to commend my Bible to the public," Webster complained in 1835), the state of Connecticut decisively took to it. A month after Webster's complaint, in December 1835, President Day and most of the Yale faculty signed a statement endorsing the new version; and for the Connecticut of 1835 this was a powerful recommendation. The Congregational church —which had only just ceased to be the established state church—never officially adopted it, but for about twenty years it was widely used in Congregational pulpits. There were large new editions in 1839 and 1841, and a special Webster New Testament for families. Then it faded quietly away.

This was the last assault on the Bible. Bowdlerism itself continued to grow, and so did demands for new Bibles to replace the King James. But by 1854, when the American Bible Society in New York put out a new revision (withdrawn again in 1858, because it was too frank), Biblical scholars were trying to get closer to the language of the original Hebrew, not further away from it. The original Hebrew being what it is, this meant more rather than less trouble for girls teaching Sunday school,* and one book running against the general Victorian trend. Of all their customs, men are most reluctant to tamper with their religious practices.

* For example, there are the two girls in Ezekiel—they're part of a metaphor, of course—who have their "breasts pressed," as the King James puts it. Webster says vaguely that they get "corrupted." Biblical scholarship has driven relentlessly toward the Hebrew, and now they have "their virgin bosoms handled."

****

CHAPTER SIX

Destiny and Mr. Plumptre

****

*I commonly read with a pen or pencil in my
hand, and either expunged or altered such
expressions as struck me to be objectionable. . . . Some I tried by that excellent test,
the reading of them aloud to ladies.*

JAMES PLUMPTRE, 1812

IN THE SPRING OF 1819, Isaac D'Israeli, the father of
Benjamin Disraeli and the author of *Curiosities of Literature*, was living in Bloomsbury Square, London,
busy gathering additional curiosities for the sixth edition.
He was thus home the last week in April to receive a
parcel from the country, sent by a man he had never
heard of. Instead of a dozen fresh eggs or a comb of
honey, its contents turned out to be a printed sermon on
the subject of ghosts, a book called *Original Plays*, and a
whole sheaf of penny songbooks, their contents rather
freely adapted from Burns, Marlowe, Shakespeare, and a
dozen others. A covering letter explained that all this was
sent as a token of esteem for a fellow author. The letter
went on to praise D'Israeli's books at some length.

D'Israeli seems to have figured out the true motive for

his present with no trouble at all. When he wrote his new admirer a pleasant if rather mannered letter of thanks ("I feel myself highly gratified by your notion of my trifles"), he ended it by saying he hoped to find room to mention him in the next edition of *Curiosities*. The admirer replied with a jubilant letter and three more of his books.

As it turned out, D'Israeli didn't find room. The sixth edition of *Curiosities* came out, the seventh, the eighth, but never a word about the author of *Original Plays*. This was not only a blow to the Rev. James Plumptre, it seems also a blunder by D'Israeli: Plumptre and his works rank among the true curiosities of English literature. There is some excuse for D'Israeli, to be sure. Curious as the books are that Plumptre sent, they aren't nearly as curious as some of the ones he didn't send. And the oddity of his own character couldn't really be deduced from the two letters. They were, for him, unusually self-effacing.

As a matter of fact, Plumptre's character wasn't odd in most ways. In most ways he was a completely normal upper-middle-class Englishman of his time—a little more education than the average, perhaps, and a little less money. He came of a distinguished family. His grandfather had been in Parliament; his father had been the President of Queens' College, Cambridge; his brother-in-law was Dean of Gloucester. He himself taught at Cambridge for nineteen years before getting married and settling down as vicar of Great Gransden, Huntingdonshire. At the time of writing D'Israeli he was a vigorous man of forty-seven.

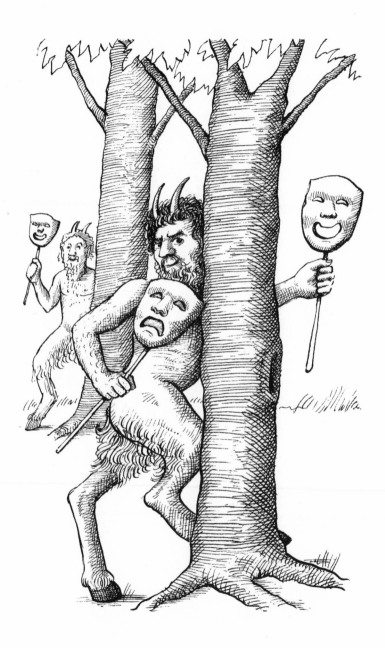

In just one way was this well-bred clergyman curious. Ever since he was a youth of twenty-two, he had believed himself destined to change the whole course of English literature. Before him it had been gross, often irreligious, and often obscene. After him it was to be a pure sparkling stream of good. He was to be the filter. Obviously a man with such a destiny cannot afford to be modest about calling attention to himself, or at least to his work. Plumptre was not modest. In fact, for sheer gall in touting his own publications he probably holds the British record. Men like Byron, Wilde, and Shaw were shrinking violets by comparison. It is true that they were and are famous, while Plumptre had only a small reputation at his peak, and now is totally obscure. But if blowing his own horn could have achieved it, he would be more celebrated than all three put together.

As for his books, D'Israeli could reasonably have devoted a full chapter of *Curiosities* to them. There are eighteen in all, plus dozens of smaller works, and even their range is striking. Many writers are at home in more than one field, but Plumptre was at home throughout literature and even beyond. Theatrically, he found time to write eight plays of his own, and to expurgate seventeen by other people. (If his original plan had succeeded, he would have expurgated something like fifty times that many, and abolished the rest; and the entire repertoire of Elizabethan, Restoration, eighteenth-century, etc., drama now in existence would consist of Plumptre versions.) As a scholar, he produced a general theory of the drama, and also two books demonstrating that Shakespeare wrote *Hamlet* in order to rebuke Mary, Queen of

Scots, for getting married so often. If you accept the theory, you see Mary as Gertrude, Queen of Danes, and Lord Bothwell thinly veiled as King Claudius. Hamlet is James I.

This is merely the beginning. In the field of religion, Plumptre produced two volumes of Bible commentary, especially designed to correct lower-class morals. As a man interested in fiction, he expurgated *Robinson Crusoe.** In travel literature, he did the same thing for Anson's *Voyages*. As a poetry lover, he published two expurgated anthologies. And just to fill in the crannies, he also wrote a comic opera, and a book on how to be a successful small-town butcher.

For the modern reader, at least, almost every one of these books is packed with curiosities. His study of dramatic theory, for example, deals with problems that Shaw and Pinter never dreamed of. Take the problem of comedy. In order to justify its very existence, Plumptre thinks he must first deal with the objection that nowhere in the New Testament is it recorded that Christ laughed. He accordingly shows that it's also not recorded that He *didn't* laugh, and that since the Old Testament is full of instances of His father laughing, there can't be anything wrong with humor *per se*. Theater audiences may laugh as much as they please, Plumptre eventually rules, provided they fail to be amused by "low buffoonery, obscenity, and what we call *double meanings*."

But though comedy may be lawful, an extraordinary number of things are not. No play can be permitted

---

* His most successful book. Sixty years after publication, it was still selling both in London and in New York.

whose characters put any trust in saints or angels (there goes Shaw's *Saint Joan*), or where prophecies turn out correct. (That rules out *Macbeth*, as Plumptre himself points out.) Neither can any which side with children against their parents (goodbye, Ibsen and O'Neill), or in which marriage produces "satiety, disgust, or aversion." This more or less wipes out nineteenth-century French drama, plus Edward Albee, two losses which Plumptre would have taken calmly.

Then there are the two anthologies. Besides some quite unusual versions of the great English songs,* both have prefaces which discuss the principles of song-expurgation. D'Israeli missed good material here. A tavern song, for example, should not be allowed to retain a line which asserts that drinking causes less harm than seducing girls. "I do not think it advisable to form a scale of the degrees of vice." In what would now be called blues—Plumptre calls them laments—there should be no talk of "cherisht woe" or "loved despair" or anything of that sort. Such lines encourage people to lead lives of emotional self-indulgence. Girls must never be described in song as goddesses or divine creatures, or called "Perfect, as celestials are." Why? "Woman was given to man 'as an help meet for him,'" Plumptre explains, "not as his deity to adore." Expurgators have literal minds.

---

* Shakespeare's, for example. "Under the greenwood tree, who loves to lie with me" becomes "who loves to work with me." "Hark, hark, the lark" becomes a sermonette on keeping early hours, the new last line reading "For shame, thou sluggard, rise." The cuckoo song from *Love's Labour's Lost* not only loses its many references to cuckoldry (which in Shakespeare were its principal point), but even drops an innocent reference to the flower the lady-smock—"smock" was a dirty word to Plumptre.

The most curious of all Plumptre's books, though, and the one that he expected to change the world, is called *The English Drama Purified*. It is probably the most thoroughgoing expurgation ever printed. The plays in it were intensely winnowed to begin with. The very first one, for example, is an eighteenth-century tragedy called *The Gamester*, and to most people it would have seemed a highly moral work as it stood. The original author wrote it as a protest against gambling. A nice young man named Beverley is taught to gamble by a villain named Stukeley, and, after losing everything he's got, is finally driven to suicide. In a thrilling last scene, he drinks poison on the stage.

Plumptre liked the bad outcome of gambling, but not the suicide, this being one of the many impermissible actions in a play. At first he planned simply to remove it, and have Beverley live. When he realized that this left the play without an ending, and couldn't think of a new one, he reluctantly compromised. In *The English Drama Purified*, Beverley still commits suicide, but he now goes off stage and poisons himself in private. This alteration makes the play less horrid for an audience to watch, Plumptre said. More important, it is "less shewing them how the act of suicide is committed."

This matter of audience education was always on Plumptre's mind. In another purified tragedy he took out all the heroic speeches of the hero, on the grounds that the language was too "ardent." (Heroes should set an example of meekness, even if they happen to be medieval Scottish earls.) In one of the comedies, a play in which a king and his court get lost out hunting, seek shelter in a woodman's cottage, and then are mistaken by the locals for a group of poachers, he cut about half the jokes. Low buffoonery and obscenity? No. Double meanings, then? The play never had any. The missing lines are cracks by the peasants at the expense of the upper classes. Lower-class people in the audience would get too excited by such remarks, Plumptre felt. Tempered criticism is one thing, but if you start allowing actual satire "against Courtiers and great men," you're asking for trouble. The groundlings will go home and snap their fingers at the squire, read Tom Paine, probably take off their culottes.

There was no danger of this sort—or, to most people's minds, of *any* sort—in the best play Plumptre included, which is Steele's *The Conscious Lovers*. The purpose of that play, as its own prologue says, is "To chasten wit, and moralize the stage." More specifically, Steele wanted to attack the custom of fighting duels. He had fought one himself as a young officer in the Coldstream Guards, had almost killed his opponent, and had been an enemy of duels ever since. In *The Conscious Lovers* he spends three acts working up to a situation in which young Jack Bevil is challenged to a duel by his friend Charles Myrtle (who thinks Jack has stolen his girl) and nobly declines. The scene was a huge success. Samuel Richardson borrowed it for use in *Sir Charles Grandison*. Fielding has it in mind when he makes one of the characters in *Joseph Andrews* say that here is the only play fit for a Christian to see. James Plumptre read the scene as an upper-middle-class schoolboy, and was so moved by it that he took a vow on the spot never to duel.

Nevertheless, in his capacity as the destined filter of English literature, he found the scene needed purifying. One of its two crucial moments occurs when Jack gets so stung by Myrtle's taunts of cowardice that he springs to his feet, hand reaching for sword, ready to accept the challenge. "You have touched me beyond the patience of a man," he says, and is about to name a time and place. Then he recovers himself, and once again nobly declines. Plumptre struck all that out, for the same reason he wouldn't let Beverley drink poison on the stage. "The giving way, even for a moment, I conceive to be a bad example."

There is also a much-changed scene between Jack and his father. As Steele wrote the play, Jack had to deceive his father. Old Sir John wanted him to marry a charming heiress named Lucinda Sealand, whereas he himself wanted to marry a girl of great beauty but obscure parentage, romantically named Indiana. (She later turns out to be Lucinda's long-lost sister, and hence entitled to half the money, anyway.) For her part, Lucinda loves Charles Myrtle, but is under parental orders to accept Jack. Hence the deception. Jack and Lucinda make a secret pact that he will propose to her after a simulated courtship, and she will turn him down. Then he can peacefully claim his Indiana, leaving her free to marry Myrtle. It is their neglect to let Myrtle in on the plan which leads to the duel scene.

Meanwhile, there are the fathers to be dealt with. The scene opens with Jack soliloquizing: "Well, then, with assurance of being rejected, I think I may confidently say to my father, I am ready to marry her. Then let me resolve upon what I am not very good at, though it is an honest dissimulation." Plumptre found two things wrong with this speech. First, there is no such thing as an honest dissimulation. Secondly, a grown man ought not to promise, even for a moment, to marry someone just to please his father. This is carrying filial duty to excess. Consequently he crossed Steele's lines out and wrote new ones in. The passage now goes: "My father I must not, will not for a moment deceive: but with a prudent reserve, without sacrificing my veracity, I will endeavour to delay matters until circumstances become more favourable." In other words, poor Jack has just become a hypocrite. And Plumptre has shown what expurgation can grow to be, given a sufficient belief in one's own high motives and narrow standards.

It is one thing, of course, to rewrite seventeen plays in this fashion, and quite another to bring them to the world's attention. In his efforts to do so, Plumptre attempted to assemble a public-relations staff including one prime minister and two foreign ministers of England, half a dozen bishops, three members of the British royal family, Tsar Alexander, Samuel Taylor Coleridge, the Marquis of Hertford, and two successive Professors of Poetry at Oxford.

The story really begins in 1809, three years before *The English Drama Purified* even reached print. Up until then, Plumptre had expurgated nothing longer than a fair-sized poem. But during the winter of 1808–09, a dramatic opportunity opened. There were in Plumptre's time only two legitimate theaters in London—Covent Garden and Drury Lane—and it so happened that that winter they burned to the ground within a few months of each other, a coincidence explained by many as a divine judgment on the kind of plays they put on. Both were, of course, going to be rebuilt; and for a while there was talk of rebuilding one of them on a smaller scale, for the production of decent plays only. After this died away, there was still talk of building a new third theater for the purpose. A philanthropic baronet named Sir Thomas Bernard was even ready to put up some of the money.

Plumptre immediately got the idea of providing a suitable repertory for the new theater.* No one had invited him to, but men of destiny don't have to wait for invitations. He wrote to Sir Thomas Bernard telling him the good news, and then he sat down to plan the work. "I shall begin with a specimen of three or four volumes," he wrote a friend, "containing our best plays with the exceptionable passages either altered or omitted." After that he intended to pick out all the other English plays worth saving—he hadn't yet decided whether Shakespeare's came in this category or not †—and after *that* he had an idea he might purify classical drama as well.

---

* The project was discussed, among other places, in a London magazine called *The Artist*. As soon as he heard of it, Plumptre sent an anonymous letter to the editor, saying eagerly, "A favorable opportunity now exists to revise all the old plays. Why should not everything be omitted that is really objectionable, and why should not the public be told that it would be so in the future?" The second question has a certain crack of the whip about it.

† "I really have not been able to make up my mind as to what should be done in respect to Shakespeare's Plays," Plumptre wrote in 1812. Great literature, of course, but for that very reason "doubly likely to mislead," unless pruned of all indecency—of subject as well as word. This he was not sure could be done.

(Two years later he was badgering Dr. Bowdler's friend the Earl of Hardwicke for free copies of translations from which eventually to work.)

Meanwhile, the whole scheme depended on the success of the specimen volumes. Plumptre's plan went like this. First Cambridge University Press would publish them, which would give the reform a good footing of academic prestige and help bookstore sales. The leading critics would jump in with favorable reviews. When interest was at a peak, the new theater would begin to put on his plays. People would find that at last it was possible to go to the theater safely. By popular demand he would go ahead and expurgate the rest of English drama. By now the old theaters would be finding there was no longer an audience for obscenity, low buffoonery, and cracks at the upper classes, and they, too, would begin to produce Plumptre versions. Within a few years, he confidently told another friend, he would have brought about "a beneficial and permanent change" in the English theater. At this point he expected to have the specimen volumes out and the change under way by the end of 1810.

Instead he got a double setback. The actual preparation of the specimen volumes was no great trouble, but when he took his completed manuscript to the syndics of the Cambridge University Press, they turned it down. Plumptre was still on the faculty then, and he had powerful friends, including the Master of Sidney Sussex. He wasted many months trying to bring pressure for a new decision. While he was doing that, the plan for a new theater collapsed. The proprietors of Covent Garden and Drury Lane had been bringing pressure, too. At this point Sir Thomas Bernard pulled out, and Plumptre was back where he had started.

A Byron- or a Wilde-sized ego might have begun to doubt itself, but Plumptre was made of sterner stuff. Within weeks he worked out a new plan. Instead of depending on one model theater to start the reform, he decided to work through all existing theaters simultaneously. And instead of relying on the comparatively feeble prestige of Cambridge University, he decided to employ the glittering cachet of the royal family. He had a sort of access to it. The first English prince ever to go to college was a person then living, H. R. H. William, Duke of Gloucester; and by good fortune he had known Plumptre's father at Cambridge. The royal M.A. had not hitherto been much involved in reforms ("Gloucester's intellectual powers were by no means of a high order," says his biographer), but he was notoriously loyal to his friends. As a start, Plumptre asked him to accept the dedication of the specimen volumes, and the Duke agreed.

There was still the problem of getting a new publisher. If Plumptre had been rich, like his friend Miss Bowdler, he could simply have hired one, as she did for the *Family Shakespeare* in 1807, or as Browning did for eleven of his first twelve books, a generation later. Not being rich, he decided to sell subscriptions, which was as respectable a method of publishing books then as it is for publishing magazines now. In early 1811 he sent out notices announcing the appearance of *The English Drama Purified* as soon as he had two hundred subscribers.

That spring and summer were a golden time. Subscriptions came in at the rate of several a week. Spenser Perceval, the Prime Minister of England and a fellow believer in clean theater, subscribed for no less than five sets. Prince William was induced to order six. Bishop Burgess ordered one, Harriet Bowdler two, the Lincoln Company of Comedians one, and so on. In August, orders passed the hundred mark.

But fall came, and they fell rapidly off. Winter came, and they dropped to nothing, even though Plumptre was now enclosing advertising brochures whenever he wrote to anybody about anything. At the beginning of 1812, only 161 subscribers had signed up, for a total of 183 copies. Plumptre could stand it no longer. He told his printer to go ahead and start setting type. The three volumes duly appeared in May 1812.

Anyone looking at the preface will find a heroic promise. Plumptre has listed some (by no means all) of the problems he has had in getting the book published. "My anxieties and labours shall not, however, rest here," he continues. "I shall not, like the Ostrich, leave my egg in the sand, to be trodden underfoot by the casual passenger, or to be hatched by the accustomed influence of the sun." In modern terms, having laid this enormous egg, he meant to hatch it himself. He almost did. May 1812 was another golden time. For about ten days the future of purified drama looked glorious.

Plumptre had had several hundred extra copies printed, and he opened his assault by sending a free set of *The English Drama Purified* and a personal letter to every theater manager in England. This was a considerable job. There may have been only two legitimate thea-

ters in London, but there were seven illegitimate ones,*
and about forty theaters in the provinces. He sent similar
parcels to all the leading actors, and to a number of what
he liked to call the literati.

At the same time he renewed pressure on the royal
family. Having discovered over the matter of the six
subscriptions that William was not basically interested in
theatrical reform, he was now after bigger game. George
III was in a private asylum and no use to him, but there
were still Queen Charlotte and her son the Prince Regent. Plumptre planned to get at them through the prime
minister. On May 12 he had sent Perceval his five sets
and an appeal for aid. "As the subject appears to me of
national importance," he wrote, "I wish the work could
be submitted to His Royal Highness the Prince Regent,
and also to Her Majesty." He was confident that the
prime minister could arrange this. So he could have. But
he had been murdered in the lobby of the House of
Commons on May 11. Destiny at the moment was
clearly frowning.

In June it began to smile again. The early returns from
the theater managers began to come in, and they were
highly promising. "Sir," wrote one from London, "I
shall use my exertion as a manager to promote the representation of plays as *purified* by you—and should you
feel inclined to pursue this laudable undertaking, I beg

---

* The two legitimate theaters had a monopoly on plays, and the
other seven were in theory limited to musical comedy, burlesque
shows, circuses, opera, and the like. In actual fact, they could put on
about what they chose, provided they inserted at least six songs and
called it a "burletta." *King Lear* was done at the Surrey in 1812 as a
burletta.

you will consider me a subscriber to the Work." This was only the manager of a burletta house, but London is London. The managers in Huntingdon and Stamford went further, and each said flatly that he intended to stage a Plumptre play right away. (Clerical support for the stage was a hard thing to get in 1812, and they were presumably flattered by so much attention from a learned university clergyman.) Better was to come. In mid-summer he heard from the new manager of Drury Lane itself. "Sir," he wrote, "There is so little integrity, ability, and justice to be found among the hired *critics* (as they are called) of the present day, that there is little hope of a reformation, unless some man sanctioned like yourself by his sacred function, should stand forward to assert the neglected rights of religion and morality. As such appears to be the plan on which you have set out, I most sincerely wish you every possible success." This letter when read twice turns out to commit Drury Lane to absolutely nothing, but it's still heady praise. If he hadn't been so busy with the royal family, Plumptre could have started on the next twenty volumes then and there.

He was terribly busy with the royal family. As soon as he had recovered from the shock of Perceval's assassination, which was still in May, he had written to the Marquis of Hertford, who was Lord Chamberlain and Master of the Revels, and hence the member of the government officially concerned with the theater, asking *him* to please get a copy to the Prince Regent. He reminded the Marquis that the late prime minister had thought well enough of the book to buy five copies.

(This was a fact that Plumptre was to mention some hundreds of times during the next ten years.) Hertford's answer was polite, but not especially helpful: "I am now to acquaint you that the presentation of books to the Regent is not in the province of the Chamberlain. It is the peculiar business of his secretary, Col. Macmahon, and therefore you will naturally address your wishes to him."

Plumptre wrote to Colonel Macmahon at once, who passed him to a Major General Turner, who did in fact agree to "lay a copy before" the Prince Regent. Whether the Prince ever picked it up is another matter. At any rate, he never made the slightest sign to Plumptre. Neither did the Queen, whom he had reached by an equally circuitous route. This is not totally surprising, at least in the case of the Prince Regent, who was extremely fond of bawdy plays, who swore constantly, who was a notorious gambler, who liked the idea of duels, who had married to please his father (from whom he wanted money at the time), who was summed up by a contemporary as a "contemptible, cowardly, unfeeling, selfish dog," and by a later biographer as "a dissolute and drunken fop, a spendthrift and gamester, 'a bad son, a bad husband, a bad father, a bad subject, a bad monarch, and a bad friend.' " The vision of a small plaque on the vicarage at Great Gransden—BY APPOINTMENT, JAMES PLUMPTRE, ROYAL EXPURGATOR—did not materialize.

Things were even darker on the theater front. After those first few—about six out of the fifty—none of the theater managers even acknowledged receipt of his free books. Not a word came from any of the literati, not

Coleridge, not Mr. Conybeare, the Professor of Poetry at Oxford, none. And the leading actors, while most of them politely wrote notes, were not very cordial. Kemble, who had gotten a previous gift parcel of books from Plumptre in 1809 and seemed very pleased ("I promise myself great pleasure and instruction from them, because I am not totally unacquainted with their author's reputation for learning and liberality"), was much chillier this time. Mrs. Siddons was ice-cold. She said nothing about using her reputation as an actress to promote the representation of purified plays.

By the middle of 1813 Plumptre must have known that he had failed. None of the five or six encouraging theater managers had come through with a production, or seemed likely to. (Probably none of them had looked to see what a Plumptre play was actually like, before dashing off his note. It is hard to imagine anyone offering to produce one if he *had* read it.) The Prince Regent was busy patronizing Byron. The Queen was in seclusion reading Jane Bowdler. Plumptre himself was now fairly secluded in Great Gransden, having gone down from Cambridge in late 1812.

He therefore fell back on a theory which has always been popular among unsuccessful authors, and still is. He decided he was too far ahead of his time. The nineteenth century, despite all its progress, wasn't quite ready for really avant-garde drama—Bowdler, yes; Plumptre, no —but the clear spirits of the twentieth century would hail him as ancestor and pioneer. His expurgations would be joyfully resurrected. Provided, of course, they were known. Plumptre spent some time in 1813 sending free copies of *The English Drama Purified* to libraries, so they would be on the shelf for later ages to discover and be inspired by.

But the great flaw of this theory is that if you have to wait a century for recognition, you aren't there to enjoy it when it finally comes. Furthermore, he soon ran out of suitable libraries, this being the pre-Carnegie era. By 1814 he was ready for a theory that offered him more scope in his own time. He seems to have had trouble finding one, and for a couple of years he spent most of his time writing model plays of his own, and getting *them* rejected by theater managers. Then it occurred to him that when a prophet is without honor in his own country, it makes sense to look abroad. This he set about doing.

It was a good moment to look abroad. The Napoleonic wars were over, Napoleon himself was on St. Helena, and Europe was finally at peace. What better way could the victorious Allies celebrate, it struck Plumptre, than by settling down to expurgate their literature? All they needed was the example. He would provide it. He would send sets of *The English Drama Purified* abroad to kindle a reformation: one each to the national libraries of France, Russia, Prussia, and Austria as working copies for scholars and playwrights, one each to the four rulers of these countries for them to gild with royal prestige. Being smarter men than Gloucester and better men than the Prince Regent, the four monarchs would sit right down and read the plays, or would cause translators to read the plays to them. Their eyes would be opened, and orders would go out for the French,

Russian, Prussian, and Austrian theaters to cleanse themselves. Plumptre himself gave orders for eight sets to be handsomely bound. At this point a tragi-comedy begins, beyond almost anything D'Israeli has in the whole six volumes of *Curiosities of Literature,* and certainly beyond anything else in the history of expurgation.

In July 1817 a parcel arrived at the Russian Embassy in London. It contained (1) the three volumes of *The English Drama Purified,* (2) a typical wheedling letter to Tsar Alexander ("I have therefore to entreat your Imperial Majesty's indulgence and gracious acceptance of them, and hope they may be the means of setting on foot a purification of the drama in your Imperial Majesty's dominions"), (3) another set to be placed in the Academy of Sciences at St. Petersburg, and (4) a covering letter to the Russian ambassador, Count Lieven. This asked him please to forward the parcel to Russia without delay.

Instead, Count Lieven sent it right back to Great Gransden. He couldn't take it on himself, he said, to forward parcels to the Tsar. His instructions did not cover operating a branch post office for English reformers. But why didn't Mr. Plumptre have the British foreign minister, Lord Castlereagh, send the books to the British ambassador to Russia, Lord Cathcart, and *he* could present them to the Tsar.

Plumptre took this rebuff gamely. He also took the advice. On August 9 he wrote to Lord Castlereagh—this time he was more cautious and didn't enclose the books —asking if he would mind forwarding a few volumes of plays and a letter to St. Petersburg in the next diplomatic pouch, together with suitable instructions for Lord Cathcart. He added the usual reminder that the books were of sufficient importance for a recent prime minister to have ordered five sets.

The only result was another rebuff. Castlereagh didn't answer. Plumptre waited eighteen months, just to be sure he really wasn't going to, and then allowed his mind to stray back to his father's old pupil. The Duke of Gloucester had been one of the official hosts when the Tsar visited England in 1814, and Plumptre decided to hope maybe they'd become fast friends. (They hadn't.) Crested letters were doubtless going back and forth all the time. Why not a little crested package? Plumptre wrote and asked. The answer was a stiff note from the Duke's secretary, a Captain Currey. "His Royal Highness has instructed me to state to you his regret that he has no channel of fulfilling your wish with respect to forwarding a Copy of your book to the Emperor of Russia."

Once again Plumptre gave up, and turned his mind to other projects. He spent a good while in 1820 trying to reform the young poet John Clare; * he expurgated most of John Gay's fables; he made sporadic attempts to encourage the founding of an Institute of Drama, which would have been a combination expurgation office, British national theater, and museum. He even occasionally sent free copies of *The English Drama Purified* out. For example, when Mr. Conybeare finally stepped down as

* He had two main goals: to persuade Clare to give up putting oaths (like "d——d old Fortune (God forgi'e me!)/ She's so cross-grain'd wi' me") in his poetry, and to get him to concentrate on "instructive Popular Songs for the lower classes."

Professor of Poetry, his surprised successor immediately found himself with one.

Then suddenly an avenue opened. In August 1822 Lord Castlereagh committed suicide, and there was a new foreign minister, George Canning. Canning took office in September, and in November Plumptre wrote him a long and almost pathetic letter, recounting his previous attempts to get the book to Russia (he skipped the Goucester incident), and asking if Canning would now find room in the diplomatic pouch. He made it clear that he didn't blame Castlereagh, since his 1817 letter must have arrived "a day or two before, or just about the time his Lordship met with the accident with the dog in Hyde Park," and a shock like that can make anybody forget his correspondence.* Plumptre also, his pen running away with him a little toward the end of the letter, asked if Canning would mind sending seven volumes to Russia instead of six. *Original Dramas* had come out in 1818, and Plumptre wanted the Tsar to be able to read them, too.

Canning was a kind man, and a prompt one. Within a week he wrote back to say he'd do it. And on the second of December, Plumptre sent off a simply enormous parcel to the Foreign Office. Two sets of *The English Drama Purified* and a copy of *Original Dramas* make a large package all by themselves, but Plumptre did not stop there. He had not forgotten the ambassador who

---

* It was actually an accident with two dogs at Lord Castlereagh's own country estate, Footscray. His "Spanish dog" and his Wurtemberger were fighting; and when Castlereagh tried to break it up, the Wurtemberger bit him first on one hand and then the other. It must indeed have made correspondence difficult for a while.

gave him that excellent advice back in 1817. "I have taken the liberty of enclosing a smaller packet for Count Lieven, containing the 'Original Dramas' only." And since Canning had shown himself so receptive, Plumptre also enclosed a copy for him, making nine books in all. But he still wasn't done. "Would I be too much obtruding on your indulgence," the letter concludes, "were I to request permission to send similar packets to the King of France, the King of Prussia, and the Emperor of Austria?"

The answer was yes, but Canning was too polite to say so. Once again Plumptre didn't get an answer. And as Canning was still a fairly young man—he was fifty-two, and Plumptre himself had just turned fifty-one—and not at all suicidal, there seemed little point in waiting for yet another foreign minister. At least Russia would be able to enter the Victorian age. France, Prussia, and Austria would just have to take their chances. The man of destiny was giving up. Less than a year later he wrote to the Vice-Chancellor of Cambridge University. "I beg leave," he said, "to present a copy of *The English Drama Purified* to the Fitzwilliam Museum. It is one of four copies I had bound . . . for the Allied Sovereigns. But, after many disappointments, I have only lately been able to get that forwarded which was designed for the Emperor of Russia. One of the others I am anxious to deposit in the Fitzwilliam Museum." (This had just been founded, and represented a brand-new storage possibility.)

The Vice-Chancellor was agreeable, and the set duly arrived at the Fitzwilliam in September 1823. A hundred and forty-three years later, I went in to see if it was still there. It was, three volumes in full red morocco, a trifle less handsomely tooled than one would think a king or an emperor had a right to expect. As far as I could tell, I was the first person to open any of them since Plumptre first succeeded in making the deposit. He has saved his egg from the casual footsteps of the passer-by, but it is still waiting in the sand for the right sun in which to hatch.

****

CHAPTER SEVEN

The American Scene

****

*The moment a woman suffers to fall from her
tung, any expressions that indicate the leest
indelicacy of mind; the moment she ceeses to
blush at such expressions from our sex, she
ceeses to be respected; becauze az a lady, she
iz no longer respectable.*
  NOAH WEBSTER, "An Address to
    Yung Ladies," 1790

*Literature: every thing the human mind has
contemplated and brought forth in a manner
not offensive to taste or decency.*
  SAMUEL L. KNAPP, Advice in the Pursuits
    of Literature, 1837

*A generation cannot be entirely pure which
tolerates writers who, like Walt Whitman,
commit, in writing, an offense like that indict-
able at common law of walking naked through
the streets.*
  NOAH PORTER, President of Yale, 1871

AMERICANS have never had much literature of their own
to expurgate. There are two reasons. In the first place,
there *was* very little American literature before the nineteenth century, even less that seemed worth reprinting to
anyone before about 1930. Most of our major writers

162

were Victorians to begin with—and few have ever itched to bowdlerize Longfellow, Cooper, or Sidney Lanier. In the second place, the occasional American writer who ignored the standards of his age, like Melville or Whitman, was protected by copyright. This made his work immune to expurgation in the United States for fifty-six years, unless he—or, after his death, his literary executor—consented to it, which seldom happened. Almost from the time that *Leaves of Grass* came out in 1855, editors were suggesting to Whitman that a bowdlerized version for the general public would be a good idea. It wasn't until 1892 that he allowed one to appear, and only then as an act of friendship for young Arthur Stedman, whose father, the anthologist Edmund Clarence Stedman, had done him many favors. He could have held out until 1911. If Henry James's novels had seemed in need of expurgation, the final versions of most of them wouldn't have been available until 1964.

The first American contribution to expurgation was therefore quite aptly a sub-literary one, the clean dictionary. Here our contribution begins very early indeed —with the second American dictionary ever printed. In fact, the first one of all, a little scrap of a school dictionary published in New Haven in 1796, may have been slightly cleaned up, too, but it's hard to tell. For economy's sake, this left out all familiar words, and put in only those that American schoolchildren in 1796 wouldn't be likely to know. Common sexual terms are therefore missing, along with all other common words. But a certain number of uncommon ones appear: "belswagger," for example, which is a shortened form of the old word "belly-swaggerer." The little dictionary defines belswagger quite succinctly: "a whore master." This is not the style of an expurgated book. On the other hand, such hard words as "concubine"—indispensable for those who wish to understand the Bible; it appears thirty-nine times—and "onanism," the usual eighteenth-century term for masturbation,* do not appear. But in a selective dictionary containing only five thousand words, expurgation or even winnowing is hard to demonstrate.

The second American dictionary is another matter. It is demonstrably expurgated. This one came out in Suffield, Connecticut, in 1800, edited by the same man who did the first, but now working with a colleague. It is edited along the same selective lines. This time there are nine thousand unfamiliar words.

In the normal course of events, one might expect that all of the original five thousand would be repeated, and nearly all are. But a few have vanished, and these few are all of one kind. "Belswagger" is missing, along with "bigamy," "bodice," "brothel," and so on.

---

* This appears to have been the most indecent act known to the eighteenth century. Dictionaries which freely define all the four-letter words—Bailey's and Perry's, for example—nevertheless shy away from listing onanism. The few that do invariably define it as "self-pollution" or occasionally "the crime of self-pollution"; and he who looks up "self-pollution" to find what this mysterious crime is does not find the term listed at all, though plenty like "self-slaughter" are.

"Masturbation" itself is a Victorian term, though known earlier: Burton spoke of "mastuprations" in 1621, and Swift and Dickens each have a character known as "Master Bates." One of the first dictionaries to list it (Worcester's, Boston: 1860) finally lifts a corner of the veil. Worcester defines it as "self-pollution; onanism," and then he offers the following etymology: "Perhaps from Latin *manus*, the hand, and *stupro*, to ravish."

The reasons for the loss are apparent at once. One is that Samuel Johnson, Jr. (no kin to Dr. Johnson, but the son of the first President of Columbia) has been joined as co-editor by the Rev. John Elliott, Congregational minister of East Guilford, Connecticut. Puritan ministers of the established church of Connecticut were stern editors. The other has to do with sales competition. Normally an American buying a dictionary in 1800 bought an imported English one—Dr. Johnson's or any of a dozen others. Why should he buy an obscure provincial one instead? The American editors offer two reasons. "Serious objections lie against those in common use, arising from their price, but more especially from their want of delicacy and chastity of language. Many words, there found are highly offensive to the modest ear, and cannot be read without a blush."

This was true. There were school dictionaries in England, too, and to some extent they were blush-free, but most English dictionaries in the late eighteenth century were as unexpurgated as any other book. In John Ash's dictionary (1775) one could learn in perfectly dry lexical form that "to fuck" was "to perform the act of generation," that one meaning of "prick" is "the penis in low or vulgar language," that "shite" is an intransitive verb meaning "to void the excrements" (and "shit" is its past participle). In Nathan Bailey's (1782 edition) one finds old four-letter words like "yard" ("a Man's Privy Member") and bluntly defined technical terms like "priapism" ("a continued involuntary Erection of the Yard"). The leading dictionary of the age, Dr. Johnson's, was consciously literary, and therefore omitted most of the words I have cited from Ash and Bailey, not for being obscene but for being colloquial. But Johnson made up for this seeming prudery by the extensive quotations he included for the words he judged *were* literary. After defining "fart" (a highly literary word appearing in a long series of writers from Chaucer to Herrick and on down), he illustrates its usage from Swift:

> So from my lord his passion broke,
> He farted first, and then he spoke.

When the Reverend H. J. Todd, one of the royal chaplains, did a revision of Johnson in 1818, he left the word and the illustration as he found them.

There was thus ample room for change, and that change was principally brought about in America. Not only were most of our early native dictionaries winnowed, but most American reprints of English dictionaries were clearly expurgated. William Perry's *Royal Standard Dictionary* was the first English dictionary to be reprinted in America; pirate editions of it appeared in Worcester, Massachusetts, in 1788 ("First American Edition") and in Brookfield, Massachusetts, in 1801 ("First Brookfield Edition").* Both omitted the verb "shite," for example, and the noun "penis." The London 1805 edition of Perry, however, retains both. Dr. Johnson was reprinted in Boston in 1804 and in Philadelphia in 1805. In Boston he was expurgated; in Philadelphia, not.

---

* This is the first dictionary printed by a member of the Merriam family, who later took over from Noah Webster, and as Merriam-Webster publish the Unabridged right now.

The leading American purifier of dictionaries was, of course, Noah Webster. His 37,000-word *Compendious Dictionary* came out in 1806, by far the largest and most accurate American dictionary yet. Webster had other things on his mind besides purity, notably spelling reform. It is because of him that Americans spell "honor" without a *u* and "ax" without an *e*. If all his reforms had caught on, we would also have spellings like "porpess," "iland," and "groop." But he also cared greatly about purity and propriety, maybe cared more than any other American of the time. Even back in the 1780s, when he made his name with the *American Spelling Book*, much of it borrowed from an earlier English speller, he had systematically taken the name of God out (as in learning-to-read sentences like "My joy is in God all the day"), on the grounds that it was improper to retain it in what were essentially secular lessons. In his dictionaries, of course, he had much more opportunity to take things out, and it was an opportunity he seized with both hands. "There is not a vocabulary of the English language so free from *local, vulgar* and *obscene words* as mine," he boasted. He was particularly interested in purifying Dr. Johnson, a task he referred to as "cleansing the Augean stables." When, after twenty years' labor, he produced the first American unabridged dictionary in 1828, he intended it as the formal—and triumphantly pure—answer to Johnson.

A few years ago the scholar Joseph Reed compared the whole letter L in the two men. In some ways Webster turned out to have copied Johnson more than cleansed him. Johnson has fourteen hundred words under L; Webster took over all but twenty, which had become obsolete. (He also added six hundred new L-words, chiefly technical terms.) Of Johnson's three thousand definitions, he helped himself to about twelve hundred, either verbatim or with trifling changes. From Johnson's many thousands of quotations to illustrate usage, he borrowed two-thirds for his own.

But some things he did not copy. He did not copy a single one of Johnson's bawdy quotations. (He had been complaining the whole twenty years that Johnson kept picking up "ribaldry" from people like Shakespeare, and putting it in the dictionary.) There was one whole class of definitions he did not touch. For example, Johnson defines a lecher as "a whoremaster." Webster was not about to use such language. He says, "Lecher: A man given to lewdness; one addicted, in an exorbitant degree, to the indulgence of animal appetite, and an illicit commerce with females." Johnson says that to swear is "To obtest some superiour power; to utter an oath." Webster doesn't. He says, "To be profane; to practice profaneness." And then, ignoring Plumptre's warning about ranking the degrees of vice, he adds, "For men to *swear* is sinful, disreputable, and odious; but for females or ladies to *swear* appears more abominable and scandalous." Finally, if not in L, then elsewhere in the alphabet, a number of problem words do indeed vanish from the "unabridged"—all the ones I have mentioned in Ash, Bailey, and Johnson, for example. Most of them did not reappear in American dictionaries until after World War II. One or two are not back yet.

Ahead with dictionaries, America was, of course, very

168

far behind in expurgating literature. Of this I have found no trace until 1814, and then only in the feeble form of an edition of Pope published in Baltimore, with a few words partly replaced by dashes. Sometimes, but not always, "whore" appears as w---e or w***e; and "clap" (the disease) appears once as c--p. and "pox" once as p-x. Everything else appears as Pope had it, including "yard," which Pope had seized with joy from Chaucer. This edition was reprinted with the same dashes, and no more, in New York in 1828. Before then Noah Webster had popped up again, with a characteristically ambitious plan to put America at the forefront of literary expurgation. He had designs on the whole of poetry.

It is a reasonable guess that Webster found his way to poetry through his habit of correcting Johnson. If Johnson's dictionary could be redeemed in the New World, why not the *Works of the English Poets*, too? * Wherever he got the idea, in March 1823 Webster wrote to his brother-in-law Thomas Dawes in Boston, asking his opinion of a purified *Works* for Americans. It was a poor choice of consultant. For all his being a Bostonian, Dawes happened to dislike expurgation, and after being

---

* This had already been redeemed slightly in the Old World, though I don't think Webster knew it. Johnson's own edition, complete except for the castration of Rochester, came out in 1779. In 1810 a Scot named Alexander Chalmers brought out a new edition in London. Rochester is still expurgated, and, obedient to the spirit of the age, Chalmers has made some cuts of his own, such as one of John Donne's rare references to homosexuality, and his one glancing allusion to masturbation. "One result was the protection of Henry David Thoreau, thirty years later and three thousand miles away. Thoreau formed his impression of English poetry through Chalmers. He is said to have read right through the 21 volumes as a high school student, and then to have read all the way through again after he graduated from Harvard."

pressed hard enough, he told Webster so. But at first he opposed the project on strictly commercial grounds. Presumably he was hoping to avoid a prolonged discussion of morality. "I told my wife," he wrote Webster, "that I was afraid you was going to lose money by your intended publication. Her answer was, 'My dear, don't throw cold water on any of brother Webster's pious efforts,' and I had intended to obey her; as *she* had always more common sense than *I* have."

But, he continues, new information has just come to light. He has just heard that one David Hale, "a very worthy man in humble circumstances," is about to produce "an immense edition of a work similar to that which you was proposing." Webster does these things better, he admits. A Boston minister has seen an advance copy of Hale's edition, and reports, "It is not sufficiently purified." But nevertheless, large numbers of Bostonians have already signed up to buy it, and "they who have subscribed for fifty volumes may not be willing to subscribe for another edition, tho' a much better one." Quit now, he urged Webster. Apart from your own risk, you don't want to hurt Hale.

Webster hated having cold water thrown on his pious projects. He seems to have written back (the letter hasn't survived) that his goal was to purify a nation, and if this meant hurting Hale or losing money, too bad.* At

---

* Dr. Bowdler would have sympathized. That same year he was writing Lord Hardwicke about his expurgated Gibbon. "What a Bookseller will say to it, I know not; but I am so sanguine in my hope that it may prove a real and durable assistant to the cause of Christianity that I would expend almost all my little fortune in the publication."

this point Dawes brought up his real objection. "I should like to have the poets weeded, but how it can be done, I know not," he said. Bowdlerism is just not a possible act. Look up the last two lines of Canto IV of "The Rape of the Lock," he told Webster. (These are the ones in which Belinda, having just had a lock of her hair cut off by the Baron, says to him with notable ambiguity:

> Oh, hadst thou, cruel! been content to seize
> Hairs less in sight, or any hairs but these!)

"Now I would ask you," Dawes says, "whether you mean to omit that poem; or whether, if you admit it, you would omit such a couplet. If you go about to alter, the poem is no longer Pope's, but Webster's."

Considering that to omit "The Rape of the Lock" from a *Works of the English Poets* in 1823 would be like omitting "The Wasteland" or "Stopping by Woods on a Snowy Evening" from a *Works of the American Poets* now, and that to rewrite it would be as conspicuous as rewriting one of them, these were touchy questions that Dawes asked. Whether because he couldn't answer them adequately, or whether because he had second thoughts about Hale and the money, Webster did give up his plan, and turned back to the Bible.

The rival edition, meanwhile, was thriving. It is, of course, the rather quaint expurgation mentioned in Chapter III. Dawes had some of his facts wrong about it. David Hale had nothing to do with the expurgation (though his cousin Edward Everett Hale, Jr., did some, many years later); he was only the New England sales-man for the book. The actual editors were a pair of

Philadelphians, Ezekiel Sanford and Robert Walsh, and they were not very good expurgators, either. It wasn't necessary to be, in Philadelphia between 1819 and 1823.

Sanford, the original editor, had meant to publish virtually all of British poetry in a hundred volumes, but the printer's bill got so high that he settled for "the complete works of the more celebrated, and selected poems of the more obscure" in fifty. He died, aged twenty-six, with only eighteen of them finished, and Walsh did the other thirty-two. Neither man felt much need to cut. Donne is quite sharply expurgated (by Sanford), but he is almost the only poet who is. Shakespeare comes through untouched; Chaucer is lightly nicked. Gay's "The Fan," put on the Procrustean bed by Goldsmith back in 1767, is released again. All cantos of "The Rape of the Lock" are complete.

Walsh's handling of Prior may best reveal the state of affairs in America. Every line of those "impure tales" that Boswell teased Johnson about he printed complete —with the exception of the last line of "Hans Carvel," in which Mrs. Carvel is saying furiously to Hans, "You've thrust your finger God knows where!" This line Walsh bowdlerized. "You've thrust your finger --- knows where!" he printed it, not, to the real nineteenth-century mind, getting to the heart of what needed expurgating at all. And the answer, of course, is that few in America in 1823 except Noah Webster had nineteenth-century minds, or at least nineteenth-century sensibilities. There were some puritans with a timeless horror of levity, like the Rev. John Elliott and the Boston minister that Dawes quoted. The rest of us lingered in the eighteenth century. Just how old-fashioned we were appears strikingly in Walsh's prefaces. Prior he praises thus: "His language is neat, pure, and, in general, smooth; seldom stiffened by new coined or unusual terms; deformed by quaint phrases; or debased by vulgar modes of expression." These are standard Augustan views, just like Dr. Johnson's or, for that matter, Francis Gentleman's—and they were held in Philadelphia at a time when England was twenty years into the romantic revolution. Wordsworth and Coleridge were men past fifty, Keats was already dead. It is no wonder we were slow to expurgate anything except a few dictionaries.

Webster did have one fellow modernist, and this was Benjamin Franklin's grandson, William Temple Franklin, who in 1818 edited his grandfather's *Autobiography*. (There had been versions of it around since 1791, but these were all translations of a French pirate edition, and not very accurate.) Franklin did not expurgate his grandfather's manuscript, but some twelve hundred times he did make an eighteenth-century phrase into a nineteenth-century one, and once or twice this mere fact results in something near expurgation. For example, Benjamin Franklin, speaking of his hasty departure from Boston in 1723, said that some people explained it on the theory that "he had got a naughty Girl with Child." His grandson refines that into their thinking "he had an intrigue with a girl of bad character."

But the true reading of all these passages was restored in 1868, with no particular protests; * and though Franklin is probably the leading native victim of bowdlerism,

* John Bigelow, then U.S. minister to France, found Franklin's original manuscript in Paris, brought it home in triumph, and published it. He himself was totally respectable, and the whole event was mainly regarded as a victory for scholarship.

since during the nineteenth century he was almost the only American writer who was both unprotected by copyright and the author of anything expurgable, that story comes later in the chapter.

Modernists began to appear in large numbers on the American scene around 1830. Mrs. Trollope's Cincinnati friend is, of course, one of them, but most of the true nineteenth-century minds showed up first on the East Coast. A typical result is George Cheever's *Studies in Poetry*, published in Boston in 1830 itself. This was an anthology for schools, and Cheever said he used "the greatest care and nicest judgement" in picking the poems to go in it, by which he means he picked only clean ones. He nevertheless felt the need to bowdlerize the very first entry, which is a section from the Prologue to Chaucer's *Canterbury Tales*—"The Character of a Good Parson," as Cheever called it. The passage admittedly poses a problem. All of it but one word meets every Victorian test; and being in praise of holiness, and also fine poetry, it was a natural for schoolbooks. But right in the middle Chaucer says,

> And shame it is, if a preest take keep,
> A shiten shepherd and a clene sheep.

Cheever silently dropped this couplet, and in so doing set a fashion for the next hundred years. Innumerable other editors have also dropped it, or, alternatively, replaced the one word. That shepherd was "fouled" to Charles Cowden Clarke in 1835, "obscene" to Richard Horne in 1841, "filthy" to Professor Walter Bronson of Brown in 1908, "spotted" to Professor F. B. Snyder of Northwestern in 1926, "dirty" to the poet Alfred Noyes in 1946. In 1969, so progress goes, he is usually back to being shiten again.

All through the 1830s America caught up fast. The year after Cheever, something as recondite as an expurgated edition of the plays of Philip Massinger appeared in New York. It was a mere piracy from England, to be sure, but a speedy one. In this case, what was being castrated in London one year was being castrated in New York the next. (By the fifties, the process was even simultaneous, as in the actor James Wallack's bowdlerized edition of Congreve's *Love for Love*, London and New York, 1854.) In 1833 Miss Macauley's *Tales of the Drama* popped up in a place as remote as Exeter, New Hampshire, and was our first expurgated Shakespeare. That same year Webster's Bible appeared. Soon a second American man of letters joined Webster in practicing serious expurgation. The fact that this was the New York poet Fitz-Greene Halleck, primarily known for his comic verse, shows how Victorian America had become. Halleck's expurgated anthology, *Selections from the British Poets*, is a far cry from the amateur efforts of Sanford and Walsh. None of those impure tales of Prior's appears at all; in fact, the only Prior Halleck cared to print was "To the Hon. Charles Montagu," the same little poem that James Greenwood put in *The Virgin Muse* in 1717. The difference is that for an audience of English boys and girls in 1717 Greenwood did not expurgate it; for a general audience of New Yorkers in 1840, Halleck did.

From the 1840s on, American and English bowdlerism

175

advance pretty much together, and get treated jointly in the remaining chapters. Here I shall discuss only two or three native American specialties. One of them is the anthology itself, succeeding Halleck. Obviously there were English anthologies, too—Palgrave's *Golden Treasury* and the *Oxford Book of English Verse* are only the best known of many—but American anthologies stand apart for several reasons.

One is that so many of our leading men produced them. Another is that the American anthology had a strange flowering at the end of the nineteenth century (if something that means a collection of flowers to begin with can be said to have a flowering). It turned into Dr. Eliot's Five-Foot Shelf, or "The International Library of Famous Literature," or "The World's Great Classics," all of them triumphs of American merchandising, and nearly all of them shoddy goods. But the most important reason is that while the English anthology was usually only winnowed, like Palgrave,* the American anthology was normally bowdlerized. There are exceptions, like Whittier's *Songs of Three Centuries* (1875). Whittier winnowed, giving space to Thomas Bailey Aldrich but not to Swift, much room to Oliver Wendell Holmes and little to Pope. Granted this selection, he had no need to expurgate. Neither did Emerson in *Parnassus* (1876), which is a collection of Emerson's favorite passages rather than of whole poems. But the standard

* The nearest Palgrave came to bowdlerism was changing Herrick's title "To the Virgins, to Make Much of Time" to a limp "Counsel to Girls." This was fairly near, since the actual advice, to "gather ye Rose-buds while ye may," acquires its full meaning only in conjunction with the original title.

American anthology is another matter.

Charles A. Dana's *Household Book of Poetry* (1858) is the principal anthology of the first generation after Halleck. Dana had been Horace Greeley's managing editor on the New York *Tribune*, and was to be Lincoln's Assistant Secretary of War. Meanwhile, he tried his hand at bowdlerism, though without admitting it. Indeed, he specifically claimed not to be. "Especial care has been taken," he said in the preface, "to give every poem entire and unmutilated." By thorough winnowing, he was able to make this statement nearly true. But when he felt the need, he quietly bowdlerized. One of his early selections is what he calls the "Saxon Song of Summer," now usually known as "Summer is icumen in." Among the late-spring activities, "Bullock sterteth, buck verteth," "vert" being an early form of the verb "to fart." It is not an easily recognizable form,* and the inquiring reader would have gotten no help from an 1858 dictionary. Nevertheless, Dana changed the line to read, "Bullock starteth, buck departeth." We were a protected nation.

Another half generation, and William Cullen Bryant's *A Library of Poetry and Song* (1870) shows a considerable advance toward the flowering of 1900, both in the pretentious title—this "library" was one volume only—and in the bad editing. The title, at least, was not Bryant's idea. The book began as the sort, still occasionally published, which a publisher puts together himself,

* Professor Robert Gay so counted on this in his *College Book of Verse* (Boston: 1927), that he did not bother to bowdlerize, merely adding an untrue footnote: *"verteth,* browses in the forest (?)." The question mark speaks volumes.

177

and for which he then buys the most famous name he can get, to ornament the title page and spine. But, having been thus bought, Bryant got interested in the editing, and in the end took it over. He, too, mainly winnowed, but occasionally he wanted to include something that would have seemed harmless to Marianne Dashwood but which he felt would endanger the American public of 1870. For example, he wanted a scene from *Hamlet*. In "Hamlet Reproaching the Queen," Bryant arranges a scene moderately like Shakespeare's and pretends that it *is* Shakespeare's. Not necessarily for this reason, he was rewarded with sales of a hundred thousand copies in the first edition alone.

A few years later the distinguished old Boston publisher James Fields and a fellow Bostonian named Edwin Whipple jointly edited *The Family Library of British Poetry* (which is again a single volume). This is an interesting book both for the cuts, which are avowed, and for the insight the preface gives to the minds of the cutters. The cuts reflect the steady growth of American prudery, as in the removal of two lines from Prior's "Epitaph on Jack and Joan":

> And having buried children four,
> They would not take pains to try for more.

The attitude of the cutters is strikingly shown by a complaint that Fields and Whipple make in their preface. They report that it has been hard to establish correct texts for the religious poems they wanted to include, and now that they have, they are shocked to find how widely incorrect versions are used.

178

The compilers of the hymn-books used in our churches have taken the strangest liberties in altering the style, and sometimes the meaning, of the religious poets from whose works they have made their selections. A lawyer who had strict views regarding the guilt of transposing or omitting words in a written document duly signed, and of substituting different words from those which the signer used, could hardly enter a church in the land without having a strange sensation, compounded of the horrible and the comical, in listening to choirs devoutly chanting or singing verses with forged names.

Considering that Fields and Whipple have themselves just substituted a word in one of Chaucer's religious poems (they forge that shepherd "foul"), taken strange liberties with Dryden, and so on, their complaint at first rings oddly. A lawyer with strict views might want to hold *them* guilty. But the very fact that this possibility never crossed their minds is evidence of how normal and necessary bowdlerism had come to seem.

Twenty years after Fields, when the five-foot shelves began to appear, the idea that the editor of an anthology has any obligation toward his text had nearly vanished. Halleck and Dana and Bryant at least made minimal changes, Fields and Whipple at least marked theirs. Nathan Haskell Dole, the editor of the "International Library of Famous Literature," and Julian Hawthorne, the editor of "The World's Great Classics," were troubled by no such scruples. Nor was Bliss Carman, the at least

nominal editor of ten volumes of "The World's Best
Poetry," much bothered, or even Mr. Justice Brewer of
the Supreme Court, the editor of ten volumes called
"Crowned Masterpieces of Literature." (Dr. Eliot, to his
honor, was; the "Harvard Classics" are unbowdlerized.)

Sets like these were designed, rather like present-day
encyclopedias, to be sold at high prices by door-to-door
salesmen. Their appeal was based on elaborate bindings,
pseudo-medieval title pages, etc., together with a false
sense of completeness, achieved through such entries as
selections from Brillat-Savarin and Boethius (Dole) and
entire volumes of "Turkish Literature" and "Malayan
Literature" (Hawthorne). At the same time, all exotica,
as well as more local products, like Shakespeare, are
thoroughly domesticated. Few editors of these literary
package-deals mark or mention their expurgations in any
way (Justice Brewer is an exception); most make them
constantly. Perhaps the extreme case is Hawthorne's version of Aristophanes' play *The Knights*. It is at something like three removes from what Aristophanes actually wrote. Hawthorne pretends to be offering the
complete translation made by John Hookham Frere in
1839. Actually, he has expurgated it. Though Hawthorne does not mention the fact, Frere's translation is
itself expurgated well beyond normal translations of Aristophanes. And even "normal" translations are generally
a little expurgated.*

* By "normal" translations I mean ones such as that used by
Whitney Oates and Eugene O'Neill, Jr., in *Complete Greek Drama*
(N.Y.: 1938), and by the anonymous editor of *Aristophanes: The
Eleven Comedies Completely and Literally Translated* (N.Y.: [1934]).
In both of these, the Chorus says of one Ariphrades: "He gloats in

Another American specialty has been expurgation in schoolbooks, not only to protect decency but to keep illusions shiny about members of the American pantheon. Franklin makes the perfect example.

From the mid-nineteenth century on, his *Autobiography* was a much-used school text. Unlike other of Franklin's works, such as "Advice on the Choice of a Mistress" and "A Letter to the Royal Academy of Brussels," which had gone completely underground, not to re-emerge until modern times, the *Autobiography* has little in it to trouble an expurgator's mind. But it's an eighteenth-century book; it does speak plainly. For example, Franklin is perfectly open about a quarrel he had in 1725. He was then nineteen, and sharing lodgings in London with a friend from Philadelphia named James Ralph. Ralph had come to England partly to get away from his wife. There was also a young milliner in the house.

> Ralph read Plays to her in the Evenings, they grew intimate, she took another Lodging, and he

---

vice, is not merely a dissolute man and utterly debauched—but he has actually invented a new form of vice; for he pollutes his tongue with abominable pleasures in brothels, befouling all of his body." This remark, absent in Frere and Hawthorne, still doesn't represent what Aristophanes wrote. As O'Neill cheerfully explains in a footnote, "The original here contains, and the translation omits, a number of details on the new vice."

O'Neill showed, incidentally, an honesty rare among editors of Greek comedy. The editor of a more recent edition (*Five Comedies* [Cleveland: 1948]) writes in his foreword, "Needless to say, no faithful translator will emasculate his author by expurgation, and the reader will here find Aristophanes' comedies as Aristophanes wrote them, not as Mrs. Grundy might wish him to have written them." He then omits slightly more than Oates and O'Neill.

follow'd her. They liv'd together some time, but he being still out of Business, and her Income not sufficient to maintain them with her Child, he took a Resolution of going from London, to try for a Country School.

While he was away, Franklin, who had always found the girl attractive, looked in from time to time to see that she was all right. One night he gave way to impulse. "I attempted Familiarities (another Erratum), which she repuls'd with a proper Resentment, and acquainted him with my Behavior. This made a Breach between us."

There are two separate problems here. One—Ralph's affair—has no redeeming feature, but the other—Franklin's pass—points a useful moral, which is what he intended. The story does, however, show a future framer of the Constitution with distinctly clay-like feet.

How American editors reacted is instructive. A few, like D. H. Montgomery, editing the *Autobiography* for Ginn & Co. in 1888, eliminate the whole incident. There is no milliner, no grab by Franklin, no quarrel. The more scrupulous majority, however, content themselves with shielding Franklin. The Houghton Mifflin edition first printed in 1886 reports Ralph's affair faithfully, but then has Franklin say vaguely, "In the mean time [other circumstances] made a breach." Professor Julian Abernethy of Middlebury, doing an edition in 1892, says more clumsily, "In the mean time [another matter which gave him offense] made a breach." A dozen other editions do similar things. It's bearable for Franklin to have friends who live in flaming adultery, but not for him even to feel temptation. A scrubbed shepherd and a shiten sheep, so to speak.

Most of these editions of the *Autobiography* were intended for high-school students, and it could be argued that there is some justice in keeping high-school students a little ignorant. But it would be a mistake to suppose that this was made up to them when they got to college, or even to graduate school. And this was a third American specialty. In the last twenty years before World War I, we were such enthusiastic bowdlerists that even our scholarship got infected. When Professor William Browne of Johns Hopkins did a learned volume of *Selections from the Early Scottish Poets*—poems, that is, in Middle Scots, which a few college upperclassmen and many graduate students would read—he silently bowdlerized. Or, rather, he bowdlerized in a whisper, marking his changes, but in such a way that students wouldn't recognize them. Like any scholar, he put conjectural emendations in brackets, and from time to time he would insert a euphemism, and put *that* in brackets, too. If an angry hawk is clutching a man by the "*bawis*," which is Middle Scots for balls, Browne printed "[*eris*]," which is Middle Scots for ears, and, of course, a non-conjectural bowdlerism.

A long succession of similar books followed, culminating perhaps in one edited by Professors W. A. Neilson and K. G. T. Webster of Harvard in 1916. *Chief British Poets of the Fourteenth and Fifteenth Centuries* is bowdlerized openly, and to a degree that seems almost incredible. Langland, Lydgate, Skelton, Gavin Douglas, Lindsay, all are expurgated. In editing the fourteenth-century religious poem *Piers Plowman,* the two scholars show a delicacy that Mrs. Trimmer herself might have thought excessive. Langland, soberly citing the evils of drink, mentions what happened to Lot, who when drunk "Did by his daughters that the devil liked." Even this seemed to them too much for excitable Harvard graduate students, and out the line went. It hardly seems surprising that bowdlerism took a fall after World War I. If literature was to survive at all, there was no other direction for it to go.

CHAPTER EIGHT

The Great Victorian Age: I—Poetry

Prose and other Human Things may take what Turn they can; but Poetry, which pretends to have something of Divinity in it, is to be more permanent. Odes once printed cannot well be altered, when the Author has already said He expects His Works should Live for Ever.

MATTHEW PRIOR, 1718

I shall betake myself to a subject ever fertile of themes, a Subject, the turtle-feast of the Sons of Satan, and the delicious, secret Sugarplumb of the Babes of Grace. . . . in short, may it please your Lordship, I intend to write BAUDY.

ROBERT BURNS, 1796

It may be urged . . . that more delicacy and respect for the poet would have been shown in leaving blanks, where expressions have been substituted: but could this method have been adopted with a proper regard to the sense of every passage, the fear of defeating the object of the attempt by provoking in such cases an unbecoming curiosity, would have been an argument against its adoption.

WILLIAM CHARLES MACREADY, in the preface to his expurgated Pope, 1849

185

IN 1834 an anecdote appeared in an English magazine about a girl bowdlerist of tremendous ambition. This young lady turned up in a publisher's office "with a blurred and blotted volume of Byron in her bag; and being asked to explain her errand, answered that she had come to treat for the publication of a 'Family Don Juan.' " The publisher, of course, just laughed; and, in fact, the whole point of the anecdote was to ridicule the idea of bowdlerism. It seemed self-evident to most people in 1834 that *Don Juan* couldn't be bowdlerized. (Not that an occasional optimist hasn't tried.*) Byronism is an essence permeating the whole poem, not a matter of a word here and there.

Sixty years later there was a *bon mot* running around London about Canon Alfred Ainger, a well-known literary clergyman. It was said, originally by Henry Festing Jones to his friend Samuel Butler, that Ainger "was the sort of man who is capable of bringing out an expurgated edition of Wordsworth." Again a *reductio ad absurdum*—given a certain extra force by the fact that

---

* The original publisher, for one. When Byron sent home the first two cantos from Venice in 1819, Murray took advantage of his absence to bowdlerize four passages—the gaps are duly marked with asterisks—before printing. Three relate to syphilis, and one was a jeer at Byron's recently dead enemy, Sir Samuel Romilly.

This accomplished nothing. The first major review begins by saying that here is "unquestionably a more thorough and intense infusion of genius and vice—power and profligacy—than in any poem which had ever before been written in the English, or indeed, in any other modern language," and predicts a future for the poem of "complete exclusion" from decent shelves. The passages were eventually restored in 1833, changing no one's opinion of the poem at all.

The Reverend Whitwell Elwin tried a full-scale Family Byron in 1854—"with the double end, of bringing together what was best in his writings, and of excluding every syllable that could give offense to the most sensitive mind." But such attempts have been rare.

Ainger actually just had bowdlerized something as unexpected as the letters of Charles Lamb.

These two jokes outline the range of Victorian bowdlerism of poetry rather neatly. Beyond the range on one side, beyond the moral pale altogether, was a small group of poets who weren't felt to be susceptible to it. Remove what you will from Byron, or Rochester, or Sedley, or Burns in one of his moods, and the result is still not fit for families to read. Chiefly because of this feeling, there was no edition of Sedley's poems during the entire nineteenth century. There was no edition of Rochester between 1811 and 1926, only *sub rosa* editions of Burns's *Merry Muses of Caledonia* between 1800 and 1959. *Don Juan* was too popular to vanish altogether this way—but in both England and America the frequency of editions dropped by about three-quarters after 1850. There was no such falling off for more proper poems of Byron's, such as *Childe Harold*.*

Beyond the range on the other side is a larger group of poets who even to the most delicate Victorians didn't seem to need cleaning up: Wordsworth, Cowper, Gray,

---

* A comparative chart might be interesting. It should be noted that *Childe Harold's Pilgrimage* was published in three parts between 1812 and 1818, and *Don Juan* the same way between 1819 and 1825. "E" and "A" stand for "English edition" and "American edition."

	Childe Harold	*Don Juan*
1810–1819	17 (13 E, 4 A)	6 (4 E, 2 A)
1820–1829	3 (3 E)	48 (46 E, 2 A)
1830–1839	6 (4 E, 2 A)	7 (6 E, 1 A)
1840–1849	3 (3 E)	1 (1 E)
1850–1859	4 (2 E, 2 A)	4 (3 E, 1 A)
1860–1869	4 (4 E)	0
1870–1879	4 (4 E)	2 (2 E)
1880–1889	10 (6 E, 4 A)	2 (2 E)
1890–1899	10 (8 E, 2 A)	0

Sidney Lanier, and so forth. In between, however, need-
ing it and susceptible to it, come about half of all poets
who have written in English. To report on every victim,
from the very obscure like Peter Motteux (he wrote the
roundelay "Man is for the woman made") to the very
famous like Spenser and Milton, would make this chapter stunningly long. To report every edition would make
it a five-foot shelf. I shall therefore discuss only a dozen
poets, and them selectively. My aim is to keep a balance
between the typical Victorian suppression, which is
quiet and businesslike, and colorful special cases, of
which there are quite a lot. And rather than driving the
whole mass of expurgations up the century together, like
a flock of clean sheep, I shall take each poet by himself. I
shall begin with Chaucer and end with a man who was
not ever expurgated but who, if innocence was really to
be shielded, should have been, Robert Browning.

Chaucer, as noted, is second only to Shakespeare in the
amount of expurgation his work has undergone. In variety, Shakespeare is second to him. The reason for this is
simple. Chaucer wrote in Middle English. For several
hundred years even educated people have needed either
special training or a translation in order to read him.
They have utilized both, and there early developed two
streams of Chaucer texts, one in Middle English and one
in modern English. The two have quite different histories as objects of bowdlerism.

The translations presented, of course, the greater
temptation to bowdlerize. As one Victorian editor of
Chaucer said, there are a good many lines in the *Canter-*

bury Tales which, if translated with reasonable accuracy, are "calculated to startle a modern reader and make him doubt his eyes." Few Victorians wanted to do that, especially on their own (as opposed to Chaucer's) responsibility. It is one thing to stand by with footnotes while Chaucer tells gross tales in quaint Middle English, and quite another to retell them in one's own words, using modern equivalents for Chaucer's archaic obscenities. After all, the equivalents very often turn out to be the obscenities themselves, spelled a little differently. "Quaint" itself ("queynte" in Chaucer) is a case in point. The word had two meanings in Middle English, which have since diverged in orthography. About half the time an accurate translator of Chaucer would render it "quaint," and about half "cunt."

Expurgation consequently appears first and disappears last in modern English versions. Pope translated a little Chaucer in 1711, and didn't tone down a thing. Neither did George Ogle, who edited a group of translations in 1741. But when the Rev. William Lipscomb reprinted Ogle's work in 1795, he prudently left out the Miller's and Reeve's Tales, and a scattering of lines elsewhere. This was for Chaucer's sake as well as the reader's, he said. "Our veneration for his great and various excellencies is rather the more testified, by purging him from his impurities, and by exhibiting him to a more refined age a safe as well as a brilliant example of native genius." Just what William Henry Ireland said the next year about Shakespeare.

In Middle English, however, Chaucer went on serenely for some time. It is true that Ezekiel Sanford abridged the Miller's Tale in Philadelphia in 1819, but even there the intent to expurgate would be hard to prove, since Sanford was only printing selections from the *Canterbury Tales*, anyway. The first demonstrable expurgation of Chaucer in his native Middle English was done by Robert Southey, poet laureate of England, in 1831. Even that partly failed.

Southey was not a career bowdlerist. Nor was he personally shocked by Chaucer. On the contrary, as a young man in 1807 he was urging his friends to learn Middle English so that, like him, they could enjoy all of Chaucer's quaint medieval jokes. But, as all students of the period know, Southey grew more refined as the nineteenth century itself did, or maybe even a little faster. When he came to edit *Select Works of the British Poets from Chaucer to Jonson* in 1831, he no longer approved of quaint jokes. One of the nicest documents in the history of bowdlerism is the indignant letter the laureate wrote his publisher in March of that year:

Dear Sir,

When I sent you the Preface to the "Select Poems," I had not examined the book further than to look at the biographical notices. I am now greatly surprised, and not less greatly vexed, both on my own account and yours, at discovering that among Chaucer's poems there are some inserted which most certainly I did not, and could not, have marked for publication, because of their indecency. For upon this point I was so scrupulous, that in one of the poems which I did mark (the "Man of

Lawe's Tale"), I very well remember striking out the single stanza which might have been deemed exceptionable.

If I were to edit the works of Chaucer, I should not think it right to castrate them, because whoever buys Chaucer knows what he has to expect. But in making selections, it was my duty to be careful that nothing should be admitted which might deter a parent from putting the volume into the hands of his children. This I owed both to myself and to you.

How it has happened that the most offensive of Chaucer's poems should have thus been inserted, it is in vain for me to guess. But I know that I did not mark them for insertion; and I am sure also that it will be less loss for you to cancel them, than to let the volume be liable to the reproach which they will bring upon it.

All that I have myself to blame for, is for not having discovered this sooner; but I am very much occupied; and upon accidentally looking into the book, it has come upon me like a thunder-clap.

Yours very truly,
Robert Southey

It is a matter of opinion which are "the most offensive of Chaucer's poems"; in our own time, quite possibly, the Prioress' anti-semitic tale of Hugh of Lincoln offends most. But in terms of ribaldry, the Miller's, Reeve's and Summoner's Tales and the Wife of Bath's Prologue probably offend most. None of these appears in Southey's anthology, and one may assume that Longmans did indeed do some rapid canceling. The stanza from the Man of Law's Tale, however, stayed in print. Presumably it would have cost too much to reset the whole poem. Southey could at least comfort himself with the cool little note he had put in the general preface: "It is not to be supposed that I could afford either time or eyesight for correcting the proof sheets of such a volume."

Translators of Chaucer were meanwhile spending their time and eyesight much more freely. Two successors to Lipscomb came out in the ten years after 1831, both expurgated meticulously. One is by Charles Cowden Clarke, later so active in castrating Shakespeare. The other, edited by Richard Horne, is the principal version of the time. It is studded with famous names. There are sections done by Wordsworth, Elizabeth Barrett, and Leigh Hunt, as well as by Horne himself. By now native genius has had all claws pulled. Wordsworth and Miss Barrett had both rendered passages that were safe to begin with (in fact, most of what Wordsworth translated has since turned out not to be by Chaucer at all), and neither one bowdlerized. But Hunt and Horne, who had the hard parts to do, omitted and rephrased with great dexterity. Leigh Hunt wouldn't even let the Manciple snarl at the Cook, "Thy breath full sour stinketh," but has him say with elegant indirection,

> and sure I am
> Thy breath resembleth not sweet marjoram.

All ribaldry has vanished, not to begin reappearing until about 1930.

192

Expurgations of modern and medieval Chaucer now chase each other through the rest of the century, with the modern usually staying well ahead. Alfred Pollard's expurgated Middle English version of 1886 is the principal advance for that side, Pollard having been a quite remarkable prude. He wouldn't even allow the Pardoner to say,

> Nay! I wol drinke licour of the vyne,
> And have a joly wenche in every toun.

But F. J. H. Darton, modernizing in 1904, easily outdoes him. Darton not only omits everything Pollard does, and more; he manages to deflavor what he does print. Here, for example, is his entire version of the Reeve's Tale:

> "Well, sirs," answered the Reeve, "you have heard this Miller's rude tale about a carpenter: now hear one about a miller."
>
> With that he began the story of Simkin, the miller of Trumpington, who was cheated and laughed at, in spite of all his cunning, by two students from Cambridge.
>
> "That was a good trick they played upon the Miller," said the Cook, clapping Oswald on the back when the tale was ended. "But let us not stop our tales here."

It's not just that Darton's Cook is a totally different person from Chaucer's (" 'Ha! ha!' quod he, 'for Cristes passioun/ This miller had a sharp conclusioun' "), but the reader has no more idea *what* the trick was than the reader of Boothroyd's Bible has of what Onan did. Darton was one of a score doing such paraphrases.

A few years later the two Chaucer traditions came together and mated. In 1908 the *Canterbury Tales* came out in the Everyman Library, then a new venture. Seventeen of the tales are translated into modern English and expurgated, seven are left in Middle English and not expurgated. "They are so broad, so plain-spoken, that no amount of editing or alteration will make them suitable for the twentieth century," the editor explains. Why bother to print them in the twentieth century, then? Apparently as an act of piety toward complete editions, and in the comfortable awareness that to the average reader they will be incomprehensible.

This strange but not unprecedented edition—there was a Victorian version of the *Decameron* in which ninety-eight of the tales were in expurgated English and two in bawdy Italian—marks the beginning of the end of tampering with Chaucer in Middle English. The actual end was still twenty years off. As late as 1928, Professor J. M. Manly of the University of Chicago brought out a brand-new and very thorough expurgation of the *Canterbury Tales* in Middle English. That edition was still in print in 1960, but was then a last eunuch shuddering amid the medieval virility. In translation, however, bowdlerized Chaucer is going strong to this day. The prim version done in 1912 by Professor John Tatlock of Michigan and Percy MacKaye, for example, is still available in a choice of three editions, one of them put on the market as recently as 1966. Newer translations are obviously a good deal more complete, but none wholly avoids bowdlerism. Take the Wife of Bath's famous

194

promise to her husbands: "Ye shul have queynte right ynough at eve." Most Chaucerians feel that the leading modern translation is Nevill Coghill's for Penguin. He renders the line, "You'll get your evening rations right enough." The *Viking Portable Chaucer*, on the other hand, puts it "you, for one,/ Can have all you can take when day is done." Both convey the meaning; both avoid the word. Again, in the Miller's Tale, a young Oxford don named Nicholas is making advances to a girl named Alison. Chaucer says forthrightly, "He caught her by the queynte." Robert Lumiansky, translating, says, "He slipped his hand intimately between her legs." This is not a change that would have satisfied Dr. Bowdler, but it is still bowdlerism.

William Dunbar, the Scots poet who is Chaucer's contemporary and near-equal, is here for the sake of one edition only. This contains one of the great Victorian acts of daring.

In 1860 a man named James Paterson brought out a works of Dunbar in Edinburgh which was supposed to make him completely available to the nineteenth-century reader. Paterson implied, without actually saying so, that the edition was unexpurgated; and he guaranteed that there would not be a single line which anyone would have trouble understanding, "difficult words and obscure passages being amply explained in footnotes." Having promised so much, Paterson was confronted with the choice of either explaining Dunbar's frequent obscenities or of expurgating after all. By a great leap of daring, he managed to do neither. A very few words he did omit.

They are ones like "erse" which would have been comprehensible to the nineteenth-century British reader (who said "arse" rather than American "ass") even without footnotes. He scrupulously marked the places. But most obscenities he printed, and he really did explain them. He just explained them falsely. Speaking of a group of sinners, Dunbar wrote, "Ilk ane led another by the tersis"—"terse" being Middle Scots for "penis." Paterson duly has a footnote; he says the word means "tail." This perhaps is euphemistic rather than actually false. Others are actually false. For example, there is the passage which gave Lord Hailes so much trouble in 1770, the minstrel exclaiming,

> the fiend me ryfe
> Gif I do ocht but drink and swyfe.

"Swyfe," as noted, is a five-letter Middle Scots and English word for "copulate." Unlike Lord Hailes, Paterson allowed it to remain in the line, and he provided a footnote as promised. It means, he said, to "sing and play."

Paterson's method is the rarest of all forms of bowdlerism. The only other example I know is Professor Gay's note on "verteth," claiming it means to browse in the forest. This rarity is not surprising. If you leave the weeds to fester in the garden, simply relabeling them all as lilies, one student botanist can spoil the whole thing.

Donne, who seems such an obvious candidate for it, nearly escaped expurgation, simply by being unpopular at the right time. After the bowdlerized versions by Chalmers and Sanford in 1810 and 1819, there were only four editions of his poems during the nineteenth century, two each in England and the United States. All four were uncut. What that leaves is the six-volume edition of his "Works" published in London in 1839 by the Rev. Henry Alford. "Works" here means all his sermons, all his religious poems, and half a dozen of the lower-keyed love poems. Even about this mix Alford was apprehensive. He feared blame as the "professed selector" of so much seventeenth-century plain-speaking in the prose, and in the end produced one of the fairly rare editions of expurgated sermons. The poems he left alone.

In his twentieth-century revival, Donne has also nearly escaped expurgation. Charles Eliot Norton of Harvard did bowdlerize him in a private edition in 1905,* perhaps as penance for his unbowdlerized private edition in 1895. No one has since. It is true that the revival has been strikingly selective, and that a look at college anthologies shows progressively franker poems tiptoeing back into the canon over a period of several decades.† But he has not been bowdlerized.

* "This little volume contains all of Donne's Love Poems, save such as offend by a license of speech more pardonable at the time when they were written than it is to-day, and one or two of inferior worth," Norton began his preface. The offensive poems include "The Sun Rising," "The Flea," and "To His Mistress Going to Bed" (Elegy XIX).

† The three poems mentioned in the preceding footnote make fair examples. None of them has yet been in the *Oxford Book of English Verse*, from its beginning in 1900 to the latest printing in 1966, nor in the *Oxford Book of Seventeenth Century Verse*. Other anthologies began to admit them after the First World War. "The Sun Rising" was often and "The Flea" occasionally printed in the twenties, though not yet Elegy XIX. It first appeared in an Ivy League anthology in 1946, and in a more popular one in 1956. It is still excluded from most of the big anthologies used in mass survey courses. An easy test of what kind of college a student goes to is to quote the single line "License my roving hands and let them go," and see if his eyes light up.

After Sir Walter Scott made the heroic decision to print Dryden complete in 1808, no one risked this act again until 1882, and after that no one until 1956. Some of those who printed him in part regarded themselves as expurgators. For example, John Warton did in 1811, when he finally published *The Poetical Works of John Dryden,* the edition his father had started in 1798. "Some omissions have been made, which it is presumed, will not be regretted," he wrote dryly in his brief preface. By my standards, however, he merely winnowed out some of Dryden's bawdier translations from Latin, as many later editors did, too.

This leaves, between 1808 and the First World War, about a dozen editions confined to Dryden's own poetry. I have found five that were expurgated. The first, published in 1852, consists of about three hundred pages of openly snipped snippets, since "his entire poems cannot be given to women, or to young persons with a view to education." Open snipping seems a perfectly fair action. The other four editions are another matter. All four bowdlerize covertly—and all do it identically, which figures, three of them being American piracies of an English original. This original, called, like Warton's, simply *The Poetical Works of John Dryden,* came out in London in 1854. Between 1856 and 1910 one New York publisher after another reprinted it—first Appleton, then Leavitt and Allen, and finally Crowell.

The edition thus stolen is a standard mid-Victorian expurgation: effective, dishonest, and dull. Dryden has a gift for invective, as when the Hind tells the Panther that after her death her sons will hold a rather crude celebration: "The wanton boys would piss upon your grave." They dance in these four editions, just as Shadwell, in "MacFlecknoe," hears echoes from a new street called Passing-Alley. But, like Donne, Dryden was too little in favor to be an important victim.

Herrick, on the other hand, was extremely popular during the Victorian age, and thus came to be one of the most frequently castrated poets in English. After his *Hesperides* came out in 1648, it was almost completely ignored for a century and a half. Then, in 1810, as Donne's star was setting, his began to rise, just in time to meet the onrush of delicacy. The second edition *Hesperides* ever had was an expurgated *Selections,* published that year. A complete edition followed in 1823, which in turn gave way to another expurgation in 1839. Samuel Singer boldly printed him complete again in 1846.

All these early Victorians understood what sort of poet Herrick was, so that Singer, defending his decision not to bowdlerize, admits readily that "the work certainly contains much that might have been omitted without injury to the fame of the author." But, he says, readers have a right to decide for themselves how much of a man's work to skip, and therefore editors must print it all.

W. Carew Hazlitt, William Hazlitt's grandson, took the same line in 1869. He went out of his way to denounce Herrick's "outrageous grossness," pointing out that it can't be overlooked as mere youthful high jinks, since Herrick was fifty-seven when he published *Hesperides.* "The title," he adds tartly, "is perhaps rather apt to mislead, for besides golden apples, this garden assuredly contained many rank tares and poisonous roots." But then, having said all this, Hazlitt feels he has earned the right to publish Herrick complete.

Over the next forty years, however, both the tone and the practice change. The later Victorians and the Edwardians tended to talk about Herrick as a gentle flower poet, at the same time quietly omitting all the words and poems that conflict with this view. The turning point seems to have come with Francis Palgrave's expurgated edition in 1877. Palgrave makes clear that he is bowdlerizing, but he does not get into the matter of poison roots. He just says gently, "Much that was admissible centuries since, or at least sought admission, has now, by a law against which protest is idle, lapsed into the indecorous."

This sentence exemplifies what can be called Palgrave's First Rule of Expurgation. Do it, but don't talk about it much. If your right hand, busy polishing golden apples, doesn't even notice your left hand quietly sorting tares, that's best of all. People shouldn't know about tares, anyway. Dozens of editors obeyed the rule during the ensuing Herrick boom. A cluster of particularly good examples occurs just after 1900.

The first is an edition published by Newnes in London and by Scribner in New York in 1902. (Scribner also published Henry James's *The Wings of the Dove* that year.) The edition is called flatly *Herrick's Hesperides and Noble Numbers*, a title implying completeness. Instead of a preface or notes or any comment on the text whatsoever, it has charming typography. The book fairly bursts with flower borders. Inside the borders, however, there are many fewer poems than Herrick actually wrote, and some that are printed have been quietly bowdlerized. No reader who didn't know *Hesperides* already could guess either of these facts. If girls were innocent in 1902, they had help.

The poet Alice Meynell, editing a selection from *Hesperides* in 1905, also helped preserve innocence. She did write a preface, but hardly to point out poison roots. She spent most of it assuring the reader that Herrick was pure spirit, like Shelley's skylark. Discussing his age, she wrote, "It is as though English, in those few decades of years, had only to speak in order to say something exquisite; but then it must be with Herrick's tongue." English, in those few decades of years, was actually saying the usual range of things—exquisite, gross, funny, and so forth. "Let me feed full till that I fart, says Jill," in one of the many Herrick poems that Mrs. Meynell omitted, and that the Newnes-Scribner editor altered.

John Masefield published an edition in 1906 called *The Poems of Robert Herrick.* Again the title is a little misleading, since the definite article usually implies that all of a man's work will follow, not just sixty per cent of it. In his preface Masefield talks in a manner similar to Mrs. Meynell's about Herrick's "dainty verses" and about the Watteau shepherds and Fragonard nymphs who inhabit them. Then he enables the statement to be true. Poems like "In the Dark None Dainty," in which Herrick can be heard remarking, Kipling-style, that "Jone" and "my Lady" are sisters after sunset, he omitted. In poems like "Oberon's Palace," which in part support and in part conflict with the dainty view, Masefield printed the sections that support and left out those that conflict, not marking the omissions.

It would not be true to say that all editors of Herrick after 1877 hid behind a flower and pretended they weren't doing anything. He was too popular and there were too many editors for that. A minority expurgated openly, and were proud of it. Edward Everett Hale, Jr., is the extreme case. Hale edited a volume of Herrick in Boston in 1895. *His* preface is mainly devoted to tares. Among other things he compares his choice of poems with those of two rival editors (and fellow bowdlerizers): John Morley and Alfred Pollard. Neither of them, he felt, was sufficiently selective. "Mr. Morley omitted whatever he considered licentious, and retained much that most people would consider nasty. Mr. Pollard seems to have omitted what was nasty, and has retained a good deal that is licentious." He himself, he boasted, cracked down on both categories, besides omitting "a few lines here and there" in poems that were neither. About a third of *Hesperides* survives.

Only with the Oxford University Press edition of 1915 did Mr. Herrick begin to recover from all this. In college anthologies, of course, he has not fully recovered yet, any more than Donne has.

Prior here makes a last appearance, not so that I can record still further expurgations—there are several—but to report the response once when he wasn't bowdlerized. That was in 1871.

Prior is a master of what the Victorians liked to call *vers de société*, a genre we ourselves have merged into the broad and not very useful category of light verse. Its special characteristics are (1) urbanity, and (2) wit. "Prior tells a story in verse the most agreeable that ever I knew," an admiring peer said in 1705, and a good many people have thought this ever since. Even a four-line epigram will give some idea of his tone:

> No, no; for my Virginity,
> When I lose that, says Rose, I'll die:
> Behind the Elms, last Night, cry'd Dick,
> Rose, were you not extreamly Sick?

The Victorians had two writers of *vers de société* themselves, Winthrop Mackworth Praed and Frederick Locker-Lampson. In 1872 Locker-Lampson brought out a new version of his *London Lyrics*, just as Praed (who died young in 1839) was having a revival, and right after the complete edition of Prior had appeared. Several reviewers seized the occasion to compare the three masters of urbane wit, and to decide which of them was best.

The *Edinburgh* voted for Praed. It preferred him to Locker-Lampson on literary grounds: he was wittier, more urbane. But it put him ahead of Prior for quite a different reason. He had more decorum. Or as the *Edinburgh* put it, Praed had and Prior hadn't "the high tone which should give a flavour even to light and unpretentious verse."

The *Contemporary Review*, which preferred Locker-Lampson, made both its judgments like this. The reviewer conceded Prior's great technical ability, adding quickly that he can't quote any examples from the new edition, because they're all indecent. He records his astonishment that Prior could see humor in "the theme of woman's frailty, especially the infidelity of wives," and he pats Praed on the head for avoiding such subjects. Then he awards the blue ribbon to Locker-Lampson, because to him can be applied "two epithets which no one dreams of applying to Prior, and which we think must be denied to Praed—earnest and tender." In an age when these were the demands made even on society verse, bowdlerism was almost inevitable.

Every *Works* of Pope between 1797 (when Warton produced his, and got into trouble) and 1939 (when John Butt began to edit the present standard edition) has been expurgated except two. This is not quite as dramatic as it sounds, since those two were available for a very long time. One is Alexander Dyce's Aldine Edition, published in London in 1831 and reprinted in 1866. (It had a third printing in 1891, but this time it *was* expurgated.) The other is its American copy, in print from 1855 to 1920. All other supposedly complete editions, numbering about fifty, shrank away from a poem called "Sober Advice from Horace." *

The fifty editors do have an excuse, in that Pope never

* Sometimes printed under the title "The Second Satire of the First Book of Horace." It was early famous. For example, in 1806 the Rev. William L. Bowes published his ten-volume *Works of Alexander Pope in Verse and Prose*. In the preface he says familiarly, "The offensive epistle is excluded; and if the chapter of the 'double Mistress,' after some hesitation, has found a place, it has been on account of its exquisite humour, and because, though offensive to delicacy, it is not seductive or dangerous to principles."

formally admitted having written "Sober Advice." As Dyce said when printing it in 1831, "The piece in question our poet did not choose to acknowledge on account of its indecencies, but that it is a genuine production has never been doubted." Certainly not by the eighteenth-century editors who freely printed it. (And not that Pope thought the poem was all *that* indecent. When he actually wrote it, in the summer of 1734, he told a friend he had "chosen rather to weaken the images than to hurt chaste ears overmuch.")

Leaving "Sober Advice" aside, about a third of all nineteenth- and early twentieth-century editions of Pope, complete or partial, have been bowdlerized. They include the little Baltimore edition of 1814; the monumental ten-volume *Works* edited by a man named Roscoe in London in 1824; the somewhat less monumental *Works* published in Princeton in 1828; the edition edited by William Michael Rossetti in 1874; an American college text published in 1906 (Professor Parrott couldn't bring himself to print lines 97–98 of the "Epistle to Dr. Arbuthnot"), and so forth. Of them all, the edition any student of bowdlerism would naturally turn to is one done anonymously in Edinburgh in 1859. This is a production rather like Chambers' and Carruthers' Shakespeare, but still more ingenious. The editor took advantage of Pope's weakness for fancy typography, and in particular of his habit of putting key phrases in small capitals. In the "Essay on Man" there are a dozen couplets like this:

> Just as absurd, to mourn the tasks or pains
> The great directing MIND OF ALL ordains.

Keeping Pope's for camouflage, the editor added a couple of hundred capitalized words of his own. Each represented a discreet expurgation. In Pope, for example, "A Farewell to London" begins,

> Dear, damn'd, distracting town, farewell!
>   Thy fools no more I'll tease:
> This year in peace, ye Critics, dwell,
>   Ye Harlots, sleep at ease!

As revised for the nineteenth-century reader, it begins,

> Dear, DROLL, distracting town, farewell!
>   Thy fools no more I'll tease:
> This year in peace, ye Critics, dwell,
>   Ye NOBLES, sleep at ease!

Since this mode of expurgation seems to have given the editor an extraordinary sense of freedom, his edition can be studied, like Carruthers' and Chambers' Shakespeare, for really detailed evidence of what Victorians didn't like. "Damn'd" and "harlots" are conventional cases; anyone from Henrietta Bowdler to John Masefield might have removed them. But some of the changes are wonderfully revealing, like this in "Windsor Forest." Pope wrote:

> In the same shades the Cupids tun'd his lyre,
> To the same notes, of love, and soft desire;

and the anonymous editor emends: "To the same notes, of love's RESISTLESS FIRE." "Soft" and "desire" are in themselves perfectly innocent words; what makes them

206

obscene here? The answer seems to go something like this. Desire is usually, by analogy, hard in men. Soft desire must therefore be feminine. Sexual desire on the part of women was an indecent idea in 1859.

Class feeling, on the other hand, seems to govern the change in "The Temple of Fame" from "Of unknown duchesses lewd tales we tell" to "STRANGE tales we tell." "Lewd" is again a harmless word—Webster regularly used it as a euphemism in his Bible—so it seems to be its application to the upper class that the editor disliked. This theory is strengthened by a change in the "Moral Essays." Pope has a line, "When Caesar made a noble dame a whore," which the editor turns into "When Caesar's DEEDS THE noble dame DEPLORES."

It also comes clear that some of the changes are not made on grounds of indecency or profanity at all, or even to promote respect for the peerage, but simply because Pope, like Prior, was sometimes not sufficiently earnest and tender on serious subjects. Writing a youthful ode "On Silence," Pope said,

Thine was the sway ere Heav'n was formed, or earth,
Ere fruitful thought conceived Creation's birth
Or midwife word gave aid, and spoke the infant forth.

His bowdlerist makes it, "Or THE CREATIVE WORD gave aid," spoiling the passage slightly by the too-quick repetition, but removing any suggestion of levity.

Most of all, it comes clear that once bowdlerism begins, there is no logical point whatever at which it stops. There is always some new, more subtle danger to protect the public from. A really thorough editor might even wind up objecting to Eloise's solemn prayer for Abelard, that when he dies,

> From opening skies may streaming glories shine,
> And saints embrace thee with a love like mine,

as making saints too physical and ardent. And, indeed, this very editor did object. He felt it better to say primly, "And saints RECEIVE thee with a love like mine." The Bible, it's true, describes saints as embracing freely,* while Milton says that angels not only embrace, but do it in a way that makes sexual intercourse seem formal and reserved.† A bowdlerist, of course, would retort that this just shows how richly the Bible and *Paradise Lost* deserved to be expurgated.

Burns, the darling of the Victorians, was occasionally altered by them. In 1887, for example, Charles Annandale edited the so-called Standard Edition in five fat volumes. By "standard" he did not mean the same thing that modern editors do. "The text of the poems is complete in the best sense, only a few rather coarse passages being suppressed," he wrote in the advertisement for the edition. But most Victorian editors of Burns did not suppress even these few passages—of the then usual canon of Burns's poetry.

---

* For example, Acts 20:1. "And after the uproar was ceased, Paul called unto him the disciples, and embraced them, and departed for to go into Macedonia."

† In *Paradise Lost*, Adam has a long, frank talk with the Archangel Raphael. Among other things, he asks whether angels have any pleasure corresponding to the "genial bed" he shares with Eve. Raphael blushes "celestial rosy red," and answers, "Easier than air with air, if spirits embrace,/ Total they mix" (VIII, 619, 626–27).

What they did do, to a man, was to stand aside from a shadowy volume that co-existed with official Burns throughout the nineteenth century. This volume, published posthumously in 1800, consists of eighty or ninety ballads and songs on sexual themes, some original with Burns, some adapted by him from earlier Scottish versions.* A few are extremely funny. All authorities on Burns have known about *The Merry Muses of Caledonia,* and each one has had to decide in his turn how far in the background to push it. A few early ones tried to push it right over a cliff. Wordsworth, who was wrong in thinking Chaucer wrote "The Cuckoo and the Nightingale," was also wrong in thinking Burns didn't write the contents of *The Merry Muses.* "He must be a miserable judge of poetical composition," Wordsworth wrote in 1816, "who can for a moment fancy that such low, tame, and loathesome ribaldry can possibly be the production of Burns." But Lockhart, preceding his biography of Scott with one of Burns in 1828, knew better. "I am grieved to say," he wrote, "he was also in the occasional practice of composing songs, in which he surpassed the licentiousness, as well as the wit and humour, of the old Scottish muse." Lockhart went on to report that these songs had reached print, "and I am afraid they cannot be recalled." But he was careful not to say where they had reached print, or under what title, lest the

---

* To be fair to Victorian editors, most of them didn't know that *all* the songs were connected with Burns. They didn't because Burns's first editor, Dr. James Currie, interpolated the sentence "A very few of them are my own" into a 1792 Burns letter, as part of the into-the-shadows movement. De Lancey Ferguson discovered this when re-editing the letters in 1931.

reader of his *Life* be tempted to seek out a copy. Even so, he was not careful enough. One result of his merely mentioning that licentious songs by Burns existed was that his *Life* was itself sometimes expurgated to remove the information. It was removed, for example, from the Murray edition of 1870.

The actual editors of Burns were meanwhile taking two courses. A majority pretended that *The Merry Muses* was never published, and its contents never written, just as an occasional editor of Chaucer has pretended that there is no Miller's Tale. Annandale of the Standard Edition pretended there was no *Merry Muses*, as did President Eliot of Harvard (who gave Burns one of the fifty volumes of the Five-Foot Shelf to himself). So did J. Logie Robertson, editing *The Poetical Works of Robert Burns* ("the text is presented entire") for Oxford University Press in 1910.

A minority of editors were not willing to practice this deception, and preferred to state plainly that an obscene book lurked in the shadows behind Burns. The American editor James Hunter is typical of the minority. Editing *The Complete Works of Burns* in Philadelphia in 1886, he put a footnote on page 65 of the second volume which names *The Merry Muses*, hints at its contents, and concludes, "To reproduce such pieces in a work dedicated to the genius of Scotland's bard would be sacrilege."

Finally, one Victorian biographer and one editor wanted to look into the shadows. The biographer was William Scott Douglas, who in 1882 put out a revised edition of Lockhart's *Life*, not only supplying full details in a footnote to Lockhart's cautious sentence, but devoting one of his five appendices to a leisurely history of *The Merry Muses*. The editor was William Ernest Henley, captain of his soul and good Victorian. In 1896 Henley and a man named T. F. Henderson did what really was a standard edition. Henley rather liked Burns's bawdy side, and wanted to print it—not as a regular part of the edition, to be sure, but as a sort of private last volume for friends only. Furnivall had done the same when he edited the Percy Manuscript in four public volumes and one private one (*Loose and Humourous Songs from Bishop Percy's Manuscript*) in 1867–68. In the end Henley was persuaded not to be so rash, but he still spoke lovingly in *his* footnote of "the unique and precious collection now called *The Merry Muses of Caledonia*."

In our own century the precious collection has very gradually crept back into view. Not counting a number of semi-literate versions sold under Victorian counters, the first edition after the original one in 1800 came out very quietly in 1911. Duncan McNaught, editor of the *Burns Chronicle*, brought it out in a private edition of one hundred copies. It was forty years since Grosart had begun publishing his private editions of poets like Donne, and signing them, and winning praise; even so, in Edinburgh in 1911 McNaught thought it prudent to remain anonymous.

Some of the hundred copies soon made their way out of Scotland, with the eventual result of a much larger private edition in the United States in 1926, and a whole rash of selections in obscure and rather smudgy magazines. Finally, in 1959 *The Merry Muses* burst out into the sunlight with a public edition edited by two respectable Scots under their own names. And it has now, in the late sixties, been admitted to the standard Burns canon.

Whitman is one of America's rare contributions to English bowdlerism, a modest return for Chaucer, Shakespeare, and the rest. In the United States he has suffered very little. *Leaves of Grass* has been winnowed many times, and it has been very mildly expurgated perhaps three times. But copyright law and a determined author can do much. Whitman was so profoundly opposed to expurgation—even when advised to do it by Emerson, as he was—and his literary executors were so watchful after his death that Americans have never really felt free to bowdlerize *Leaves of Grass*. Our solution was to ban it altogether, as New York and Philadelphia bookstores did informally during the 1870s, and as Boston once did legally in the eighties.

In England, however, *Leaves of Grass* has been bowdlerized from the start. That start was in 1868, thirteen years after the book first appeared in America, and it was in many ways a curious one. For one thing, the editor of the first English edition was not personally shocked by Whitman—on the contrary, he thought *Leaves of Grass*, sex odes and all, was "incomparably the largest poetic work of our period." He was just trying to print the parts most acceptable to Victorians, with the idea that they would soon be tempted on to the whole book. For another, his edition denounces itself in its own preface, one of a tiny handful of expurgations to do so.

The editor said firmly that he did not aspire to "Bowdlerian honours," and explained that he was omitting about half the poems only because he and Whitman had the misfortune to live in "this peculiarly nervous age." Furthermore, he said, looking defiantly around at people like Frederick Locker-Lampson and Mary Cowden Clarke, "I have not in a single instance excised *parts* of poems." *It's the sort of preface a liberal poet might write if he happened to get involved in bowdlerism—and, in fact, the author was William Michael Rossetti, the pre-Raphaelite, art critic, ex-bohemian, liberal poet, and future expurgator of Pope.

Bowdlerism is an inherently deceptive practice, though, and hard to do clean-handed. The sad irony is that Rossetti wound up being almost as devious as the true believers. As claimed, he did not excise any parts of poems. Prose was different. He began by printing Whitman's preface to the original 1855 edition of *Leaves*, thinking it a major critical document. Here he bowdlerized freely, even excising as mild a term as "prostitute." The distinction between bowdlerizing Whitman's poetry and bowdlerizing his prose will not, of course, stand up. It might work for Prior, but not for a free-verse writer like Whitman. Whitman himself printed the 1855 preface as prose only once, and then turned most of it into the poem "By Blue Ontario's Shore," where phrases improper as prose remain improper as poetry.

---

* He could look defiantly at Locker-Lampson because this poetic rival had excised a great many parts of poems only the year before in his anthology *Lyra Elegantiarum*. Sheridan, Moore, Dr. Johnson (and Peter Motteux) were among the victims.

Furthermore, Rossetti forgot his original intention of tempting Victorians on to read Whitman complete. His expurgation was so successful that he kept it in print all the rest of his long life (he died in 1919, aged eighty-nine), and even after that the book went on for another decade. Most other English editors followed his example. Even Ernest de Selincourt, doing *Leaves of Grass* for Oxford's "World Classics" series in 1920, did a little quiet weeding.

In his own old age, Whitman looked across at the then solid phalanx of bowdlerized *Leaves* that represented him in England, and made a recantation. It is quite unlike the Earl of Rochester's, or the one Dr. Bowdler imagined for Gibbon.

> Rossetti expurgated—avowed it in his preface . . . and it was much the same with Rhys * . . . Rossetti said expurgate and I yielded . . . Emerson said expurgate—I said no, no. I have lived to regret my Rossetti yes—I have not lived to regret my Emerson no. . . . Of course I see now as clearly as I did then how big and fine Rossetti was about it all . . . But I now feel somehow as if none of the changes should have been made: that I should have assumed that position: that's the only possible, final, logical position.

---

* Ernest Rhys, first editor of the Everyman Library, of which the first 152 volumes all came out in 1906. By 1908 Rhys was arranging for the expurgation of Chaucer, personally expurgating Herrick, etc. His (basically just winnowed) Whitman came out in 1886, in the Canterbury Poets series.

Browning was a product of the age of delicacy, and a firm upholder of its standards.* That he himself should need expurgation at first seems odd. But it was entirely without intention that he wrote the most indecent single line of Victorian poetry. He didn't know what he was saying. The whole incident is evidence of the genuineness of Victorian innocence.

In 1841 Browning published the long dramatic poem *Pippa Passes*, now best known for the lines "God's in His heaven/ All's right with the world." Toward the end of it, he sets up a kind of Gothic scene, and writes:

> Then, owls and bats,
> Cowls and twats,
> Monks and nuns, in a cloister's moods,
> Adjourn to the oak-stump pantry!

The second of these lines created no stir at all, presumably because the middle class had truly forgotten the word "twat" (just as it has still forgotten "quaint," so that Marvell's pun on the two meanings in "To His Coy Mistress" has fallen flat for six or eight generations now). A few scholars must have recognized the word, but any who did behaved like loyal subjects when the emperor wore his new clothes, and discreetly said noth-

---

* "I was at a House four days ago, where an English young bride of a year's standing began the dinner by getting hold of her husband's hands, with other significacies before us all—me an entire stranger; by the evening she was resting her head on his shoulder, and *I* did not stay for the little more that could well happen, and which probably *did*, for the edification of boys and girls." Robert Browning to Isabella Blagden, July 19, 1862.

ing. No editor of Browning has ever expurgated the line,* even when Rossetti was diligently cutting mere "womb" out of Whitman. The first response only came forty years later when the editors of the *Oxford English Dictionary*, collecting examples of usage, like Johnson before them, and interested to find a contemporary use of "twat," † wrote to Browning to ask in what sense he was using it. Browning is said to have written back that he used it to mean a piece of headgear for nuns, comparable to the cowls for monks he put in the same line. The editors are then supposed to have asked if he recalled where he had learned the word. Browning replied that he knew exactly. He had read widely in seventeenth-century literature in his youth, and in a broadside poem called "Vanity of Vanities," published in 1659, he had found these lines, referring to an ambitious cleric:

* Though a few have conspicuously avoided it. Augustine Birrell (Locker-Lampson's son-in-law) did a complete Browning in 1896. He promised to "explain in the margin . . . the meanings of such words as might, if left unexplained, momentarily arrest the understanding of the reader." Such words include "lutanist" ("player on the lute"), "fugue," "jerboa." They do not include "twat," presumably because if explained it would arrest the reader even more.

† There were two, actually. Bulwer Lytton also used the word in his novel *The Coming Race*, published anonymously in 1871. This case is harder to assess. His use of *twat* is as part of an imaginary language called Vril-ya, and may be pure accident. It doesn't feel accidental, though. Lytton, poking fun at evolution, invents a human race derived from frogs, and has one of its philosophers say, "Humble yourselves, my descendants; the father of your race was a *twat* (tadpole)."

Considering the aptness of the English meaning here; considering that Lytton stresses language in the novel ("The philologist will have seen from the above how much the language of the Vril-ya is akin to the Aryan or Indo-Germanic," he says near the end of a chapter devoted exclusively to Vril-ya linguistics); considering that "woman" in Vril-ya is *gy*, obviously meant to remind the reader of Greek *gyne*, English *gynecology*, etc., it seems probable that Lord Lytton was getting away with a Victorian dirty joke.

They talk't of his having a Cardinall's Hat;
They'd send him as soon an Old Nun's Twat.

If you are sufficiently delicate and sheltered, it is possible to take the last word as meaning something like a wimple, and Browning did. A fugitive and cloistered virtue can get into difficulties that even Milton didn't think of.*

---

* Browning was not the only Victorian poet to be caught this way. Arthur Hugh Clough provided the second-dirtiest line in Victorian poetry when he published *The Bothie of Toper-Na-Fuosich* in 1848. This is a Scottish pastoral. The words of the title are Gaelic, "bothie" meaning hut or booth, and "toper-na-fuosich" meaning Clough didn't exactly know what. (He got it off an old map.) About three months after the poem was published, someone told him what it did mean, with the result that he lost all pleasure in what is a very good poem. (See his *Correspondence*, ed. F. L. Mulhauser, II, 498.) It was never reprinted during his lifetime.

What the phrase means is "twat"—or, literally, "bearded well"—and this astonishing fact spread fairly rapidly through Victorian literary circles. It was even hinted at in reviews. When the poem was reissued in 1862, it had been renamed *The Bothie of Tober-Na-Vuolich*, according to Clough's posthumous instructions. Reviewers still couldn't resist going back and giving hints about the original title. (See *Blackwood's*, Nov. 1862, p. 589.)

The tittering was guarded enough, though, so that the editors of the present standard edition of Clough (Oxford U.P., 1951) apparently had no more idea than Clough himself what the phrase meant, and reported, "It is difficult now to guess what the supposed impropriety was."

CHAPTER NINE

The Great Victorian Age: II—Prose

I shall read Sterne's Sentimental Journey *to you soon after we are married. It wouldn't quite do for a lady to read it by herself, I am sorry to say.*
          THOMAS HUGHES (age 23), future author
          of *Tom Brown's School Days*, to his
          fiancée (age 20), 1845

Mrs. Clemens received the mail this morning, and the next minute she lit into the study with danger in her eye and this demand on her tongue: Where is the profanity Mr. Howells speaks of? Then I had to miserably confess that I had left it out when reading the manuscript to her.
          MARK TWAIN to WILLIAM DEAN HOWELLS,
          1874

PROSE WAS even more frequently bowdlerized than poetry during the nineteenth century. It shows less. There are no rhyme words, no line numbers, comparatively few memorable passages to testify to change. In all but the best-known prose, a bowdlerist could (and still can)

alter about what he pleases, secure from detection by any but really close critics, or an occasional outraged author. Victorian editors took full advantage of this fact.

The three-part division—works too gross to be saved, works ripe for saving, and works sufficiently innocent as they stand—applies in prose as in poetry, but for prose the whole pattern shifts in the direction of greater prudery. The class of prose too gross to save is perceptibly larger than the comparable class of poetry. No one attempted, for example, to expurgate the plays of Wycherley, though these were still read: There were several complete editions for "strong" readers. No one attempted to expurgate either the novels or the plays of Aphra Behn. (Sir Walter Scott's great-aunt had suggested that they simply be burned.) No one even mentioned the novels of John Cleland, a condition that persisted, in public, until quite recently. In the case of the *Oxford Companion to English Literature*, a work committed from the start to mentioning novels on a really massive scale, it persisted through the first edition in 1932, the second in 1937, the third in 1946. Cleland appears, blinking, in the fourth edition, 1967—just in time to greet the movie *Fanny Hill*.

On the other side—prose immune to expurgation because not felt to need it—the limit is sometimes hard to find. A novel as non-erotic as *Tom Brown's School Days* was expurgated by at least two nineteenth-century American publishers. The objections of one of them extended to all references to beer, and even to the word "nasty," which he felt was. *Moby-Dick*, crossing the Atlantic the other way in 1851, was bowdlerized by its first English publisher. *His* objections extended to a reference to Queequeg's underclothes,* to the word "obstetrics," even to Melville's saying that Ahab had a "crucified" look. (It got changed to a look of "apparently eternal anguish.") Nor did books have to travel to get this sort of treatment. Robert Surtees' lively but perfectly innocent fox-hunting novel *Handley Cross* (1843) was expurgated in its native England in 1891. *Huckleberry Finn,* that novel of pre-adolescence, was expurgated in New York as early as 1885, the year after its publication. Under the guidance of Richard Watson Gilder, Huck ceased to say things like "in a sweat" and "hogwash," and began to say things like "in such a hurry."

The immune group in non-fiction is equally hard to find. This is true even of books which are literally saintly. St. Augustine's *City of God,* for example, was

* How to speak of underclothes had already been a problem for two generations. "A fine lady can talk about her lover's inexpressibles, when she would faint to hear of his breeches," the *Farmer's Magazine* reported in 1809. Plumptre was expurgating the word "smock" in 1808. Bowdler permitted "smock," but not "breeches," and not usually "linen," which is the word Melville had used.

Three generations later, the problem was worse than ever. After the first performance of Synge's *Playboy of the Western World* in 1907, Synge and Lady Gregory sent a telegram to Yeats: "Audience broke up in disorder at the word shift." These disturbances continued. The Dublin satirist Susan Mitchell then wrote a poem, the second stanza of which reads,

They tell me no one says it now, but yet to give me ease—
If I must speak they bid me use a word that rhymes with "sneeze."
But, oh! their cold permission my spirits cannot lift—
I only want the dear old word, the one that ends in "ift."

The one that rhymes with "sneeze" is, of course, "chemise." For a claim that smock, shift, and chemise are *all* obscene—"nor [may] the garment itself be alluded to by any decent writer"—see Leigh Hunt's *Autobiography,* 1928 edition, p. 501.

regularly expurgated in England after about 1870. Some editions, such as one done in London in 1890, do not actually omit any of Augustine's words, to be sure; they just leave a certain number in Latin. That particular edition, in fact, reprinted the Healey translation of 1610—and shoved back into Latin quite a lot that Healey had carefully Englished. Other editions, like F. S. Bussell's in 1903, bowdlerize in the strict sense. Bussell omits, for example, most of St. Augustine's remarks about the human body, and what control we have over it. Less than Adam, but still considerable, he felt. "There are that can break wind backwards so continuously, that you would think they sung," he reported of fifth-century man. A Renaissance editor like Luis Vives joyfully supported this with a note about a similar Renaissance man at the court of the Emperor Maximilian. Bussell cut the whole passage. Sir Thomas Browne's *Religio Medici* also frequently lost passages in late-Victorian editions. So did Burton's *Anatomy of Melancholy*. So did Charles Lamb's letters. Canon Ainger's edition in 1888 was not the first but the third time they had been bowdlerized.

There is, of course, *some* prose that no Victorian editor altered. Jane Austen's novels, for example, have never been bowdlerized by anyone except Jane Austen herself—and her expurgation amounts to no more than removing one sentence about bastards from the second edition of *Sense and Sensibility* (1813).* The other sen-

* "Lady Middleton's delicacy was shocked; and in order to banish so improper a subject as the mention of a natural daughter, she actually took the trouble of saying something herself about the weather."

tence about them she left alone. The essays of Addison and Steele, so far as I am aware, have not been bowdlerized at all.

Since prose, unlike poetry, can readily be shortened, simplified, adapted for children; and since he who digests a book can hardly help changing its flavor a little, or even quite a lot,* there has been a certain amount of semi-deliberate purification of English prose going on since at least the seventeenth century. As a fully deliberate practice, however, clearly distinct from abridgment, it appears simultaneously with the Bowdlers. Henrietta Bowdler published the first *Family Shakespeare* in 1807. Leigh Hunt began to edit *Classic Tales, Serious and Lively,* in 1806. Three of its five volumes contain unaltered stories by Dr. Johnson, John Hawkesworth, etc. But in the other two, Hunt wanted to include classic tales by Sterne and Voltaire. He decided that on these it would be necessary to practice what he called "chastening."

Despite Goldsmith, Ramsay, and Bishop Hurd, Hunt plainly considered himself to be a pioneer. In the preface to the second volume, which is solid Voltaire, he won-

---

* For example, an 1868 abridgment of *Clarissa.* E. S. Dallas, the rather distinguished abridger, had no intention of bowdlerizing. Though he dutifully apologized for Richardson's choice of topic—"It shocks us to know that any novelist has dared to wreak his genius on a subject so dreadful as the violation of a virgin"—in fact he left the details of the violation pretty well intact.

But Richardson was almost as interested in Clarissa's finances as in her virginity. Here Dallas cut radically. Consciously or not, he abridged Clarissa and her friend Anna Howe into a pair of high-minded Victorian girls. No longer do they eagerly discuss inheritance laws, will-making, dowries. If economics instead of sex were obscene, this would be a bowdlerized book.

ders out loud if readers will mind the chastening—and concludes that they won't even notice it. "Loose description is seldom missed when it is not found," he wrote with the self-assurance of twenty-two; "for the generality of readers insensibly become too intent upon what their author is saying, to fancy what he might have said." This being the case, one may snip away in perfect freedom.

With Voltaire, Hunt was fairly lenient. He excluded *Candide* altogether, as being too indecorous, and he removed an occasional continental leer elsewhere. But he went out of his way to approve Voltaire's prose as basically virtuous, quite unlike Swift's ("that vilest of all vile ribaldry") or Rabelais' ("inconceivably disgusting"). Sterne was another matter. Hunt's headnote to him in Volume V sounds rather like an Edinburgh clergyman describing Allan Ramsay. "Terms evidently occurred to his mind," the young editor wrote indignantly, "which being never written in works of taste, nor tolerated by a decorous public, were for that reason only rejected by him; and asterisks, in due literal or syllabic numbers, are substituted, which, with more explicitness than the celebrated eastern star of antiquity, guide the simple as well as the wise to the specific popular phraseology." * In the

---

* The charge is true. Sterne was addicted to sentences like this one from *Tristram Shandy:* "The chamber maid had left no ******* *** under the bed:—Cannot you contrive, master, quoth Susannah, lifting up the sash with one hand, and helping me into the window seat with the other,—cannot you manage, my dear, for a single time to **** *** ** *** ******?"

Curiously enough, Hunt was also addicted to them, though his method was periphrasis rather than asterisks. Nothing amused him more than to report that a seventeenth-century duchess, meeting a friend, "saluted him by the plainest title of affiliation with which the

end, Hunt felt able to include only three snipped-up passages from Sterne. These were what readers were still getting in 1895, when Hunt's whole five volumes were lifted bodily into a "Nuggets for Travellers" series.

From this modest beginning in 1806, the flow of bowdlerized prose grew rapidly into a flood, which ran at spate for a century. The sheer quantity is so great that in this chapter it will be possible to describe only a few specimen cases. I shall, in fact, deal entirely with three: *Gulliver's Travels*, Pepys's *Diary*, and the twin case of Defoe's *Moll Flanders* and *Roxana*. Each shows a different aspect of the Victorian mood.

Swift's vile ribaldry has generally been located, by those who track it down, in his poems and to a lesser extent in the prose satires. *Gulliver* is work of another kind. "No better style in English prose was ever written, or can be," said the novelist William Dean Howells, writing a preface for a new edition in 1913. "A few supreme things please from age to age on the same terms as at first," he added, and then reverently placed *Gulliver* in this high class—books so great as not to be affected by any mere change in literary taste.

In actual fact, however, *Gulliver* was anything but immune to the change of taste that occurred just after 1800. Howells was certainly right that the book was too good simply to be stood in a corner, like *Fanny Hill*. In fact, if anything it grew more popular in Victorian

---

illegitimate of the mercenary are wont to be greeted." This is a roundabout but perfectly clear way of expressing the phrase "whoreson bastard." Presumably Hunt would retort that it is clear only to people with large vocabularies ("the wise"), and what matters is protecting the simple. He and Grosart thought alike.

times. *Gulliver* went through about sixty editions from the time it was published in 1726 until 1800—and it went through a hundred and fifty more between 1800 and 1900. But while the eighteenth-century editions were all complete,* something over half the nineteenth-century editions were bowdlerized. So have many been in the twentieth century, including the one introduced by Howells. (This detail does not emerge in his preface.) There are still expurgations in print now.

Two factors combine that made bowdlerism of *Gulliver* almost inevitable. One is that while Swift may not be ribald in it, in the sense of leering at man's animal nature, he certainly does insist on its presence. If the Victorians tended to put not only their women but all human beings on pedestals, Swift dug pits. Not only does he insist on pointing out that otherwise repulsively hairy male yahoos are bald on their buttocks ("except about the *Anus*"), while the sagging breasts of the females "often reached almost to the Ground," he will go out of his way to specify that when the Lilliputian army marched, twenty-four abreast, between Gulliver's legs, some of the younger officers were unable to resist looking up to see if they could catch a glimpse of his genitals through his ragged breeches, or inexpressibles. (They could, and were about equally divided between "Laughter and Admiration.") This sort of thing was intolerable.

The other reason is that *Gulliver's Travels*, like

---

* In England, that is. The very first French edition, 1727, is bowdlerized. Its editor, the Abbé Desfontaines, explained that a complete version "would have revolted the good taste which reigns in France." *Gulliver* had no eighteenth-century editions in America, except two brief (but unexpurgated) abridgments.

Lamb's *Tales*, has always been appealing to readers younger than those it was written for. Most of the expurgated editions have been for children—though there have been plenty for adults, too, such as the version put out by Pocket Books in 1939.

Expurgated *Gulliver*'s come, in fact, in about five different forms. Two of these are specifically for children, two are for adolescents, one is for the general reader. For young children the changeless book is normally cut to the first two voyages—Lilliput and Brobdignag—thus disposing of the yahoos, and it is drastically abridged, which always causes the junior officers to keep their eyes down. Or else it is retold, in Swift's words where these are bland, in the editor's elsewhere, thus getting rid of all problems at once. Alfred Blaisdell, the publisher, had great success with such a retelling in 1886. Padraic Colum had even greater success with one in 1917, which is still in print. Juvenile writers continue to retell *Gulliver* now.

For adolescents, there are fancy illustrated editions, such as the one Howells wrote his preface for, and school editions. Both forms appeared about a hundred years ago, and both still exist. But by and large the openly bowdlerized school edition was characteristic of the Victorians, and the covertly bowdlerized picture book is characteristic of the twentieth century.

Both give an interesting picture of what knowledge has been thought too dangerous for teenagers. In the more severely bowdlerized versions, all references to the human torso are gone (hands, feet, head, arms, and legs are all right), and also nearly all reference to activities that involve the torso. Oral activity remains, genital and anal vanish. Gulliver may still swallow a Lilliputian turkey whole, or gag on a quart of Brobdignagian cream. He may not urinate, on palaces or elsewhere, defecate (or even notice the fly-specks of Brobdignagian flies); he may not watch a baby being nursed, or learn that houyhnhnms limit the number of their foals. He may not notice the body-lice on a beggar, or the body odor of a maid of honor; he may not tell a fascinated houyhnhnm about the English medical practice of giving laxatives.

In milder expurgations the same rules apply, but more loosely. There are several editions, for example, in which Gulliver does see a Brobdignagian woman nursing a baby. He is permitted to react. "I must confess no Object ever disgusted me so much as the sight of her monstrous Breast, which I cannot tell what to compare with, so as to give the curious Reader an Idea of its Bulk, Shape, and Colour." But these editions then cut the two following sentences, in which it turns out that Gulliver actually does have some ideas for comparison. He no longer says, "It stood prominent six Foot, and could not be less than sixteen in Circumference. The Nipple was about half the Bigness of my Head, and the Hew both of that and the Dug so varified with Spots, Pimples, and Freckles, that nothing could appear more nauseous." In short, the *idea* of a huge breast being disgusting was tolerable to the more liberal editors, but not the reality. Their teenage readers must not learn what the breast actually looked like.

This was obviously not because Swift's description

was likely to arouse lust. Neither can it have been simply because pimples, etc., are too disgusting or too shocking for the teenage mind, since the same editions leave other shocking details untouched. This is especially true in the context of death. None of the bowdlerized editions for adolescents, even the strictest, feels it necessary to eliminate the Lilliputian worry about "the Stench of so large a Carcass," if they kill Gulliver. Nor Gulliver's own description of battlefields in Europe, with the dead soldiers "left for Food to Dogs." More striking, none removes the scene in which a Brobdignagian criminal is beheaded, tied in a chair, and Gulliver watches his blood spout thirty feet in the air, and his severed head bounce on the scaffold floor. (Recent expurgations, such as the Heritage Illustrated Bookshelf edition, New York: 1940, generally *do* eliminate this passage. Our day is less concerned with innocence, and more with bad dreams.) What was the motive, then? No bowdlerizer of Swift has left a note to explain, but presumably they wanted to preserve the romantic illusions of their readers, even about freckles on breasts. In short, to keep humanity on pedestals.

There is, of course, a considerable case for bowdlerizing *Gulliver* for children or even adolescents—though there may be an even better case for not giving them the book until they are old enough to read it the way Swift wrote it. What there is not a case for is pretending that Swift wrote it some other way than he did. Scores of editions do pretend that, however, the extreme case perhaps being an unusually severe expurgation published by Rand-McNally in 1912. It omits two hundred passages instead of the usual one hundred—not merely body hair on yahoos and the curiosity of Lilliputian junior officers, but also the information that scandal about ladies' reputations sometimes springs up at courts, that there is a thing in the world called dung, and so on. The anonymous editor has previously contrived to give the impression that Swift himself avoided such matters. "His name echoes through history," the brief preface concludes, "as the clerical exposer of human frailties in a manner to call forth only innocent mirth." First you tell the lie, then you make it true.

Finally, there are a considerable number of expurgations of *Gulliver* for a general audience. These range from a scholarly expurgation done by the Vice-President of the Royal Irish Academy in 1862 to the slapdash one supervised by Harriet Beecher Stowe in 1873 ("Swift's genius commands our admiration, but his works should never be introduced into the home-circle save in such revised and cleanly editions as the present one") to the 1939 Pocket Book. This type has now died out; examples of the other four may still be found throughout the English-speaking world.

"It has gone rather hard with the purchasers of Pepys's Diary," an American critic wrote in mock-pity in 1893. He was looking at the new edition published that year, and marveling at how very expurgated the thirty or so preceding editions had been, and therefore what a swindle. He was not the first man to marvel at this. An earlier generation of Pepys readers had been similarly startled by the new edition of 1875, and a still earlier generation got its shock from the edition of 1848. Nor have things changed much since. Next year, too, a new edition of Pepys will start to appear, and once again it will show up all preceding editions—by now over a hundred—as bowdlerized. (The future will be duller. The 1970 edition will actually be complete.)

The history of Pepys's diary thus runs counter to the general trends reported in this book. Pepys made a pre-Victorian debut, almost incredibly expurgated. Three times, as the nineteenth century moved on and the level of prudery increased, portions of the text were restored. Queen Victoria got older and Pepys got franker simultaneously. Now, after seventy-five years of holding steady in its final Victorian state, the diary is finally in the process of appearing as Pepys wrote it. It all makes a nice study in the conflict between the will to decorum on one hand, and human curiosity on the other.

Pepys actually kept his diary during the 1660s, secretly and in cipher. Along with the rest of his books and papers, he willed it to Magdalene College, Cambridge, where it sat quietly on a shelf until 1818. That year the diary of his contemporary John Evelyn was first published,* and had a success. This stimulated the Hon. and Rev. George Neville, the Master of Magdalene College, to haul out Pepys's manuscript, and eventually to have it deciphered by a bright undergraduate. The job took three years. Neville then turned the transcript over

---

* Bowdlerized, of course. Evelyn first appeared unexpurgated in 1955. Still another Restoration diary, the one kept by the naval chaplain Henry Teonge between 1675 and 1679, has the same history: first edition, 1825; first unexpurgated edition, 1927. *Most* diaries begin life bowdlerized and abridged.

to his elder brother, Lord Braybrooke. Braybrooke was the college Visitor, a role amounting to a sort of one-man board of trustees. (Neville's father, the preceding Visitor, had appointed him Master in the first place.) Lord Braybrooke then personally edited the transcript for publication, and Samuel Pepys first began telling quaint stories in print in 1825. The book was soon being hailed as the most delightful of all English diaries.

The delights had, however, already been twice refined, once by the undergraduate and once by Lord Braybrooke. The undergraduate's transcript still survives, and it turns out that he chose not to decipher quite everything. A few of Pepys's more unabashed accounts of sex in the 1660s, a few scatological touches he omitted. Lord Braybrooke then proceeded to omit all the rest, along with a couple of thousand passages which he regarded as trivial rather than indecent. His first edition includes roughly half of what Pepys wrote, and it is a bowdlerized abridgment.

Braybrooke freely admitted the abridgment, but said nothing of the bowdlerism. Readers were supposed to think he had removed a lot of boring Navy Office material and entries like "Had a cold today," and retained everything else. Most did think this, but not all. Sir Walter Scott, for example, who by now had edited Swift as well as Dryden, and knew what to expect of old writers, was extremely suspicious. Scott wrote one of the first reviews of the diary, and he began it by giving some tepid praise to Lord Braybrooke's plan to omit trivia. But he went on to voice his suspicion that "something has been kept back, which would have rendered the whole more piquant, though perhaps less instructive." If so, a bad idea, "even when decency and delicacy may appear . . . to demand such omissions." Editors should print their texts in full, he concluded, echoing Wordsworth's advice to him.

Scott heeded Wordsworth; Braybrooke ignored Scott, at least for twenty years. But for the third edition of his Pepys, which came out in 1848, he did read all the way through the undergraduate's script again, to see if he had really been too harsh in 1825—and he decided he had. He formally promised to "insert in its proper place every passage that had been omitted, with the exception only of such entries as were devoid of the slightest interest, and many others of so indelicate a character, that no one with a well-regulated mind will regret their loss; nor could they have been tolerated even in the licentious days to which they relate." * In short, he admitted having expurgated, and he promised restitution to the possible Victorian limit.

Critics have short memories, and probably don't read older critics, anyway. Scott might never have spoken. When the new edition came out, they were torn between indignant surprise at finding they had been deceived—"the most valuable characteristic portion of the Diary was often that which was suppressed," the *Edin-*

---

* This, of course, is nonsense. Braybrooke continued to omit lots of things which were freely tolerated in Pepys's day. Pepys once described, for example, a Restoration-style political cartoon. "Mr. Moore told me of a picture hung up at the Exchange of a great pair of buttocks shooting of a turd into Lawson's mouth, and over it was wrote 'The thanks of the house.' Boys do now cry 'Kiss my Parliament' instead of 'Kiss my arse.' "

Boys and stock-brokers, at least, tolerated these things. Even the 1893 edition of Pepys tolerates all but one word. (It has "Kiss my [rump].") Braybrooke killed the whole passage.

burgh complained—and joy at the restitution. This they supposed to be almost total. After all, they had Lord Braybrooke's word. "The work may now, we presume, be regarded as complete," said *Blackwood's*. What he had actually done, however, was to increase the proportion of the diary he printed from 50 to 60 per cent.

This second swindle came to light only well after his death. By then there was a new Master of Magdalene, and a new President—Magdalenese for second-in-command—whose name was Mynors Bright. Bright was fascinated by Pepys's diary, learned the cipher, and made a whole new transcription. In 1875 he published it, loudly proclaiming that he had added one new word for every three Braybrooke had printed, and a little more quietly saying that now the reader had the whole thing ("with the omission of but a few passages").

Once again reviewers were divided between delight at getting Pepys complete (by Victorian standards) at last, and indignation at their past deception. "For nearly sixty years the Diary of Samuel Pepys has been a household word in English literature; it may therefore seem almost paradoxical to say that we now read it for the first time," the *Edinburgh's* reviewer said, sounding much like his predecessor in 1849. He was also like his predecessor in being wrong. Bright had only advanced the proportion of the diary in print from 60 per cent to 80, and one word in every five was still missing. This fact emerged, to fresh cries of outrage, in 1893.

Henry Wheatley, the man responsible, was Pepys's first honest editor. When he in turn made his claim to have printed the whole diary "with the exception of a few passages which cannot possibly be printed," he was very nearly telling the truth. Thirty pages of omissions may be more than "a few passages," but it is a trifle compared to Braybrooke and Bright. Wheatley jumped the total of Pepys in print from 80 to 99 per cent, and he even marked the places where the missing one per cent ought to have gone. The effect was like holding a letter written in invisible ink up to a fire. A whole new side of Pepys emerges. It begins on the very first page. Pepys started his diary on January 1, 1660. The first entry is a brief summary of his condition on that day. In all previous editions he had been content to say that he was in good health, moderate fortune, and lived in Axe Yard with his wife and servant Jane, "and no more in family than us three." Actually, Pepys had plenty more to say, notably about why there were only three in the family. Wheatley didn't restore the whole passage, but he did print enough to let the reader know. The addition reads (the dots and bracketed material are Wheatley's): "My wife . . . gave me hopes of her being with child, but on the last day of the year . . . [the hope was belied]."

Or again, a little later Pepys and his wife had a quarrel about her dog, a quarrel eliminated by Lord Braybrooke perhaps as trivial and by Mr. Bright definitely as improper. Wheatley, retaining all but one word, allows Pepys to note that he swore to fling the dog out the window "if he [dirtied] the house any more," thus giving a sharp little vignette of seventeenth-century housekeeping. In 1893 it really did take courage to print entries like these and the great pair of buttocks.

The appearance of Wheatley by no means ensured that purchasers ceased to be swindled. Publishers of secondary editions of Pepys in general went right on using the Braybrooke and Bright texts. The Globe Pepys, an edition born in the twentieth century and in print until just recently, has a note by its editors regretting "that they dare not go further than the most valiant have already ventured." They then venture as far as Lord Braybrooke's final or 60-per-cent version. The Everyman Pepys, revised in 1953 and in print right now, is a selection from Bright. So is the Washington Square edition published by Simon and Schuster in 1964.

Even editors who followed Wheatley usually followed at a safe distance. Another standard book of selections is a Wheatley-based volume called *Everybody's Pepys*, first published in 1926. O. F. Morshead, the editor, is very respectful of Wheatley. That brave Victorian, he told his readers, printed the "full text, with the exception of an occasional word or phrase which it is safe to say will never be put in print." (It *has* taken forty-four years to prove him wrong.) Is he then true to brave Wheatley's text? He is not. Not on the opening page. Especially not in sexual episodes, such as the one in the fall of 1668 when Mrs. Pepys discovered her husband with his hands on and perhaps in their maid Deb. Deb got fired, but Pepys managed a last sight of her, and a few last kisses, on November 18. I don't know what he actually entered in his diary for that day, since the new unexpurgated edition won't reach 1668 until about 1976, but I do know part. Wheatley permits this much:

She come into the coach to me, and je did baiser her. . . . I did nonetheless give her the best council I could, to have a care of her honour, and to fear

235

God, and suffer no man para avoir to do con her as
je have done, which she promised. Je did give her 20
s[hillings].

(Pepys used not only cipher but also polyglot when he
especially didn't want his wife to see a passage.)

Morshead altered the entry in two ways. He took out
the ellipsis marks and the "nonetheless" to conceal
Wheatley's expurgation, and he took out the last part of
Pepys's advice, to protect his sheltered jazz-age readers.
In *Everybody's Pepys* the passage reads:

She come into the coach to me, and je did baiser her.
I did give her the best council I could, to have a care
of her honour, and to fear God. Je did give her 20
s[hillings].

A cure for all this was announced in 1932. A minor
storm had brewed up in the *Times Literary Supplement*
over Pepys, with readers writing in to complain of
Wheatley's "omission of passages considered to be unprintable forty years ago." Francis Turner, the Pepysian
Librarian at Magdalene, then announced that he was at
work on a new definitive edition, "as complete and accurate as possible." (Lord Braybrooke, of course, had
said the same.) The London publisher Bell had already
contracted to publish it.

Twenty-eight years slipped by with no sign of the
new edition, and then it was 1960. In America, Harper's
was reissuing Morshead's expurgated abridgment of expurgated Wheatley as a Harper Torchbook. In England,
the fellows of Magdalene College were still trying to

decide how complete the new edition ought to be. In June the Master called for a vote. The most distinguished fellow, C. S. Lewis, was away, but he left a written proxy, which survives. It contains one of the few serious modern discussions of bowdlerism. There were two questions to decide, Lewis said, one prudential and one moral. Prudentially, completeness was a risk. A group of sober Cambridge dons might make themselves look ridiculous by restoring Pepys's scatology and Deb-fondling; reviewers might laugh. It would be "pusillanimous and unscholarly," Lewis wrote, "to delete a syllable on that score."

There remained the question of morality. By merely admitting there *was* a moral issue, Lewis showed himself more akin to Dr. Bowdler than to most literary men in 1960. He and Dr. Bowdler saw the issue in quite different terms, however. Confronted with any given passage in Shakespeare, Dr. Bowdler asked himself, "Can it be read aloud? Will it cause the innocent to blush?" These are essentially questions of propriety.* Confronted with

---

* Though also of Lockean psychology. As Professor Robert Siegel of Dartmouth has pointed out, people like St. Augustine and Milton were untroubled by the idea of innocent young men and women reading frank sexual passages, provided they *did* blush. As Milton puts it,

> Evil into the mind of God or Man
> May come and go, so unapprov'd, and leave
> No spot or blame behind. [*Par. Lost*, IV, 117-19.]

Input doesn't matter, only outgo. But Locke insisted that anything that comes into your mind, whether you consciously approve of it or not, can't help leaving spots. You therefore do well to control input. Lockean psychology is presumably one of the bases on which the idea of delicacy rests.

Pepys, Lewis asked himself, "Is it probable that the inclusion of these passages will lead anyone to commit an immoral act which he would not have committed if we had suppressed them?" This is entirely a question of behavior—and, said Lewis, an unanswerable one. "No one can foresee the odd results that any words may have on this or that individual. We ourselves [he and Sir Henry Willink, the Master], in youth, have been both corrupted and edified by books in which our elders could have seen neither edification nor corruption." But if one can't know, one can guess. And considering the deliberate aphrodisiac effect of much of modern life, Lewis concluded, to say that "any perceptible increment in lechery will be caused by printing a few obscure and widely separated passages in a very long and expensive book, seems to me ridiculous, or even hypocritical. . . . I am therefore in favour of printing the whole unexpurgated Pepys."

Ten more years now pass by, and it is 1970. Bell in London and the University of California Press in Berkeley publish the first three volumes of their long, expensive, unexpurgated Pepys. It has been a hundred and fifty-two years since the Hon. and Rev. George Neville took the first steps to put the diary in print. It is a pity the *Edinburgh Review* does not survive to point out that we are really reading Pepys for the first time.

Defoe's *Moll Flanders* and *Roxana* had still a third kind of career. *Gulliver* and Pepys were stock Victorian works—familiar, beloved, and usually expurgated. Not so the two Defoe novels. Throughout the nineteenth century both teetered on the edge of that limbo into which *Fanny Hill* wholly vanished.

Moll, which came out in 1722, was originally a popular novel. It had three editions its first year, and another every few years for the next sixty. Then, for more than a century, there is a blank. The lone nineteenth-century edition didn't appear until 1896, and even that was printed in Holland, though sold in London. It was not expurgated; it was also not reviewed. A more respectable edition came out in 1907. But *Moll* actually re-entered literature with a rush during the 1920s. There were three editions in 1924, as in 1722, nine during the decade. None was expurgated. *Roxana* repeats the pattern on a lesser scale. Its first five editions are spaced out between 1724 and 1775; the sixth was a joint one with *Moll* in 1907; the seventh through tenth cluster in the 1920s. No new edition from before the American Revolution until after 1900; no expurgation.

If this were the whole history, neither book would deserve mention here. But the editions I have listed were merely all the occasions on which the two novels were printed as separate entities; and the Victorians had other ways of allowing themselves to encounter forbidden books by major novelists. One was to include them in expensive sets of a man's whole work, so that only wealthy "strong" readers could get hold of them.* *Moll* and *Roxana* were both included, unexpurgated, in the

---

* If they bought the set new. "When I was a boy, it [*Moll Flanders*] was not an easy book to come by; it was on the moral index. From second-hand sets of Defoe's works that volume was frequently missing." Desmond MacCarthy, *Criticism* (London: 1932), p. 216.

collective Defoe begun by Hazlitt in 1841, in the twenty-volume set edited by Sir G. C. Lewis at the same time, in the complete novels edited by George Aitken in 1895. (A fourth collection, called *The Works of Daniel Defoe*—Edinburgh and New York: 1869—omits them both, at some cost to the accuracy of the title. This was a cheaper edition for weaker people. John Keltie, the editor, said plainly in the preface that he had stuck to those Defoe novels which "required no emasculation to fit them for perusal by all classes.")

The other and more interesting Victorian solution was to print portions of such books in one-author anthologies, or ur-Viking Portables. Here expurgation occurred freely. A typical ur-Portable is *Selections from Defoe's Minor Novels* (he means everything but *Robinson Crusoe*) edited by George Saintsbury in 1892. Saintsbury was no common bowdlerist, but a leading man of letters. He had already re-edited Scott's Dryden without being tempted to expurgate, and he later helped to edit the complete poetry of John Donne without harming *that*. Defoe he quietly castrated. The difference is not that Defoe is any more shocking than Donne,* but that the bowdlerism was in a volume of selections. Volumes of selections are for the masses, at least comparatively. One Victorian double standard said that for women innocence was necessary, while for men experience was tolera-

---

* Less. Donne speaks of dildoes, Defoe never. Donne could and did write scenes of real passion, as in Elegy XIX. Defoe, like Richardson, preferred money. Moll and Roxana may be whores, but they are probably the least sensual pair in literature. Willa Cather, introducing Americans to *Roxana* in 1924, said flatly, "The book is as safe as sterilized gauze."

ble, sometimes even desirable. Another said that an editor owed the mass of readers a safe text but not necessarily an honest one, while he owed the educated minority an honest text, even if it were a little dangerous.

Moll being Defoe's best book after *Robinson Crusoe*, Saintsbury naturally included selections from it. But first he got out his gelding knife. Having picked a group of the blander scenes, he lopped out all racy paragraphs. No marks to show this. Many a digest-maker does the same. Then he went through again, cutting out individual sentences, such as one about two friends of Moll who told a lie in order to avoid being executed as pickpockets. "They both pleaded their bellies, and were both voted quick with child; though my tutoress was no more with child than I was." This appeared as a line of dots. Respectable anthologists do the same, though not often for a single sentence. Finally, he poked through word by word—and fell abruptly to the ranks of the lower-grade bowdlerists. In one of those bland sections, Moll happens to say, not of a customer but of a lawful husband, "We supped together, and we lay together that night." To readers raised on the King James Bible, the second verb would be utterly familiar, from much hearing in church. Saintsbury still decided to have Moll and her husband merely "abide" together, and to pass off the new word as Defoe's.

The conflict between his usual role as man of letters and his new role as bowdlerist is very apparent in Saintsbury's preface. As man of letters, he valued *Moll* very highly indeed. "In my opinion, *Moll Flanders* is not only the most remarkable of Defoe's minor novels, but the

most remarkable example of pure realism in literature."
Set any of Zola's novels next to it,* and you will see "the
difference between talent misled by theory, and genius
conducted by art." When art takes genius by the hand,
an editor's job would seem to be to tiptoe away, strewing
footnotes. Saintsbury, of course, had done no such thing.
Consequently he also wrote, still with a certain show of
"strong" authority, "Susceptibilities which deserve respect, if not full sympathy, have required a very little
'editing' here and there, and have still more conditioned
the selection." This is superb euphemism. In actual fact,
Saintsbury's "editing" comes to quite as much as Dr.
Bowdler's bowdlerism. Maybe more. Bowdler was perfectly willing, for example, to let *The Merry Wives of
Windsor* end,

Sir John,

To master Brook you yet shall hold your word;
For he tonight shall lie with Mrs. Ford.

He was willing to have Bassanio in *The Merchant of
Venice* say to Portia, whose disguise as a doctor of law
he has just penetrated,

> Sweet doctor, you shall be my bedfellow;
> When I am absent, then lie with my wife.

* No easy thing to do in England in 1892. The English publisher
Henry Vizetelly had had some of Zola's novels translated between
1884 and 1888. He was then arrested for publishing "brutal obscenity," and fined a hundred pounds. He won his release by agreeing to
withdraw them from circulation. In 1889 he started putting them
back out again, lightly expurgated. This time he was sent to jail for
three months.

242

Saintsbury showed no such courage.*

But then, to be fair, it should be added that books like *Moll* were beyond the power of almost any Victorian to confront squarely in public. Perhaps the quickest way to show this is to quote the account of it given in a Victorian equivalent of the *Oxford Companion*. W. Davenport Adams published his comprehensive *Dictionary of English Literature* in 1878. In it there is a brief entry for *Moll*. Defoe himself had summarized the book in the original title, which reads, "The Fortunes and Misfortunes of the Famous Moll Flanders, who was born in Newgate, and during a Life of continu'd Variety, for Threescore Years, besides her Childhood, was Twelve Year a *Whore*, five times a *Wife* (whereof once to her own Brother), Twelve Year a *Thief*, Eight Year a Transported *Felon* in *Virginia*, at last grew *Rich*, liv'd *Honest*, and died a *Penitent*." Adams also summarized it. His entry reads, "*Flanders, Moll:* The title of a novel written by Daniel Defoe; the heroine of which is a female of questionable reputation, who afterwards becomes religious." The one thing Moll's reputation isn't, of course, is questionable. Adams was using a Victorian code phrase. A code which can squeeze Moll into that pallid sentence seems doomed to appear first repressive and then hypocritical.

---

* Even Bowdler was not wholly consistent. When the royal family was at issue, he did saintsbury a little. A man in *Henry VIII* who had seen Queen Anne Boleyn's coronation tells a friend,

> Believe me, sir, she is the goodliest woman
> That ever lay by man.

In Bowdler, she only sits.

CHAPTER TEN

The Fall of Bowdlerism, and After

****

> *In 1911, a book was widely sold named* Three
> Weeks *in which the obscene passages con-*
> *sisted only of pages of asterisks at appropriate*
> *places. The book was passed from hand to*
> *hand in every college. Certainly it is un-*
> *healthy to be stimulated by asterisks.*
> THURMAN ARNOLD, 1965

> FUCK COMMUNISM.
> *The Atlantic Monthly* (quoting John
> Wayne's cigarette lighter), March 1968

WHEN THE First World War ended, bowdlerism turned
out to be among the casualties. Or at least it seemed that
way.* Actually, the forces that destroyed it had all been
present before the war, and its years were numbered

---

* "I grant you the Victorian Age is closed: definitely closed, if you
will, by the late War." Sir Arthur Quiller-Couch, 1922.

"But out of that swinishness [the war] there was bound to come
reaction, and out of the reaction there was bound to flow a desire to
re-examine the whole national pretension—to turn on the light, to
reject old formulae, to think things out anew and in terms of reality.
. . . The war, first and last, produced a great deal more than John
Dos Passos' 'Three Soldiers.' It also produced Lewis's 'Babbitt,' and
Cabell's 'Jurgen,' and Fergusson's 'Capitol Hill,' and O'Neill's 'The
Emperor Jones.' And producing them, it ended an epoch of sweetness
and light." H. L. Mencken, 1924.

244

anyway. The war merely shook patterns of all sorts loose enough so that new ones formed rather more rapidly than they would have otherwise.

The forces that destroyed bowdlerism are, of course, the same ones that brought on the present age in all its aspects. The rise of Freudian psychology has meant many things; among them it has had to mean that bowdlerism as a form of repression would come to seem not only ludicrous, but dishonest and dangerous. The women's-rights movement had hundreds of effects on the shape of society; one of them had to be a distrust of the double standard in delicacy, as well as in sexual behavior or voting rights. The appearance of the new mass media, notably radio and television, has caused thousands of changes, from a decline in piano lessons to an altered silhouette for most houses. One of them had to be the demotion of books from the mass medium they were from, say, 1800 to 1920, to an extensive but minority medium. If the masses are going to the movies in 1928, you expurgate the movie and let the book go free. Longfellow was a family poet, but now there aren't family poets, there are family TV programs.

The approaching end of bowdlerism begins to be apparent (to a modern eye—no one foresaw it then) in the 1890s. A certain irreverence appeared, the kind of irreverence that usually develops when a movement is so solidly entrenched and so powerful that its demands have become a burden. In 1894, for example, two girls of the newly educated suffragette class produced an English version of the *Journals* of the brothers Goncourt. Naturally they expurgated; it would have been unthinkable to do otherwise. But the reviewers were not altogether grateful. "Miss Belloc and Miss Shedlock have shown almost an excess of zeal in our interests," one of them complained, going on to say that of what the Goncourts wrote, "there remains only that which even a man may read." This sounds like the joke of a man who is a little nervous that in another twenty years there won't be any unexpurgated books left at all, and who is beginning to wonder if the whole movement is really such a good idea.

At the same time, an occasional editor began to break the prevailing code of silence. It was always correct for a Victorian editor to bring out an unexpurgated edition of a classic, if he was discreet about it, but it was not correct for him to identify, much less point the finger of scorn at, the rival bowdlerized editions. To do so was wickedly to tempt innocent women, children, and lower-class men. But someone like G. Ravenscroft Dennis, editing a complete *Gulliver's Travels* in 1899, behaved as if he had never heard the rule. "The more recent illustrated editions are all expurgated to a very considerable extent," he wrote contemptuously in his preface, "though the publishers do not seem to consider it their duty to mention the fact." Considering that many publishers in 1899 honestly felt their duty lay in *not* mentioning such facts, here is perhaps a distinct change in attitude.

A third sign that an age was ending was that the old indecent books began to creep out of their corners. This occurred even as the volume of bowdlerism continued to increase, which it did right up until the war. In 1905, for example, a reputable scholar named Ernest Baker brought out an edition of the novels of Aphra Behn. The first circles in London may have read them with delight in the eighteenth century, but, except once, they had been sternly ignored ever since. That once was a reprint edition in 1872, which was a real publishing disaster. The response was almost hysterical.* Now, however, Mrs. Behn was received placidly; and when Ernest Baker said that though her novels were decent, "a general reprint of the plays would hardly be justified, at least, in anything like a cheap or popular form," the *Athenaeum* answered at once, "Her plays, a further reprint of which would be welcome, constitute her chief claim to literary rank."

Even John Cleland moved an inch or two out of limbo. That same year the *Athenaeum* published an article about *him*—the first in a reputable magazine in more than a century. It was not even a denunciation. The writer, R. P. Karkaria, began by quoting Lord Macaulay's brief dismissal of Cleland as "the author of an infamous book." He then, as coolly as Dennis, broke rules by telling what the book was; and after that

---

* The *Saturday Review,* under the heading "Literary Garbage," explained that its critic had burned his review copy, and therefore couldn't discuss the edition. Mrs. Behn's work, it added, is "protected against critics as a skunk is protected against the hunters; it is safe because it is too filthy to handle."

The *Athenaeum* did pick up the skunk, but with notable gingerliness. "Beneath a slab of grey stone," its review begins, "marked by an almost illegible inscription, in the Cloisters of Westminster Abbey, lie the remains of the woman known as Aphra Behn. If it had entered the mind of any one of the present day to tear open the grave, and carry about, for the inspection of the public, the rottenness of that infamous person, he would have conceived an act only second in revolting loathesomeness to that of digging up this unwomanly creature's literary remains."

he began a guarded defense of Cleland. "Now this 'infamous book,' *Fanny Hill; or the Memoirs of a Woman of Pleasure*, published 1750, is well known [besides word of mouth, there were underground editions] and I need not here debate on this regrettable episode in its author's life. But to call him a 'disreputable person,' as the Dictionary of National Biography does, is, I make bold to say, very unjust to him."

When literary journals are worrying about being just to John Cleland, the foundations of bowdlerism are trembling. Soon they began visibly to collapse. That is, the ideal of delicacy itself—hitherto paid at least lip service—began to be openly attacked. At first scattered, and at first wholly English, these attacks soon took on the character of a movement. Three examples:

In 1913, a young scholar named C. B. Wheeler edited a volume of Thackeray's essays for Oxford. "Despite the disgust which all decent people feel at selections and expurgated editions," he wrote in the preface, "I have almost at times wished that someone would edit an edition of Thackeray without these terrible excrescences" —but he is only talking about Thackeray's habit of saying "dear reader," and in order to complain about that matter of aesthetics, he must first make it clear that he is not one of those doddering Victorians who support expurgation on moral grounds.

In 1915, Aphra Behn got another twentieth-century edition, and this time it included plays and all. The editor exhibited no sober caution, as Ernest Baker had in 1905. On the contrary, young Montague Summers spent a good deal of his preface quoting Victorian views of Mrs.

Behn ("tainted to the very core," etc.) and then laughing heartily. "The absurdities and falsities of this extreme are of course patent now, and it was inevitable that the recoil should come," he concluded more seriously. It should be added that the recoil was still very partial, and Summers knew it. His liberating edition was limited to 50 copies de luxe and 760 cheaper ones.

In 1916, the *English Review* laid profane hands on Dr. Bowdler himself. It was the first time anybody had since early in Victoria's reign. Bowdler was not, of course, a prominent figure in 1916; but the *Family Shakspeare* was still in print, and its editor remained the eponym and to some extent the sacred ancestor of English expurgation. (Even less well known in America, he was still the nearest thing *our* bowdlerists had to an ancestor, and Douglas Bush of Harvard did the comparable American desacralization in 1929.)

Richard Whiteing, the *English Review* writer, alternated between tweaking Bowdler's nose with a good deal of relish, and making serious statements about the importance of frank and open publication. He even raised the root issue: what effect would the end of expurgation have on children? "The question must be faced," he said; "should there be *any* age of innocence?" (Italics mine.) He concluded that there should not, at least as regards sex. "We prepare the child mind for most things in life; why hold back in the most important of all?" And he made a strong plea for the debowdlerization of schoolbooks along with all the rest. As will emerge at once, English schools have been reluctant to heed this call. But the age of delicacy was almost ended.

The history of the fifty-three years from 1916 until now is one of barriers steadily falling, and of expurgation steadily diminishing. It diminished faster in the United States than in England, so that at some point in the thirties we caught up with and then passed the parent country. Any precise date for this passing is bound to be a false one, since there are so many strands in the literary life of a country, all changing at different rates. But if the root issue is really what you let children read, the year would probably be 1939, when George Lyman Kittredge, our then greatest living Shakespeare scholar, began to edit the plays complete and unexpurgated for use in American high schools, and almost immediately won the market away from Rolfe and Hudson. Students in English schools, by contrast, continued to read their expurgated Pitt Press Shakespeare from Cambridge and their expurgated New Clarendon Shakespeare from Oxford. (This was re-edited in the forties, and emerged a good deal more complete, but still bowdlerized. The Pitt Press was set in new type in the fifties, and emerged as expurgated as ever.) Even in 1960, the London publisher Heinemann found it profitable to put out a brand-new expurgated school Shakespeare.

A later but still historic date would be 1950, when Princeton University Press brought out the first unexpurgated edition of Rochester to appear in modern times. Discreet as this book was,* it was still too daring for

---

* It was a mere photographic reprint of the edition of 1680, which cut Princeton's guilt considerably. The first unexpurgated edition actually edited in modern times didn't come along until December, 1968—also in America. Even that may be intended just for the "strong." At any rate, the new Yale University Press Rochester costs $10 in America, and four pounds, ten shillings in England. The de Sola Pinto edition costs $1.50 in America, eight shillings and sixpence in England.

England. When Professor de Sola Pinto published the first definitive edition of Rochester in London, three years later, he had to advise readers in a note to send to New Jersey if they wanted to read the two poems his publisher insisted (and still insists) on omitting.

And though this is long past the date when we moved ahead, 1957 might even be worth mentioning, when the same American dictionary that helped to usher delicacy onto the American scene helped to lead it off again. As recently as the revision of 1952, Webster's Unabridged was still defining masturbation in the old opaque way as "onanism; self-pollution." Not so in the revision of 1957. That year our leading dictionary decided to say plainly what the veiled act was, namely, "Production of an orgasm by excitation of the sexual organs, as by manipulation or friction." By 1961, when Webster's Third appeared, plainness has turned to scientific precision and even to a sort of short course in how to go about it. The 1961 definition reads, "Erotic stimulation involving the genital organs commonly resulting in orgasm and achieved by manual or other bodily contact exclusive of sexual intercourse, by instrumental manipulation, occasionally by sexual fantasies, or by various combinations of these agencies." No delicacy lingers there. The comparable English dictionary, however, the Shorter Oxford, still said primly in its 1964 printing, "Masturbate: to practice self-abuse."

Why America debowdlerized so much faster than England is not easy to say. A quick explanation would be that we are simply more volatile in all respects. Having adopted bowdlerism later than England, we moved faster then, too. Starting well behind in 1820, we had caught up by 1840. In the second half of the century we were probably even more enthusiastic expurgators than England. These violent extremes have violent reactions.

But a more analytical look at the reasons would lead rather quickly to class structure. England has practically always tended to maintain two cultures at once. In terms of books, this means the limited edition and the private press for the educated minority, and the popular edition for everybody else. In the wake of the Vizetelly trial for publishing Zola, for example, two events occurred. One was that Chatto and Windus took over his translations, expurgated them a bit more, and published Zola for the masses. (These are the translations of Zola still to be found in most libraries, English and American.) The other was that a group of high-culture men, notably Havelock Ellis, Arthur Symons, and Ernest Dowson, got together and produced new and completely unexpurgated versions of six Zola novels. The Lutetian Society of London printed them as a set, for private distribution only, in 1894–95. In 1968, by way of non-contrast, Mac-Gibbon and Kee of London published the collected poems of E. E. Cummings in two large volumes. One page of this work is simply blank—except in the much more expensive limited edition. In that, Cummings' poem "the boys i mean are not refined" appears.

American publishers also print limited editions, of course. That same Cummings poem originally appeared in a volume called *No Thanks*, New York: 1935. Nine copies were priced at $99 each, and contained "the boys i mean." Nine hundred and ninety others were priced at either $7.50 (the nine hundred) or $12.50 (the ninety), and didn't. But on the whole America tries to be one nation, even literarily. With us the limited edition is more likely to be a sales gimmick than a cultural divider. T. E. Lawrence's *The Mint* is a case in point. When it finally appeared in 1955 (Doubleday, the copyright owner, had been waiting twenty years for phrases like "Fucking bar's shut" to become acceptable), it stepped demurely out as an expensive limited edition, both in London and in New York. But whereas in London this was accompanied by a much cheaper expurgated edition, in New York, after a suitable interval, the entire text appeared as a paperback for $1.25.

What this comes to is that in England and America both, by the third decade of this century, intellectuals had firmly rejected the concept of delicacy, and hence expurgation. National culture has steadily changed and is still changing in both countries as a result. But because English intellectuals are more inclined to address each other over the heads of the polloi, and American intellectuals are more inclined to want to carry every last high-school student with them, ours has changed faster.

In both countries, in 1969, bowdlerism seems to be defunct. In fact, a certain amount of anti-bowdlerism has begun to appear. Refinements that seemed permanent not merely to the Victorians but even to people two hundred years ago are being steadily undone. The history of Smollett's novel *Peregrine Pickle* makes a good example. When Smollett published it in 1751, he was violently criticized. In part this was because the book contained a thinly veiled account of Lady Frances

Vane, a peeress of really stunning indiscretion, but mostly it was because people felt some of the other scenes were in bad taste, such as the one in which Peregrine bores holes in his aunt's chamberpot. When Smollett brought out a second edition in 1758, he took out both the account of Lady Fanny and the low scenes, something like eighty pages in all. He then wrote a triumphant (and quite untruthful) preface, saying that he had "expunged every adventure, phrase, and insinuation that could be construed by the most delicate reader into a trespass upon the rules of decorum."

This second edition was taken as definitive, and no one even thought about the first edition again until our century. Then about thirty years ago Lady Fanny and the chamberpot quietly reappeared in a limited edition. And in 1964 they climbed boldly into the current general edition. Contemporary Smollett is franker than the Smollett of Smollett's time. So, in a small way, is contemporary Hawthorne than original Hawthorne. Modern scholars have succeeded in deciphering some of the phrases inked out by Mrs. Hawthorne in his journals before they were printed, and therefore unknown to his time. In our day they have bounced onto the page, considerably enlivening the American-pantheon or pale-puritan view of Hawthorne.*

---

* One example out of many: When Hawthorne was consul at Liverpool, he met an American sea captain named Devereux and his gigantic but handsome wife, Oakum. Oakum's size greatly amused Hawthorne, and he spent about a page in his journal playing around with the possibilities. "In case of a mutiny, she would be a host by herself," etc. Playful, but proper. Actually, the play went on. Mrs. Hawthorne had inked out four lines immediately after the sentence just quoted. In 1941 Professor Randall Stewart was able to perceive and for the first time to print eight of the inked-out words: "What a vast amount of connubial bliss she . . ."

Actually, however, bowdlerism is far from defunct, even in America. It still has a vigorous effect on our life as well as on English life in a number of ways, and seems likely to for some time to come. The most obvious of these is the continued and deliberate printing of new expurgations. As mentioned, even now London publishers bring out new editions of Shakespeare for schools, lightly but indisputably bowdlerized. No American publisher does this for separate editions of Shakespeare, but many do it when they put his plays into school anthologies. When James Lynch and Bertrand Evans published *High School English Textbooks: A Critical Examination* in 1963, they reported that of the eleven textbooks that include *Macbeth*, usually abridged, all eleven bowdlerize it. (Just like Pitman in 1822, they go first to the Porter's scene and cut his joke about sex and drinking.) For that matter, Lynch and Evans also found expurgated work of every kind—short stories, essays, sections of novels, poems. Almost always the cuts were *à la* Meiklejohn— that is, concealed to the best of the editor's power.

But even six years have made a difference, and their findings would not be the same in 1969. Just as college anthologies underwent debowdlerization twenty or thirty years ago,* high-school anthologies are undergoing it now. Most new ones will be honest. So will the huge majority of other books. There is an expurgated edition of *Candy* newly printed in England, and there

---

* A study of editions of college texts between 1920 and 1950 would provide a good deal of amusement. Silent changes went on all the time. Chaucer's shepherd was discreetly "spotted," for example, in Franklin Snyder's *A Book of English Literature*, 2nd ed. (Macmillan: 1924). By the fourth edition in 1942, Snyder by now being the President of Northwestern, he has returned to being shiten. There must be thousands of these small grapples with conscience.

may yet be more expurgations of Lord Rochester. But new expurgation has plainly almost ceased—until the next cycle, anyway.

A second and more important present effect is the deliberate reprinting of old expurgations. Cambridge University Press does not plan to print any new bowdlerized editions of anything—but neither does it plan to drop the Pitt Press Shakespeare. "The Press will presumably go on reprinting Verity as long as there is a demand for his editions (and the demand is still surprisingly, perhaps shockingly, large)," its Secretary wrote a couple of years ago. "I see no reason why the series should not sell well in schools for a considerable number of years yet," an Oxford official wrote about the partially expurgated New Clarendon Shakespeare. Ginn & Co. of Boston, who introduced the Kittredge Shakespeare in 1939, did not drop therefore their castrated New Hudson Shakespeare. On the contrary, it's still in print now, selling briskly, though much less briskly than it used to. If only to avoid paying royalties, most selections from Pepys printed in the next twenty years will be from Braybrooke, Bright, and Wheatley. It will probably be close to the twenty-first century before the last existing expurgation vanishes.

A third present effect is the unconscious or accidental printing of bowdlerized texts. This is fairly rare, but not as rare as one might expect. In 1968, for example, a new Penguin translation of Castiglione's *The Courtier* appeared. The translator, George Bull, spent part of his preface condemning previous bowdlerized translations, especially the one done by Leonard Opdycke in America. He himself intended to translate with absolute fidelity, and he did, working from the great critical text edited by Professor Cian of Florence in 1884. But delicacy has an international history. "It is ironic," said the first major review, "that Mr. Bull should condemn Opdycke's bowdlerization yet present the translation of a bowdlerized text."

Another case would be the German edition of Nikos Kazantzakis's novel *The Greek Passion*. The first character one meets in that book is a homosexual. As the book opens, he is sitting on a balcony in a Greek-speaking village in Anatolia, and next to him is "a beautiful plump young Turkish boy," his current favorite. In the German edition, what's next to him is *"ein hubsches rundes turkisches Mädchen,"* a plump young Turkish girl. There is no evidence that the German translator in 1951 was afraid to mention homosexuality; it's just that he was translating not from Greek but from Swedish, and therefore couldn't know it was a boy. Börje Knös, doing the Swedish translation in 1950, was the conscious bowdlerizer. But the boy is still a girl in Germany in 1969.

Or again, almost any contemporary editor who quotes letters printed more than fifty and less than a hundred and fifty years ago is likely to bowdlerize whether he means to or not. Charles Francis Adams expurgated the letters of his grandmother, Abigail Adams. Edmund Gosse expurgated Swinburne's. When William Wilberforce's sons wrote their father's life, they apologized on the one occasion they *didn't* bowdlerize.*

---

* Their father had been profane. "At last they are gone, and the devil go with them," he wrote, referring to a bundle of business letters he had just dealt with while on vacation in France in 1784. The

Or again, sometimes a bowdlerized phrase gets carried
forward through sheer inadvertence. When E. E. Cummings published his war memoir, *The Enormous Room*,
in 1922, he had a character named Jean Le Nègre exclaim, "My father is dead! Shit. Oh, well. The war is
over." This greatly upset John S. Sumner, the Secretary
of the New York Society for the Suppression of Vice;
and in order to calm him, a girl in the publisher's office
inked out the word "shit" in every copy left in stock.
When the second edition came along in 1927, Cummings
found a typical cummingsesque solution, and put Jean's
remark into French. He now says, *"Mon père est mort!
Merde! Eh b'en! La guerre est finie."* (In America, even
French provides the decent obscurity of a learned language, and Sumner was still satisfied.) When *The Enormous Room* came out in a Modern Library edition in the
thirties, this form got carried over. It is still there, though
the New York Society for the Suppression of Vice no
longer even exists. Nor would it be any use turning to
the other current edition of *The Enormous Room*,
which is apparently printed from the original plates. In
this the passage reads, "My father is dead!   Oh,
well. The war is over."

The fourth and probably most important hangover
from the age of delicacy is the enormous number of
expurgated books still on library and home shelves. The
turn-of-the-century sets, like Dole's International Li-

---

sons print the complete sentence in 1832, and then explain why in a
footnote. "The propriety of inserting this letter unaltered will be
manifest from the sequel," they say, which means that their father
underwent religious conversion shortly afterwards, and they want a
sample of his behavior beforehand, for contrast.

brary of Famous Literature, have mostly vanished; and the expurgated, or any other, textbook of even thirty years ago is something of a rarity. But editions of Herrick or Ben Franklin or Zola or Castiglione are quite another matter. Most libraries probably don't have any unbowdlerized English version of Zola or Castiglione. Most have a spotty mixture of Herrick and Franklin. It can be amusing to see a contemporary student reading a bowdlerized edition of Franklin and wondering what made Franklin such a prude, to see him go on to D. H. Lawrence's *Studies in Classic American Literature* with its famous sneer at Franklin for being a grey nag trotting inside a paddock, and to know that neither student nor Lawrence is even aware of one whole aspect of Franklin's mind. It will be a long time still before our picture of the past has its warts fully restored.

Finally, there remains a good deal of bowdlerism in what is left of print as a mass or family medium. *The Atlantic Monthly* was a family magazine a hundred years, and it edited extensively. William Dean Howells wanted the swear words out of *Life on the Mississippi*, for example. ("I think the sagacious reader could infer them," he wrote Mark Twain.) And the mate of the steamboat *Paul Jones* duly curses in the form "dash-dash-dash-*dashed*." Its readers still thought of it as a family magazine twenty years ago. When it printed extracts from *Mister Roberts* in 1946, and there was the captain of the U.S.S. *Reluctant* saying over the loudspeaker, "All right now, goddam it, listen to this. Some smart bastard has been up here and thrown my palm over the side," the effect was striking. Some readers were delighted at such frankness, but many others felt betrayed. "When a magazine such as the *Atlantic Monthly* stoops to gutter profanity, to whom or what shall we look?" one asked.

But ten years ago the *Atlantic* no longer behaved like a family magazine. In its hundredth-anniversary issue in November 1957, which was a time for setting new directions, it printed a couple of stories by Hemingway, in one of which there was dialogue like this:

> "Oh, Philip—"
> "Shit," he said.

There were not even any protests. And in 1965 a third boat officer becomes audible. This time it is Hemingway in command of the *Pilar*. "Put her on the fucking course," he says.

The New York Times, on the other hand, still regards itself as a family publication. In 1967 its Sunday magazine reprinted (as penance for having misquoted it) a poem that first appeared in *Canadian Dimension*. The second stanza, as the *Times* ran it, appeared like this. "You" is the United States.

> Seed-blaster
> harvest-ghoul
> are you finally choked
> on the fat of your land
> and have you run out of your
> > own poor
> to *** upon and are you ready
> now to burst out

Those three asterisks represent "shit," of course—a word which the *Atlantic* takes in stride, a word which is back in unabridged dictionaries, but not in collegiates. The collegiate is a family dictionary.

Comic strips are also a mass medium in print, and it is perhaps there that Victorian delicacy most strikingly survives. Scenes of violence are all right in comic strips, just as the spurt of blood at the beheading was all right in Victorian *Gullivers*. Some visual frankness (*e.g.*, vivid rendering of the female bust) is also all right. But the language is bowdlerized. A random issue of the funnies in the New York *Sunday News* supplies the following chastened examples:

General Hasp, USA, of "Terry and the Pirates" says to a Sicilian archeologist, "Blast you, Palma! You know danged well I don't care about your busted crockery."

An angry Indian in "Little Orphan Annie" exclaims, "Uglyface got ugly tongue, by golly!"

Beetle Bailey's sergeant says to his platoon, "All right, you *#&! jerks!"

A native of Slobbovia says to some Americans—they seem to be Peace Corps workers—who have come to introduce Mother's and Father's Day, "By us is already every *!!# day a holiday."

This phenomenon, too, seems likely to pass. New expurgations will cease, and so will printings of old ones. Libraries will gradually clear their shelves of bowdlerized editions, except those they keep deliberately as part of the history of taste. The age of innocence for children is already extremely compressed, and still shrinking. When witty children again call "whore" and cry "bas-

tard," as some at least did in Ben Jonson's time, there will
be small point in expurgated comic strips, or even in
protectiveness on the part of *The New York Times*.

What then? Then it may be time for the new cycle to
begin. Or a different cycle may by then be in full swing.
Delicacy has never died, and never will. (So great is the
fear of false predictions in our time that I find myself
starting to change that to "and seems unlikely to." But
one should sometimes go out on limbs, especially a limb
as sturdy as this.) It merely takes new forms. At the
moment, as everybody knows, the vocabulary of race
relations has become a delicate matter. The result is a
new little growth of expurgation, and not merely in
nursery rhymes like "Catch a tiger by the toe." Lynch
and Evans found a high-school text in which *Huckleberry Finn* was expurgated new-style. "A nigger
woman" became "one of the servants"; "a young white
gentleman" became simply "a young gentleman," and so
on. If the rise of "black" continues, "Negro" itself may
become obscene; perhaps it already has. If so, those of
us who avoid the word will not seem prudish to ourselves, but sensitive—just as Americans in 1875 who
avoided the word "crotch," say, felt perceptive.

Delicacy will never die, because it is an essential part
of romanticism. A race of computers (unless pro-
grammed to be human) would not be moved to expurgate, because a computer does not have illusions about
itself, or want to keep a young computer from knowing
too much ugly truth too soon. Men do. We don't even
want too much just commonplace truth. No computer
is disgusted at learning the precise girth of a 1401, or

bothered by the sight of a repairman cleaning dirt out of one, but many a human being would rather not know the bust and thigh measurements of his queen or the wife of his president or perhaps his own mother; many would actually avert their eyes to avoid seeing the family pastor seated on a toilet.

Harriet Bowdler certainly did not express it that way, but her basic aim in 1807 was to preserve for the adolescents of England some of the mystery and opaqueness of human behavior without which we are likely to regard ourselves as either animals or machines. Her method was laughable, and it may even be doubted that the human mystery requires deliberate preservation, but the aim was an honorable one.

****

CHAPTER ELEVEN

The Current Scene

****

> *When Thomas Bowdler produced his* Family Shake-
> speare, *he was concerned to cleanse the Bard of all
> indecent language and frivolous allusions to Scrip-
> ture. Today, what is apparently thought to poison
> our minds, and especially the impressionable minds
> of the young, is the concept of "white sexist hetero-
> sexual Eurocentrism."*
>
> THE TIMES (*of London*), 1988

> "*Redneck*" *is the only opprobrious epithet for an
> ethnic minority still permitted in polite company.*
>
> C. VANN WOODWARD, 1989

TWENTY-TWO YEARS have passed since I wrote the preceding chapter. It is curious to look back from so great a
distance at the predictions I made in 1969. I wasn't exactly
wrong as a prophet, but I wasn't entirely right, either.

I had thought that bowdlerism as Dr. Bowdler knew
it would be almost entirely gone by now. "New expurgations will cease, and so will printings of old ones," I wrote,
thinking that this would happen before the end of the
century.

It is now clear that it won't. Certainly expurgation on
sexual or religious grounds has continued to diminish—

and in some arenas the decline has been stunning. For example, back in 1969 general circulation magazines had barely begun to follow the example set by *The Atlantic*. Some, like *The New Yorker*, had not begun at all. Its editors continued to cut out any word even faintly vulgar; the magazine was famous for its delicate fastidiousness. But now? Now their theater critic can calmly quote a refrain from a new English play—"Fucking long life, i'n't it"—and then praise the line as providing "music in the writing." In 1969 the editors would probably have argued that reliance on words like "fucking" is not only unmusical but evidence of a linguistically stunted mind.

The New Yorker, of course, is read by what the Rev. Alexander Grosart called the "strong." But things have changed just as radically for the "weak." Speaking of fiction written solely for teenagers—and it was the vulnerable innocence of the young that led to bowdlerism in the first place—speaking of the teenage novel, a commentator wrote this in the mid-8os: "During the preceding two decades, taboos had been falling like dominoes. . . . No subject was too lurid, no language too explicit, no outlook too bleak."

And yet even as the taboos crashed, sexual bowdlerism has continued to exist and even modestly to thrive. Many old expurgations that I had thought would be phased out by now are still present. For example, Oxford's expurgated *New Clarendon Shakespeare* and Cambridge's expurgated *Pitt Press Shakespeare* remain in print, still preserving some British students of high-school age from a full knowledge of Shakespeare.

What surprises me more is that many high-school stu-

dents on this side of the Atlantic continue to be thus protected; not as thoroughly protected as they were in 1969,
but still quite a lot. Back then American teenagers got their
Shakespeare—and most other literature—from large anthologies, one per year of high school. They still do. Back
then, editors of such anthologies invariably expurgated
them. Most still do, but now there are some exceptions.

The first of these dates back at least to 1975. That year
a doctoral candidate at the University of Tennessee named
Dorothy Weatherby completed her dissertation, which
was a study of the twenty-two most commonly used
high-school anthologies. Only twenty-one of them turned
out to be expurgated. My own samplings suggest that a
comparable study now would turn up as many as four or
five unexpurgated high-school anthologies.

And even the vast majority that continue to be bowdlerized are cut less than they used to be. In 1986, the De-
partment of Education of the State of Virginia asked one
of its employees to make a study of expurgation in the
leading anthologies. He was to pay special attention to
Shakespeare.

When J. Kenneth Bradford finished his study, he was
able to report that bowdlerism for the benefit of high-
school students was noticeably less thorough than in the
past. For example, the publisher he came to admire most
for fidelity to texts—Scott, Foresman & Co.—had cut only
320 lines in its entire ninth-grade reader. The figure was
down from 440 lines just a few years earlier. And though
Scott, Foresman nowhere told the ninth-grade students
they were getting expurgated literature (the teachers do
learn this in the accompanying manual), twelfth-graders

were now considered strong enough to confront the fact. In the anthology they got, Scott, Foresman used ellipses to indicate cuts. So far as I know, this was the first time since Hudson's Shakespeare in 1872 that an expurgating textbook publisher in America was either open or truthful.

Openness and truth remain rare, however, among those who publish for the high-school market. Bowdlerism is simply not conducive to truth. One story Bradford tells, without using names, is of a consulting editor for one of the larger textbook publishers. He assured an audience of high-school teachers that his firm did not tamper with texts. Bradford described him as "genuinely surprised when they showed him he was mistaken."

In a second story, Bradford does use names, though he remains temperate in his charges. "When an editor-in-chief at McGraw-Hill does not at first appear to know that *Romeo and Juliet* and *Macbeth* have been altered," he writes, "one may wonder if publishing companies have not become too unwieldy for their editorial tasks."

The other stronghold of traditional bowdlerism since 1969 has been in school book clubs. These clubs buy reprint rights to popular books for children, publish them in inexpensive editions, and then sell them directly to school classes, using the teachers as agents. Some of them do original titles as well.

Up until about six years ago all of them expurgated. If the original book used a highly colored word like "damn" or "thigh" (these are actual examples), out it went. If there was one gaudy incident in a book the club editors otherwise liked, they either eliminated it or toned it down.

For example, in a young adult novel by Frank Bonham there was a scene in which a girl loses the top of her bathing suit while diving, and a boy misinterprets this accident as provocative behavior. One of the book clubs owned by Scholastic wanted to publish the book, but not with that scene. When their version appeared, the contretemps had shrunk to a misunderstood kiss.*

The school book clubs naturally did not call attention to their expurgations, and the authors involved seldom said much, either. Almost no one outside of the publishing industry was aware of the practice. Even many insiders were as ignorant as the editor-in-chief of McGraw-Hill had been.

But then a small scandal arose, in a case where a school book club broke the unwritten rules. It expurgated a book not only without any public admission but without even telling the very-much-alive author. And the book that Ballantine picked to alter in this way was a truly remarkable choice.

Back in 1953, the science fiction writer Ray Bradbury published a novel called *Fahrenheit 451*. It's a work in some ways like *1984*, about an oppressive society in which books are forbidden objects. When one is found, firemen are called to burn it. (Hence the title: paper ignites at

---

* There is one big difference between Harriet Bowdler's expurgation of Shakespeare in 1807 and Scholastic's expurgation of Bonham in 1981. Miss Bowdler obviously could not get Shakespeare's consent before doing what she called "purifying" him and what Sir Walter Scott called "castrating" him. Scholastic not only obtained the consent of authors like Mr. Bonham, it also engaged them to perform what *it* preferred to call "revision" of the text, and paid them for their efforts. As Mr. Bonham said, a couple of years after purifying/castrating/revising his own book, "I didn't want to make the change, but it was that or nothing."

451° F.) Bradbury means, of course, to be shocking, since he really considers books sacred objects. One oughtn't to burn a sacred object—just as one oughtn't to tamper with its wording.

The book was an instant success. There have been fifty-some editions so far, and the book has been extensively used in schools. Teachers tend to regard it as an eloquent plea for a free literature.

In 1967 Ballantine Books published a special edition of *Fahrenheit 451* to be sold in high schools. The editors must have been aware of the irony of expurgating this particular book; they must also have been aware that some school boards and perhaps some teachers would be troubled by a few of Bradbury's words. In any event, someone or some group at Ballantine tampered with about a hundred passages. No one noticed. Suspecting nothing, Bradbury had no reason to check the new edition. The students who actually read it (there were a lot of these: the expurgated edition ran to ten printings) did not know the original, so they had no basis for comparison. The copyright page of the book, of course, made no mention of the changes.

Ballantine meanwhile continued to print Bradbury's original version as well; it was what you found in a bookstore. We "strong" adults thus had to encounter words like "hell" and "abortion." We also encountered a drunk man, who in the expurgated version is merely sick. And putting our maturity to a stern test, we encountered the human navel. The students did not. These young Americans in 1967 were spared almost as much reality as Rosa Baughan had excused English girls from a hundred years

earlier. Miss Baughan, expurgating *Romeo and Juliet* in
1863, took out Juliet's father's joke about ladies with
corns on their toes, because she thought it indelicate. The
anonymous expurgators at Ballantine took out a reference
to cleaning fluff out of the human navel, presumably for
the same reason. They replaced it with a reference to
cleaning ears.

For six years the two versions existed simultaneously.
Then, in 1973, the adult version vanished. Whether
through sheer carelessness, or because someone at Ballantine saw a chance to reduce warehouse costs by replacing
two editions with one, the expurgated edition took over
completely. That was what adults got in bookstores as
well as what students got in schools.

Six more years went by. Then in 1979 someone told
Bradbury what had happened to his book. He was not
pleased. He demanded that Ballantine withdraw the expurgated edition, and replace it—in schools as well as
stores—with what he had actually written. Ballantine
meekly agreed. The book has been complete from 1980
to the present.

Such a story is hard to keep quiet. It occurred to some
of those who heard it that if even a book like *Fahrenheit
451* got expurgated for schools, it was probably not alone.
Among those who developed such suspicions were those
natural protectors of books, librarians.

The American Library Association has a division entirely concerned with teenagers (who are an age cohort
known to publishers and librarians alike as Young Adults).
This division in turn has an Intellectual Freedom Committee. In 1981 the committee was asked to look into expurgation by school book clubs. It launched a formal

investigation, which lasted a year. Then it reported back that all the major clubs did it, though not with all their books.

The president of the division then sent a letter to the editors of all the major clubs. It was no mere fluttery protest. The letter had teeth.

People who buy children's books love to get commended ones, especially winners of the Newbery or the Caldecott medals. (Both are awarded by the American Library Association, the Newbery for text, the Caldecott for illustration.) Buyers are almost as attracted to books which have been given a "Best Book" designation by the Young Adult Services Division of the ALA—and what attracts them are the words "ALA Best Book" in prominent type on the cover.

The president now warned that any Best Book which got bowdlerized (several had been) would instantly have those words stripped from its cover. Nor did the ALA stop there; the librarians also told teachers' unions what they had learned. In 1983 the American Federation of Teachers passed a resolution urging its members to include a letter of protest about bowdlerism along with any order they might send to a club.

The results were prompt and impressive. The four clubs run by Scholastic are the most prominent in the field, and the only ones which sell their special editions in bookstores as well as to schools. By the end of June, 1983, the top editors at Scholastic had formally promised to make it clear on the copyright page whenever a book was expurgated. As it turned out, they didn't need to keep the promise, because they decided on more radical reform. In 1984 they ceased to expurgate at all. The clubs even went back and restored the cuts in all the books still in print which they had expurgated in the past.

Some other school book clubs do continue to expurgate in 1991, but they do it less often than they used to, and almost always they now identify such editions. The identification may not be in a form recognizable to high-school students—it normally consists of the words "edited school book club edition" on the copyright page—but teachers, at least, are apt to know what that phrase means, just as Victorian parents knew what "family edition" meant.

So much for my first prediction. Traditional bowdlerism is more tenacious than I had thought it would be, but it is in general retreat, and the retreat will continue.* I also made a second prediction. I thought it likely that as sexual prudery diminished, ethnic prudery would increase —and would do so from the best and most high-minded of motives. I noted that in 1969 the word "nigger" had become a true obscenity. In most parts of the country it was then and is now more uncomfortable to hear spoken than, say, that musical word "fuck." I guessed that in time even the word "Negro" might come to seem obscene.

This has not happened. No one blushes while reading an appeal for the United Negro College Fund. Nonetheless, "Negro" has become a word that most people avoid in common speech—and it is only one of many ethnic

---

* I am speaking, of course, only of the near future, and only of the developed English-speaking countries. Quite other moves are afoot elsewhere. In some Moslem countries traditional bowdlerism is on the rise. In Egypt, after a period of relative freedom, rules are tightening. When the head of the Morals Division of the Interior Ministry recently confiscated an unexpurgated edition of *The Arabian Nights* (the second-ranking book in the Mohammedan world), he explained why. "Any part of our heritage which includes dirty words should be locked up in a museum, and an expurgated version should be made available to youth," he said, sounding much like James Plumptre.

and racial terms that sensitive people now shun. Most of these terms have begun to be expurgated, though not in all contexts. The second cycle of bowdlerism has begun.

The first cycle started at the top, with high literature, and then gradually spread out and down. The current cycle is exactly the opposite. So far, high literature has been almost entirely immune to it, though there have been several stage expurgations of *The Merchant of Venice* on racial grounds, and, as I noted in 1969, *Huckleberry Finn* was then being altered, though only in a high-school anthology or two.

But popular literature is not immune. Nancy Drew books and Hardy Boys books, for instance, are quite thoroughly expurgated on racial and ethnic grounds; some of them have been so for a quarter of a century now.

The two series have identical histories, as well they might, since both are products of the Stratemeyer writing factory. (Thirteen hundred books so far.) Edward Stratemeyer personally wrote the first three Hardy Boys mysteries in 1927 and the first three Nancy Drew mysteries in 1930. Other hands continue to produce new ones now.

From the beginning, both series followed standard factory rules. Each volume in each series contained twenty-five chapters and was 215 pages long. (There's a leeway of a couple of pages either way; writing is never quite like canned beans.) Each book after the first contained a plug for the preceding volumes in the series, placed in Chapter 2, and a briefer plug for the volume to come, placed in Chapter 25.

Starting in 1959, the factory began to update the books, at the rate of two or three volumes per series per year. This was necessary so that Nancy Drew's car would stay reasonably contemporary, and so that the Hardy Boys, when they flew west on commercial airlines to take a new case, would not be in the air for two days, in a succession of small propeller planes.

In doing the updatings, the Stratemeyer writers took the opportunity both to shorten the books and to expurgate them. Each now has only twenty chapters and is only about 175 pages long. A considerable saving in manufacturing costs there, though also some loss in whatever denseness of texture the books originally had.

There was no need to perform any traditional expurgation; these books were simon-pure to begin with. (One of the factory rules: "no smooching.") Indeed, in an age when taboos have been falling like dominoes and when no language is too explicit for teenagers to read, the factory might have been tempted to juice them up, as Dryden juiced up *The Tempest*. If so, the temptation was resisted.

But racial and ethnic expurgation is another matter. Both series, though in general friendly toward members of all ethnic groups, did use terms which seemed normal enough when the books were written, but which since have become troubling.

Take a fairly typical book from each series: the Nancy Drew mystery called *The Secret of the Leaning Chimney* and the Hardy Boys book called *The Sign of the Crooked Arrow*. Both were written in 1949, and both got expurgated in 1967. In the case of the Nancy Drew, the expurgation is slight. There are a number of Chinese characters in the book, most of whom are presented not just favorably but with real warmth. There are also two villains,

274

brothers who are partly Chinese and partly white American. In 1949 the brothers were freely called half-breeds and half-castes. In revision, both words vanish from otherwise unchanged paragraphs. Both had become mildly obscene, as pointing too much to the question of ancestry, and more specifically as having a built-in implication that racial "purity" is somehow a good thing.

The Sign of the Crooked Arrow, on the other hand, is quite heavily expurgated. Here the non-white characters are Navajo Indians, and they, too, are presented favorably, if somewhat stereotypically. (*All* characters in the book are stereotypes, so there's nothing either pro- or anti-Indian about *that*.) The next-ranking hero to the Hardy Boys themselves is a fearless Navajo cowboy named Pye.

The expurgation in the book takes two forms. First, the offensive word "Injun" is removed, and replaced by "Indian." "Injun" used to be defined in dictionaries as a facetious spelling. It was clearly so intended in the original version of *The Sign of the Crooked Arrow*, being put in the mouth of an elderly garage owner in New Jersey, a slow-witted fellow whose mind lingers somewhere back in the nineteenth century. But "Injun" has also come to seem patronizing, and out it went.

The other form of expurgation is more complicated and interesting. There is an early scene in a chemist's lab, where the Hardy Boys have taken a wristwatch band for analysis. The chemist remarks that it must have been worn by an Indian. How does he know? By smell, he says. Indians have a characteristic smell? Yes, a light pleasant smell, rather like hominy. And then the chemist goes on to give the budding detectives a quick fill-in on human scents in general. Some races, he says, without specifying which, smell strong and musky.

In the revision, the information that Indians smell like hominy remains; the rest is all cut, in an otherwise complete chapter. Here there were probably two grounds for offense. One is that, though the chemist doesn't *say* the odor is or could be disagreeable, and certainly doesn't connect it with blacks, the passage is playing on American stereotypes that do. And secondly, musk is connected with sex—in perfumes quite favorably so. But that calls up the stereotype of allegedly strong sexuality in blacks; and one of the phenomena of the late twentieth century is the increasing offensiveness of any human streotyping at all. In an age that values human groups as much or more than individuals it might be a compliment to say "spoken like an Englishman" or "she's a true New Zealander"; such is not now the case. And it is downright insulting to suggest that all blacks are musical, or all Poles brawny, or all Wasps inhibited.

No one takes the Hardy Boys books very seriously, and no one would claim that expurgating them is harming sacred texts. But other and much better popular works have also been bowdlerized, a few even earlier than the Hardy Boys. For example, George Gershwin's *Porgy and Bess*, a musical that approaches the condition of opera, was bowdlerized as early as 1951. That spring, Goddard Lieberson made a historic recording, helped by Ira Gershwin. The principal singers came from the City Center Opera. Lieberson took enormous care with the score and restored numerous passages that had been cut, back in the thirties. He made the high claim that *Porgy and Bess* belongs "among the great operas of the world." In short, he treated it as an at least partially sacred text. But he nevertheless wrote in the album notes, "It seemed proper . . . to eliminate certain words in the lyrics which, in racial terms, had proved offensive."

The most offensive of those words was, of course, "nigger." That word continues to send shudders throughout popular culture, but it is not yet automatically excluded. For example, in 1989 EMI Records gave to the musical *Show Boat* the same kind of splendid and definitive recording that Lieberson gave to *Porgy and Bess. Show Boat* does not aspire to operatic stature, but it does occupy a high throne, as the greatest of all popular American musicals. One thus takes its text seriously. John McGlinn, who edited the new recording, took it so seriously that he chose to retain the word as being an authentic part of Jerome Kern's lyrics. One result was that his chorus walked out, as did one of the principal singers. With the rumored encouragement of Eartha Kitt, another singer stepped into the role, and the recording did get made. As these two cases show, there is as yet no consensus on the proper way to deal with offensive racial and ethnic terms that are part of serious art. Or even just part of the language, for that matter. The recent history of such terms in dictionaries is a striking instance of how unclear the path is, even to professional linguists.

Expurgation has a long history in American dictionaries. As I noted some chapters back, it started at almost the same moment that the dictionaries themselves did, nearly two hundred years ago. Without exception, Amer-

ican dictionaries were expurgated from the year 1800 up
into the 1950s. Then the taboos began to topple, at the
same moment that lexicographers began to see their job as
descriptive rather than prescriptive. That is, they thought
that instead of telling people what was right or wrong,
they should merely report with great care what was being
said. Since what was being said included "bad" words of
several kinds, dictionaries needed to start making room
for them. There followed a period of about twenty years
when most dictionaries were prepared to admit any word
or usage that was part of our language, merely because it
existed. But then came racial expurgation.

In American dictionaries, it began about 1980, when
most racial and ethnic terms had become so totally offensive that dictionary-makers found themselves confronting
a painful dilemma. Did they include a word like "nigger,"
or one like "polack"? If they did, they not only helped to
perpetuate it, but they might also seem to be giving it their
stamp of approval. Or did they leave it out, as being a word
no decent person would have a use for, anyway?

Either way, there were problems. If lexicographers
printed those words, they contributed to the human po-
tential for giving pain to others. If they omitted them,
they were untrue to the language.*

The dictionary-makers came up with two solutions.
Neither has proved fully satisfactory. One is to include

---

* And also unhelpful to the reader who might come across a strange
word in an old book, and simply not know what it meant. There are
readers right now who are unsure what Thoreau means in *Walden*
when he refers to "a young Patrick," and even more who could not say
what Emerson intended in this description of a building crew: "The
men were common masons, with paddies to help." There are perhaps
even a few who without dictionary help would not know who or what
the angry "Micks" are that Mark Twain brings up in *Roughing It*.

racial and ethnic obscenities, but not to bless them, or even be neutral—on the contrary, to mark them prominently with a stamp of disapproval. The other, of course, is to omit them. Both are prescriptive actions.

At least five dictionaries decided to resume, or in one case to begin, expurgation: *The American Oxford Dictionary* in 1980, *The Macmillan Dictionary for Students* in 1981, *Webster's II (New Riverside University Dictionary)* in 1984, and *Webster's New World* in 1986. Even one dictionary that claimed to include the total language, *Webster's Encyclopedic Unabridged*, castrated itself in 1989.*

Three of these five followed the normal practice of bowdlerizers: they omitted words and said nothing. The editors of *Webster's New World* and of *Webster's II*, however, clearly felt troubled by what they were doing. They took two steps to ease their scholarly consciences (and possibly also to court sales among those who wished taboos *weren't* falling so fast). First, they resumed traditional expurgation at the same time as they began racial. Second, they acted openly. As the editors of *Webster's II* state in their foreword, "We have omitted certain offensive words whose meaning is hardly ever retrieved from a dictionary." And as the editors of *Webster's New World* say, they have cut not only the old vulgar words but "those true obscenities . . . the terms of racial or ethnic opprobrium."

---

* All these Websters are confusing. None of the three has any connection with the other two, and none has any line of descent from Noah Webster. *The Encyclopedic Unabridged* is in fact an expurgated cheap-paper reprint of the real *Webster's* big rival, the *Random House Unabridged*. In dictionary circles "Webster" is a talismanic word, like Rolls Royce when applied to cars, or "Viennese" for a waltz.

Meanwhile, the majority of dictionaries were taking the other course. They eliminated nothing, but they frowned. And since some racial and ethnic terms are clearly more opprobrious than others, most of them wound up frowning on three or even four levels of severity. The results are sociologically fascinating.

The Merriam-Webster Collegiate (1987) manages to stay the most nearly neutral, but it still creates four classes. Words like "polack" and "wop" are the least bad. They are, *Merriam-Webster* says, "usually used disparagingly." The implication is that the speaker is being unfriendly, but that Poles and Italians do not care much. "Mick" is worse—"often taken to be offensive." (Some Irish people do mind.) "Greaser" and "frog" are worse still—"usually taken to be offensive." (Most Mexicans and French people feel insulted.)

The fourth class is a very small one indeed. It consists of one word. The term "limey" for an Englishman is neither offensive nor disparaging; *Merriam-Webster* reports that it is merely slang. How can this be? Presumbaly because England was so self-confident for so long (and much of America so anglophile) that even now the English remain virtually insult-proof.

The editors at *Merriam-Webster* tried hard to avoid judgement. They claim merely to give the facts. The facts are that some people use words with the intention of putting other people down on the basis of the group they belong to; and quite often the other people don't like it. This dictionary never says it's *wrong* to employ racial or ethnic put-downs. But many other dictionaries do.

The extreme case is one you might not expect. *Webster's New World Dictionary*, as I mentioned, was expurgated in 1986. For whatever reason—a drop in sales, a wave of criticism, an attack of conscience—the editors then reversed course. In 1988 they put all the expurgated words back in. But now they're not just labeled; they're practically branded.* There is no question of neutrality now.

"Honkie," for example, is defined as "a white person; a term of hostility and contempt." And that's just one of the milder words. It would be much worse to say "yid," that being "a very offensive term of contempt." And then there is one word that cannot be said at all, at least not by honkies. "Nigger," being "a viciously hostile epithet," is "virtually taboo." If you speak black English, you may use it; otherwise it is forbidden.

Has a new taboo come into existence even as the old ones have crashed? I think so. So far *Webster's New World* is the only American dictionary to fence off a racial term as literally unspeakable, but I think it will have company soon. It already does in England. There the *Longman Dictionary of Contemporary English* (1987) isolates half a dozen words ("wop" rather surprisingly among them) as words so terrible as to be taboo—and not just "virtually," either. There will be more: words and dictionaries both.

One other change is occurring in the incidence of racial and ethnic expurgation. Slowly but surely it is moving into the classics of children's literature—that is to say, into the foothills of high art. In this country, Roald Dahl's *Charlie and the Chocolate Factory* has recently been ex-

---

* All but one, and that is the one ethnic term that had been in the dictionary right along. It is defined identically in 1986 and 1988: "limey: an Englishman."

purgated, and so has *Mary Poppins*. In England there have been recent expurgated editions of children's books by Walter de la Mare and by Kipling. Probably best known, Hugh Lofting's *The Story of Doctor Dolittle* was heavily bowdlerized in both countries in 1988, having been lightly cut—nicked, really—twenty years earlier. Hugh Walpole once said of *Doctor Dolittle* that it was "the first real children's classic since *Alice* [*in Wonderland*]." I think Hugh Walpole exaggerated, but the book is unquestionably a good one, which makes its recent history both exemplary and shocking.

Lofting published *Doctor Dolittle* in England in 1920. At that time English children were almost invariably white, and most of them, like their parents, had various unexamined feelings of racial superiority. Thus when Doctor Dolittle and his animals sail for Africa on an errand of mercy and meet a black prince who wishes he were white, there was no offense. On the contrary, there was a good deal of gentle comedy about the prince's attempts to achieve his desire. Prince Bumpo is an appealing character, even though slightly ridiculous. The same could be said of almost everyone in the book. Doctor Dolittle himself is white, English, appealing—and slightly ridiculous.

By the 1960s, though, with the world beginning to coalesce into one international, multiracial society, there were readers who were offended by the idea of a black person wanting to be white, and offended also by the ethnic terms occasionally used by Doctor Dolittle's 182-year-old parrot Polynesia, herself a native of Africa. Polynesia does not say the word "nigger" in *The Story of Doctor Dolittle* (though she uses it in several later Dolittle books).

But she does once say the word "darky," and once the even more offensive word "coon."* In the middle 1960s, Lofting's American publisher, Lippincott, quietly took both words out.

By then the Council on Interracial Books for Children had come into existence. An article in that organization's bulletin said coldly in 1968 that no curbing of Polynesia's tongue was going to make *Doctor Dolittle* decent, not with Prince Bumpo still present. The book was racist to the core, and beyond saving. This view parallels the one held in England in 1831, that Fielding's *Tom Jones*, being indecent to the core, was simply not susceptible to bowdlerizing.

Publishers listen to librarians, as I noted in the matter of Scholastic. Librarians listen to committees. They listened hard to the Council on Interracial Books for Children. And after 1968 the Doctor Dolittle books gradually began to disappear from the recommended lists of books to be bought for school and public libraries. That needn't have prevented Lippincott or anyone else from continuing to publish Lofting; this is a free country. But it did make it both financially and morally less appealing to do so. All

---

* This has not always been an offensive word. Nor, when used for human beings, has it always denoted black ones. It came into general use in American speech during the political campaign of 1840, and then it meant a member of the Whig party. Later it became a humorous frontier term, meaning just "person." A (usually white) frontiersman in deep trouble would say of himself, "I'm a gone coon."

Even when it came to be applied mostly to blacks, which was in the late nineteenth century, it was not necessarily offensive, any more than it had been for Whigs or frontiersmen. The second play by a black author with a black cast ever to appear on Broadway was called *A Trip to Coontown*. That was in 1898. In short, when Hugh Lofting used the word in 1920, he could as easily have intended to be humorous as insulting. But by 1960 there was nothing funny left.

twelve Dolittles went out of print in the United States, and stayed out for a decade and more.

As I reported many chapters back, the Victorians eventually discovered that it was not impossible to bowdlerize Fielding, after all. He was expurgated many times, once by his own great-granddaughter. So with Hugh Lofting. In 1988 he was thoroughly and successfully expurgated. The changes and cuts were made by a committee of three: two editors at Dell and Lofting's son, Christopher. The changes were extensive, and they were probably necessary. Prince Bumpo survived them, though he is a considerably different person than he used to be. For one thing, he is neither black nor white, but colorless. That changes the plot a good bit. The prince's interesting medical treatments, for example, have vanished entirely. It also affects the illustrations. Colorlessness is hard to depict. And therefore all the illustrations in which Prince Bumpo (or the king and queen, his parents) figured have been dropped.

Lofting did his own artwork, and his style was caricature. It is fair to say that he drew the royal family absurdly. But then he also drew Doctor Dolittle and *his* family absurdly. That's the kind of book he was writing. It remains that kind of book as far as limeys are concerned.

This expurgation is well known in literary circles, because both the editors and Christopher Lofting have been quite honorably open about their changes. Mr. Lofting even wrote an afterword for the first volume, not so much justifying the expurgation as explaining it. His main point is that his father would have been appalled at the idea that any child could be hurt by reading a book of his, and would therefore gladly have seen the changes made.

It is hard, though, to be sure what someone else would have liked. Dr. Bowdler's theory that Gibbon would have been glad to look down from heaven and see Bowdler making changes in the *Decline and Fall*, because as originally written it gave pain to some Christians, is highly doubtful. Nevertheless, Christopher Lofting seems to me to make a convincing case for his father's probable response. At the same time, I am clear that the new *Story of Doctor Dolittle* has been purged of racism only at the price of denying its characters race altogether. They are neutral human beings. Words such as the most fastidious dictionary would permit—the phrase "black man," the phrase "white man"—are without exception cut. That is a very high price to pay.* If one imagines, say, C. S. Lewis's Narnia books expurgated in the same way—and there is no question that Lewis openly prefers the fair-skinned Narnians to the dark, Muslim-sounding Calormenes—one sees a book like Lewis's *The Horse and His Boy* pretty well destroyed. Will that be on the agenda for the 1990s? Will *Huckleberry Finn* get a major slashing, followed by the works of Booth Tarkington, Rudyard Kipling, Bret Harte (the Chinese characters), and so on? It begins to seem probable.

Pendulums do swing, and they usually swing too far. That is the nature of pendulums. If I think that racial and ethnic expurgation may go to extremes in this country, and I do think that, I also reflect that it will not be the

---

* Too high for many people. *The Times* of London, among others, has denounced the new edition. There has also been warm praise—in *The New York Times*, for example. Probably the most striking endorsement comes from *The New Yorker*. At almost the same moment that it abandoned traditional bowdlerism, the magazine has embraced the new form. Doctor Dolittle had become "clearly unacceptable," its reviewer wrote. "Tactful editing has solved the problem."

first time. There was a rash of racial and ethnic expurgation in the 1840s and '50s, but of the opposite kind. What got omitted was any criticism of black slavery—and it was omitted, of course, so as not to give pain to white slaveholders. For example, in 1852 *Harper's* reprinted a famous English schoolbook called *Evenings at Home*. But first they cut out a dialogue called "The Master and the Slave."

A more extreme case involves the American Tract Society, at that time perhaps the principal religious publishing house in this country. With much conscientious struggle and with pious groans, the Society expurgated a considerable number of books and pamphlets so as to avoid giving offense to white southerners. It simultaneously tried to conceal or at least to downplay what it was doing. This infuriated a writer for the *Free Presbyterian*. Mincing no words, he wrote, "To send forth a work with two or three short paragraphs on slavery omitted, and call it an abridgment of the original, is a farce and a lie."

It is true that the farce and the lie were eventually brought to a halt. At the annual convention of 1857, the members of the American Tract Society voted to stop expurgating, and they did. (They also lost some members.)

It's also true that as long as anyone believes that books have the power to influence human actions, there are going to be strong pressures for expurgation—and where governments have that power, for censorship. I don't mean just sexual censorship, as in the past, or racial, as now. There are many kinds. And nearly always one can admire the motives of those trying to bring about the expurgation, even if one questions their judgement.

I warmly approve of a California regulation that forbids California schools to endorse junk food. But I half laugh and half sigh when I hear that because of this regulation a publisher was once required "to change a story in which a boy received a birthday cake." It is hard to imagine valley boys or valley girls being corrupted by reading about some kid's birthday party in a school anthology, even if you believe that birthday cake is a danger, which not many people do.

I even more warmly approve of true and enduring equality between the sexes. But I laughed and sighed when I learned that in 1976 the Commissioner of Education in Texas removed five dictionaries from the approved list for Texas schools. He did so partly because of pressure from the National Organization for Women. What NOW objected to was the fact that those five dictionaries did not include some new words like "chairperson," and did include some old words like "womanish," which are undoubtedly derogatory—and undoubtedly real parts of the language.

I have a special hatred of drunkenness—having, among other things, lost a friend to a drunk driver. He was 22 when the drunk ran him down. But I laugh and sigh and even moan a little when I learn that a dozen years ago *Huckleberry Finn* had a special alcoholically expurgated edition for use in the schools of Tennessee. It was identical to regular editions except for one thing. It omitted the passage where the Grangerford boys (and Buck Grangerford *is* only about 13) toast their parents with whiskey each morning at breakfast. Of course I don't want to see daily whiskey toasts made normative for American children. But the Grangerfords are hardly a normative family.

In fact, history does not support Tennessee's fears. Since Mark Twain published *Huckleberry Finn*, we have had a national experiment with prohibition. We have raised the drinking age to twenty-one. We have been drinking less and less whiskey per capita for years now. It could be argued that among the myriad causes for all this, one is precisely the terrible example offered by the Grangerfords. In that hard-drinking family, nearly everyone dies young, and of bullet wounds.

I don't wish to make that argument, however, but merely to reject the simplistic converse, that the scene which was expurgated presented a threat to the book-reading children of Tennessee. Surely books do have the power to influence human actions. But they exercise that power in such complex ways that bowdlerists and censors and experts on Young Adult reading would have to be a lot smarter than most of them are, if they hope to have predictable effects on audiences by expurgating or adapting our literature.

Am I saying that bowdlerism is always wrong? No, I'm even less ready than I was twenty-two years ago to claim that. Some things are so offensive or hurtful that it is probably right to take them out even if one can't foresee the full consequences of doing so. It seems especially justifiable in books for small children.

But to get rid of everything that could hurt anybody? We might consider getting rid of cars, knives, wine, and ballistic missiles before we get rid of a free literature. How will people ever become "strong" if they are always treated as "weak"?

****

Dr. Bowdler and His Publisher

****

LONGMAN, Hurst, Rees, Orme, Brown, and Green, the publishers who took over the *Family Shakespeare* in 1818 and kept it in print until 1925, are still thriving as Longmans, Green & Co. Ltd. (hereafter referred to as Longmans). A good many of their early records survive—nearly all did until there was a direct hit on their office during the Second World War. These records include a file of letters from Longmans to Dr. Bowdler, though not his replies. (It is usually possible to figure out what he must have said.) They are here printed by kind permission of Longmans. The first letter answers Dr. Bowdler's original inquiry, after taking over from Harriet.

London, July 3, 1817

Sir,

We were duly favoured with your letter respecting the Family Shakespeare. The sale of the edition published has been so very slow that we would rather decline taking the speculation of another edition on ourselves individually; but if you will be so good as to state what sum of money you would accept for a complete altered edition of Shakespeare's plays with your name prefixed, we will submit the matter to the proprietors of the regular edition of Shakespeare. We would advise that the volumes be about the same size as those of the last edition, and not in large 8vo.

We are
Sir,
Yr most obedient
Humble Ser.ts
Longman & Co.

The "proprietors of the regular edition," it should be noted were the forty London booksellers and publishers, including Longmans (but not Hatchard, the London distributor for Harriet's 1807 edition), who owned the big trade edition of Shakespeare, published in 1811, which dominated the market. It should also be noted that Harriet's edition had apparently only just sold out, after ten years.

As to what fee to ask for preparing the second edition, Dr. Bowdler seems to have been at a loss, and apparently wrote back to Longmans begging them to name one for him. This was breaking the rules, though, and they refused.

London, July 31, 1817

Sir,

We have received your letter of the 26th inst. It will be necessary for you to consult with your literary friends on the subject of remuneration for the proposed edition of Shakespeare, and of course the more reasonable the sum, the Trade will be the more inclined to engage in the speculation. If you can conveniently favour us with your reply in about six weeks from this time, we shall have, probably, an opportunity of laying the proposal before the Partners in the work. There is still a great difference of opinion as to the manner of spelling the name [Shakespeare]; however, we believe the mode we have used is now most generally adopted.

This fight over spelling is further evidence, were it needed, that a new editor had taken over. Harriet, in 1807, used the same spelling that Longmans here argues for.

As to the fee, Dr. Bowdler still couldn't bring himself to name a figure. His problem was lack of information. He had brought out four earlier books, but experience with them was no help. Hitherto he had acted as his own publisher, and the question of what fee to pay himself didn't arise. There were no literary agents to consult, certainly not around Swansea, Wales, where he was then living. Once again he cast himself on the mercy of Longmans, and once again they insisted on playing by the rules.

London, September 30, 1817

Sir,

We were favoured with your letter of the 9th inst., and have been writing to F. C. Rivington, who has just returned to town. F. C. Rivington being the manager of the Shakespeare for the Booksellers, we requested he would summon the partners for the purpose of submitting to them your proposed Edition. F. C. Rivington observed that it would be essential he should be previously informed of the terms that would be satisfactory to yourself, on seeing which he would with pleasure immediately summon us together. We have therefore to request you will be so good as to name a specific Sum, and we take the liberty to recommend you to fix the sum as low as possible, in order that there may be no obstacle on that account to the attainment of your desired and laudable object.

Thus pressed, Dr. Bowdler finally did name a price, though the surviving records don't show what it was. Presumably low, after so broad a hint from Longmans. Even so, the next letter makes clear that he was worried sick that the sum *would* be an obstacle, and that a mere matter of money might delay the final stage of Shakespeare's expurgation. The worry was misplaced. It turned out to be expurgation itself the Trade was doubtful of. In the fall of 1817, the *Family Shakespeare* almost fizzled to an end.

London, November 26, 1817

Sir,

Mr. Rivington, the managing partner of our edition of Shakespeare, called a meeting on Thursday last and submitted to them the Family Shakespeare. The matter was considered very fully, and we are sorry to say that they considered the success of a republication of the work so very doubtful that they declined undertaking the speculation. We think it right to state that they came to this determination without any consideration as to what sum was to be given to the Editor. That point was not at all canvassed, and they decided wholly on the probability of a very limited demand for the book.

If you print the work at your own expense, we shall be happy to render you any service in our power as to the sale of it. We would advise you to confine the publication to a selection of the plays, rather than give the whole 36 or 37.

This would seem to close the negotiations. But Dr. Bowdler came of a persistent family. He apparently sent Longmans a brand-new proposal by return mail; and either his letter was unusually persuasive, or a different partner made the decision. For whatever reason, Longmans reversed themselves completely, not only accepting the book as their own speculation, but going back to the idea of a complete edition, and even making a very generous financial offer.

London, December 8, 1817

Sir,

We have been considering your last letter relative to the Family, or Bowdler's, Shakespeare; and though the partners in the Trade Edition have declined your proposals, we will, if it meet your approbation, individually undertake it on the following terms: to print the 36 plays in the manner you have proposed, and pay you for the trouble the sum of £400 when we shall have sold 750 copies. Should this proposal not meet your approbation, and should you print the work on your own a/c, we will with pleasure publish it for you. We would not advise partial publication of the plays, but that the whole should be published together, in perhaps 8 volumes, and the publication should not be deferred beyond April next.

Dr. Bowdler did accept this proposal, and well he might have. It was a handsome offer. The highest recorded payment to an editor of Shakespeare was Dr. Johnson's £1,312; the next highest was Lewis Theobald's £652; and much lower payments were common. Pope got £217 for his edition in 1725, and Isaac Reed £300 for his big twenty-one-volume annotated trade edition in 1803.* These men, of course, had the standard editorial labor of establishing and annotating a fresh text, while Dr. Bowdler took his text for granted, and was being paid merely to expurgate and to write a preface.

How much of the expurgating he already had done before the contract was signed, it is impossible to say, but plainly not all. At the very least, he still had *Measure for Measure* facing him. This was one of the sixteen plays Harriet omitted in 1807, and it had been an article of faith in the Bowdler family ever since that it was beyond redemption. As John, Jr., wrote in 1808, *Measure for Measure* has some glorious passages, "but the plot of this drama is so radically indecent, that no skill or labour can purify it." You can either print a few disconnected scenes, or you can leave the play out.

* This was about five per cent of the total cost (£5,683) of the Reed edition; by contrast, the publisher spent £3,345 on paper.

Neither of these choices was open to Dr. Bowdler for the complete *Family Shakespeare*, and what he did try to choose shows him a fairer-minded man than most expurgators. He suggested to Longmans that in this one case he print the complete text as well as the limp fragments that would be left after cutting. Longmans objected, on purely commercial grounds:

London, December, 1817

Dear Sir,

With respect to Measure for Measure, we would not advise your printing the entire play as well as in an altered state, but merely to give one copy altered according to the best of your judgement; and you are at liberty to make whatever use you choose of our Theatre edition, which was altered by Mr. Kemble. Should you find that you cannot alter the play quite to your mind, some allusion might be made to the circumstances in your preface, and your having adopted the copy which Mr. Kemble altered for the Covent Garden Theatre [in 1789]. Your printing the play with all its objectionable passages would not, we fear, be agreeable to the purchasers of such a work as the Family Shakespeare. In spelling the name, Shakespeare, we have followed Mr. Steevens, whom we have always considered to be the most able of all the annotators of our immortal Bard.

Dr. Bowdler gratefully accepted this offer, and the 1818 edition of the *Family Shakspeare* (he won on the spelling) consists of thirty-five expurgations by Bowdler, and one thirty-year-old acting version by John Philip Kemble. Kemble was not much of a prude, though, and when a new edition came out in 1820, it had a properly bowdlerized *Measure for Measure*. This note preceded it: "The editor having been blamed for inserting in the former edition of this work, the theatre copy of Measure for Measure, has in this instance, as in all the other plays, had recourse to his own pen, endeavouring to render the comedy as little objectionable as it can be rendered,* without destroying

---

* Where Kemble had the character Pompey arrested as a bawd, Bowdler has him arrested as a thief. (Shakespeare got him on both counts.) When the Duke complains that wenching is "too general a vice" in Vienna, Kemble allowed Lucio to answer, "Yes, in good sooth, the vice is of a great kindred; it is well allied; but it is impossible to extirp it quite, Friar, till eating and drinking be put down." Bowdler cuts Lucio off at "allied," a change that shows, among other things, a truly wonderful optimism about the coming

its great beauties, which are closely interwoven with the numerous defects."

Most of the later letters to Dr. Bowdler are illegible because of war damage, but the Longmans account books for the period are still readable, and they give the printing history of the *Family Shakspeare* in some detail. (I have not found the history of Harriet's original 1807 edition.)

The edition that came out not in April but in June 1818 was 1,000 copies. It sold slowly enough so that the second Longmans edition, 1820, is simply the remainder of the first edition, with a new foreword and new sheets for *Measure for Measure*. The 750th copy sold, and Dr. Bowdler got his £400, in the spring of 1822, nearly four years after publication day and a few months after the *Edinburgh* took up the cause. Henceforth, sales and salesmanship both increase. The third edition, 500 large-type copies for papas, came out in November 1822. Longmans spent £50 advertising it. The fourth edition, 750 regular copies, came out in 1824, helped along by £75 worth of advertising. Five hundred more copies for papas were printed in April 1827, and Longmans now put £200 into advertising, as befits a successful book. After that there is a new printing of 500 or 1,000 copies every few years until the 1880s, when the print order drops to 250. The final order for sets of the *Family Shakspeare* was in June 1900; 15,250 had been printed altogether—a good run for an expensive set.

This is not the full story, though. Back in 1864, Longmans began to print the plays separately, for sale to schools. These sales were never large. The standard print order was 250, and only the most popular plays, like *Julius Caesar*, got printed as much as once a year. The last single plays were printed in 1914 —a nice piece of symbolic timing—but Longmans continued to list them in its catalogue and to sell them through 1925. About 150,000 single plays were sold in all.

Even this is not quite the full story. Besides the pirate American edition in 1849, which failed, there were two British rivals. The Glasgow publisher Griffin began to put out the *Family Shakspeare*, enhanced with steel plates, as soon as the forty-two-year British copyright expired, which was in 1860. Its edition

---

Victorian age. But even in 1820 *Measure for Measure* carries the message that sex is here to stay. And to the end Dr. Bowdler considered it one of the three plays "which form exceptions to what I have advanced respecting the facility of the task that I have undertaken."

and Longmans' ran side by side until 1874, when the two publishers seem to have come to terms, Griffin keeping the Scottish market and Longmans the English, both using the steel plates. Like much Victorian printing, this edition is in type so fine that not only papas but almost anyone would need glasses to read it. Finally, in 1887 Ward, Lock & Co. of London brought out what they called a "New Edition," which is plainly printed from the same old steel plates. By this time, though Dr. Bowdler's name was still in good odor with Swinburne and others, his style of expurgation had long since been outmoded, and the pruning of Shakespeare was in the hands of Eton masters, American university professors, and other professionals. In 1908, Longmans itself brought out a "School Shakespeare," cut with a bright new knife by someone younger and more academic.

REFERENCES TO SOURCES CITED

There are two kinds of notes in this book: footnotes, which are printed in the text, and mere references, which are gathered here. I have keyed these latter by page and by catch-phrase. Reference notes refer to both text and footnotes.

EPIGRAPH

"If you'd climb the Helicon": Gilbert and Sullivan, *Princess Ida*, Act II, ii, 11–19.
"Damn the expurgated books": Horace Traubel, *Walt Whitman in Camden*, Boston: 1906, I, 124.

PREFACE

ix "*faire Eunuques*": Pierre Bayle, *A General Dictionary, Historical and Critical*, London: 1741, X, 425.
xiii "larger audience": Francis T. Palgrave, ed., *Songs and Sonnets by William Shakespeare*, London: 1879, p. 236.
xiv "winnowed editions": Richard D. Altick, *The English Common Reader*, Chicago U.P.: 1957, p. 36.
xv "spirit of the author": Thomas Bowdler, *A Letter to the Editor of the British Critic*, London: 1823, p. 12.

CHAPTER I

3 "Can it call, whore": Ben Jonson, *Every Man in His Humour*, II, iii, 21–23.
3 "A vulgar scribbler": Byron, "Hints from Horace," ll. 393–398.

3   "bolder height": Jenkin Jones, *Hobby Horses*, London: 1797, pp. 15–17.

4   "and Fielding": Fred W. Boege, *Smollett's Reputation as a Novelist*, Princeton U.P.: 1947, p. 63.

5   "for a Nurse": Georgina Galbraith, ed., *The Journal of the Rev. William Bagshaw Stevens*, Oxford U.P.: 1965, p. 186.

5   "profane expressions": J. R. Pitman, ed., *The School-Shakspeare*, London: 1822, Advertisement.

5   "are cultivated": Alan B. Howes, *Yorick and the Critics: Sterne's Reputation in England, 1760–1868*, Yale U.P.: 1958, p. 105.

6   "out of the question": *ibid.*, p. 134.

6   "his sense or his style": Stanley Lane-Poole, ed., *Selections from the Prose Writings of Jonathan Swift*, London: 1884, Preface.

6   "I would blot them": Sidney Lanier, *The English Novel*, N.Y.: 1883, p. 180.

6   "scarcely be intelligible": Frederic Harrison, *The Choice of Books*, London: 1886, p. 63.

7   "your Ladyship": Galbraith, p. xii.

8   "spitting on a peer": Harold W. Thompson, ed., *The Anecdotes and Egotisms of Henry Mackenzie*, Oxford U.P.: 1927, p. 156. Mackenzie actually wrote the anecdotes down in 1825, as an old man of eighty.

8   "accomplished, and refined": *Females of the Present Day*, By a Country Lady, London: 1831, p. 69.

9   "in times of old": J. E. Morpurgo, ed., *The Autobiography of Leigh Hunt*, London: 1949, p. 167.

9   "circles in London": J. G. Lockhart, *The Life of Sir Walter Scott*, Edinburgh: 1902, VI, 376. I am indebted to Mr. James Corson, Mossrig, Lilliesleaf, Melrose, Scotland, for dating this incident.

11   "a novelist can't say": W. D. Howells, *Criticism and Fiction*, N.Y.: 1891, p. 155.

11   "a union of hearts": *The Spectator*, #286.

11   "one editor of Henry Mackenzie": Henry Morley in 1886. Hamish Miles reprints part of the index in his edition, London: 1928, p. 28.

12   "blush'd in my turn": Laurence Sterne, *A Sentimental Journey*, Oxford U.P.: 1935, pp. 9, 32.

12   "Virtue's precious seed": Hannah More, "Sensibility, a poem." In her *Sacred Dramas*, Boston: 1801, p. 152.

12   "imperious passions": Louis I. Bredvold, *The Natural History of Sensibility*, Wayne U.P.: 1962, p. 25.

13   "sweet impulsive modesty": C. J. Rawson, "Some Remarks on 18th-Century Delicacy," *Journal of English and Germanic Philology*, 1962, p. 4. The novel is Frances Brooke's *Lady Julia Mandeville* (1763).

13   "Lady Louisa Stuart": Hamish Miles, ed., Henry Macken-
     zie's *The Man of Feeling*, London: 1928, p. 29.
13   "unbending set of features": *The Looker-On*, #62 (1793).
14   "salutary restraints": John Bennett, *Letters to a Young
     Lady*, London: 1789, II, 43.
15   "uncommonly unfeeling": Vicemus Knox, *Essays, Moral
     and Literary*, 14th ed., London: 1795, II, 322.
15   "A girl should *hear*": Bennett, *op. cit.*, II, 43.
16   "eminently unbusinesslike": Yorke, *op. cit.*, pp. 17, 277.
16   "a public petition": it was published in *The Nineteenth
     Century*, 1889, pp. 781–88.
17   "said Clara Reeve": in *The Progress of Romance*, N.Y.:
     1930, I, 31.
18   "professors at Columbia": G. P. Krapp and Elliott Dobbie,
     eds., *The Exeter Book*, Columbia U.P.: 1936.
18   "Paull Franklin Baum": ed., *Anglo-Saxon Riddles of the
     Exeter Book*, Duke U.P.: 1963. The translation of Riddle 44
     is a conflation of his and of Professor W. S. Mackie's for
     the Early English Text Society edition, London: 1934.
19   "no cause of error": Walter E. Houghton, *The Victorian
     Frame of Mind*, Yale U.P.: 1957, p. 367.
19   "a strange phrase": Ian Jack, *English Literature 1815–1832*,
     Oxford U.P.: 1964, p. 43.
19   "using quotation marks": *Blackwood's*, Jan. 1831, p. 92.
20   "300,000": Jack, *op. cit.*, p. 44.
20   "amounts to a million": George Levine, ed., *The Emergence
     of Victorian Consciousness*, N.Y.: 1967, p. 194.
21   "editions of 5,000": see Marjorie Plant's *The English Book
     Trade* ("An Economic History of the Making and Sale of
     Books"), London: 1939, esp. pp. 331, 337–38, 414–18.
21   "appetite for reading": W. O. B. Allen and Edmund
     McClure, *Two Hundred Years: History of the SPCK,
     1698–1898*, London: 1898, p. 192.
22   "equally with the 'weak' ": Grosart, *op. cit.*, pp. ix, x.
23   "handle the phallus": J. B. Peabody, ed., *Holmes-Einstein
     Letters*, N.Y.: 1964, p. 30.
24   "much 'fie-fied' ": *Poems of John Donne*, ed E. K. Cham-
     bers, intro. George Saintsbury, London: 1896, p. xxvi.
24   "the antients": Knox, *op. cit.*, pp. 319–20.

CHAPTER II

25   "To rescue from oblivion": [Francis Gentleman], *The Dra-
     matic Censor; or, Critical Companion*, London: 1770, II, 241.
25   "I have often wished": Clara Reeve, *The Progress of Ro-
     mance*, N.Y.: 1930, II, 17.

26 "obscenity dreadfully propagated": Burns Martin, *Allan Ramsay*, Harvard U.P.: 1931, p. 33.

28 "unless by themselves": Phillips, *op. cit.*, 3rd ed., London: 1727, I, 153.

30 "small Difficulty": Ramsay, *op. cit.*, Edinburgh: 1724, I, 72.

32 "these few Blanks": *ibid.*, I, 126.

33 "otherwise have been withheld": Austin Dobson, ed. *Selected Poems of Matthew Prior*, London: 1889, Preface.

35 "burned his annotated quarto": J. B. Wakeley, *Anecdotes of the Wesleys*, London: 1870, p. 319.

37 "hoarder of ancient dirt": John Pinkerton, ed., *Ancient Scotish Poems, Never Before in Print*, London: 1786, I, xv.

38 "to the unlearned": John Wesley, *An Extract From Milton's Paradise Lost*, London: 1763, Preface.

38 "he termed it": In that same dedication to the Countess of Huntingdon.

39 "in a selection of this kind": *Critical Review*, June 1767, p. 409.

39 "prevented the sale": Thomas Percy, ed., *Miscellaneous Works of Oliver Goldsmith*, London: 1801, I, 84.

39 "interdicted from general reading": John Forster, *The Life and Times of Oliver Goldsmith*, London: 1854, II, 22.

40 "strengthen that innocence": [Oliver Goldsmith, ed.], *Poems for Young Ladies*, London: 1767, p. iii.

41–2 "half a dozen cuts": these are given in detail in Jean Loiseau, *Abraham Cowley's Reputation in England*, Paris: 1931, p. 103n. The cuts are mainly of passages that offend theology rather than pudeur, as in Bowdler's Gibbon.

42 "happier works": *Monthly Review*, Jan. 1773, pp. 10–11.

43 "free from adulteration": Mona Wilson, ed., *Johnson Prose and Poetry*, London: 1957, p. 523.

43 "kindness of the friend": James Osborn, "Johnson on the Sanctity of an Author's Text," *PMLA*, 1935, p. 428.

43 "philosophical rhymer": Mona Wilson, *op. cit.*, p. 813.

44 "Prior is a lady's book": *Life of Johnson*, Oxford U.P.: 1934–50, III, 192.

45 "filthy pictures": Vivian de Sola Pinto, ed., *Poems by John Wilmot, Earl of Rochester*, London: 1964, p. xxxvii.

45 "interested in pornography": *ibid.*, p. xl.

45 "rival edition": London: Tonson, 1691.

46 "request of the publisher": Routledge & Kegan Paul of London. The book is handled in America by Harvard U.P.

49 "2 lines which follow": Hailes, *op. cit.* p. 238.

50 "drynk and rore": *ibid.*, p. 242.

50 "changed it to 'fondlars' ": James Sibbald, ed., *Chronicle of Scottish Poetry*, Edinburgh: 1802, III, 213.

50 "Dalrymple specifies": *op. cit.*, pp. 3, 8.

52 "to the most squeamish": A. F. Falconer, ed., *The Corre-*

spondence of Thomas Percy and David Dalrymple, Lord Hailes, L.S.U. Press: 1954, pp. 163–64.

52 "truly ridiculous": *ibid.*, p. 164.

52 "putting asterisks": Pinkerton, *op. cit.*, p. x.

53 "inscribed to you": Dawson Turner, ed., *The Literary Correspondence of John Pinkerton*, London: 1830, I, 197.

53 "couldn't find a publisher": Turner, *op. cit.*, I, 35.

53 "stain the delicacy": Elizabeth Frank, ed., *Memoirs of the Life and Writings of Lindley Murray in a Series of Letters, Written by Himself*, York: 1823, p. 95.

53 "cuckold carlie": Herd, *op. cit.*, II, 40.

54 "scores of castrati": Frank, *op. cit.*, p. 103.

55 "Dryden a la Hurd": J. G. Lockhart, *The Life of Sir Walter Scott*, Edinburgh: 1902, II, 242.

57 "in female hands": H. J. C. Grierson, ed., *Letters of Sir Walter Scott*, London: 1932–37, I, 264.

57 "in my power": Lockhart, *op. cit.*, II, 242f.

57 "obscure passages": *ibid.*, II, 249.

57 "drink and whore": *ibid.*, I, 257.

58 "obnoxious lines": Grierson, *op. cit.*, I, 284.

59 "you have directed me": *ibid.*

59 "our literary history": Lockhart, *op. cit.*, III, 64.

CHAPTER III

60 "The unbounded licentiousness": [Elizabeth S. Bowdler], *A Commentary on the Song of Solomon Paraphrased*, Edinburgh: 1775, p. 2.

60 "So much superior": John Bowdler, ed., *Select Pieces in Prose and Verse by the Late John Bowdler, Jun., Esq.*, London: 1816 I, 78–79.

60 "If any word": Thomas Bowdler, *A Letter to the Editor of the British Critic*, London: 1823, p. 17.

61 "Brown, and so on": Esther Dunn, *Shakespeare in America*, N.Y.: 1939, p. 288.

61 "chiefly 'young ladies'": J. C. Thompson, *Bibliography of . . . Charles and Mary Lamb*, Hull: 1908, p. 26.

61 "a leading magazine": *Critical Review*, 1807, p. 98.

63 "Francis Gentleman said": *The Dramatic Censor*, London: 1770, I, 171.

63 "torrent of feculence": Leigh Hunt, ed., *Beaumont and Fletcher; or, The Finest Scenes, Lyrics and other Beauties of these two poets, now first selected from the whole of their works, to the exclusion of whatever is Morally Objectionable*, London: 1855, p. viii.

65 "circumspect and judicious reader": Thomas Bowdler, ed., *The Family Shakspeare*, 4th ed., London: 1825, I, xviii.

66 "clear this beautiful poem": Elizabeth S. Bowdler, *op. cit.*, p. 1.

66 "would suit ill": *ibid.*, pp. 86–87.

66 "daughters of Jerusalem": *ibid.*, p. 139.

67 "name was Frances": *Family Shakspeare*, 1825, X, 362.

67 "freedom of conversation": Jane Bowdler, *op. cit.*, N.Y.: 1811 (1st American from the 11th English ed.), p. 223.

67 "three times in a single winter": the Rev. Thomas Bowdler, *Memoir of the Late John Bowdler*, London: 1825, p. 93.

67 "to the Earl of Hardwicke": Letter in the British Museum.

68 "men of delicacy are shocked": *Memoir*, p. 135.

68 "to *do good*": John Bowdler, ed., *op. cit.*, pp. xiv–xv.

69 "she could not bear to look": The Countess of Minto, ed., *Life and Letters of Sir Gilbert Elliot, 1st Earl of Minto*, London: 1876, I, 135.

69 "aversion to sick people": see *Memoir of the Late John Bowdler*, p. 301, and Dr. Bowdler's own *Letters Written in Holland*, London: 1788, p. 161.

70 "Doll Tearsheet": Elizabeth Montagu, *An Essay on the Writings and Genius of Shakespeare*, 5th ed., London: 1785, p. 125.

70 "Percy to Lord Hailes": Percy-Dalrymple *Correspondence*, p. 152.

71 "You fight hard, I see": John Bowdler, ed., *Select Pieces in Prose and Verse by the Late John Bowdler, Jun., Esq.*, London: 1816, p. 546.

73 "great abuse of the Holy Name": Virginia Gildersleeve, *Government Regulation of the Elizabethan Drama*, Columbia U.P.: 1908, p. 19.

74 "to the government censor": *ibid.*, p. 112.

75 "*Monthly Review*": 1807 (Part II), p. 212.

75 "*British Critic*": 1807, p. 442.

76 "Let it live or perish": *The Christian Observer*, 1808, p. 390. The original unfavorable review was on pp. 326–34.

76 "the name of Thomas Bowdler": James Plumptre, *Four Discourses on Subjects Relating to the Amusement of the Stage*, Cambridge: 1809, p. 222n.

76 "fiend of licentiousness": Cunningham, *op. cit.*, I, 65–66.

77 "Harriet's very obituary": *Gentleman's Magazine*, 1830 (Part I), p. 567.

77 "tried by the BBC": "The Trial of Dr. Bowdler," by Lawrence Kitchin, was broadcast by the BBC in the middle fifties and published in Mr. Kitchin's book *Three on Trial*, London: 1959.

77 "mocked by Bertrand Russell": "Mr. Bowdler's Nightmare" appears in Lord Russell's *Nightmares of Eminent Persons*, N.Y.: 1955.

77 "sole quill-driver of the family": Robert Southey, ed., *The Remains of Henry Kirke White of Nottingham*, London: 1816, I, 123.

78 "Mayow had a small suggestion": Unpublished letter in the University Library, Cambridge.

79 "Playhouse and the Players": *ibid.*

79 "Cowburn himself wrote": both notes are written in the front of Harriet's copy of Alexander Keith's *Evidence of the Truth of the Christian Religion*, London: 1826. This copy is now in the possession of Mr. Anthony P. Collins, currently a Peace Corps volunteer in Africa, who kindly showed it to me.

80 " 'cuckold' to 'wronged man' ": Charles and Mary Cowden Clarke, eds., *Cassell's Illustrated Shakespeare*, London: 1864.

83 "*Blackwood's*": 1821, pp. 512–13.

83 "*Monthly Review*": 1820, p. 433.

84 "*Edinburgh*": XXXVI, pp. 52–54.

85 "the name of the editor will be remembered": *Memoir of* the *Late John Bowdler*, p. 321.

CHAPTER IV

87 "Emendations": *The British Critic*, April, 1822, p. 372.

87 "I have no objections": Dan H. Laurence, ed., *Bernard Shaw: Collected Letters 1874–1897*, N.Y.: 1965, p. 650.

88 "prophanes and ribaldry": Hazelton Spencer, *Shakespeare Improved*, Harvard U.P.: 1927, p. 21.

88 "Now Friend": *ibid.*, p. 165.

90 "Pain full nine Months": Montague Summers, ed., *Shakespeare Adaptations*, London: 1922, p. 39.

90 "nervous about quoting": *e.g.*, Hazelton Spencer in the work cited above. He considered Dennis' version "a contemptible compound of farce and smut. . . . The dialogue in II, ii is unquotable," pp. 347, 349.

91 "identical lines away from Juliet": see George C. Branam, *Eighteenth Century Adaptations of Shakespeare*, U. Cal. Press: 1956, pp. 119–20.

92 "the Danish Macaroni": *ibid.*, p. 12.

92 "monarch run into such vulgarisms": Francis Gentleman, *The Dramatic Censor*, London: 1770, I, 99–100.

93 "a royal character": Francis Gentleman, ed., *Bell's Edition of Shakespeare*, London: 1774, VI, note to *Antony and Cleopatra*, I, v.

93 "glaring indecencies": *ibid.*, I, 9.

93 "Touchstone makes his exit": *ibid.*, I, 182.

94 "A careful pruner": *ibid.*, IV, 240.

94   *"an old black ram"*: *ibid.*, I, 215.

95   "good critics were saying this": See Herbert S. Robinson, *English Shakesperian Criticism in the Eighteenth Century*, N.Y.: 1932, p. 77.

95   "I conceived appropriate": Bernard Grebanier, *The Great Shakespeare Forgery*, N.Y.: 1965, p. 114.

96   "foistered in by the players": W. H. Ireland, *An Authentic Account of the Shaksperian Manuscripts*, London: 1796, p. 19.

96   "yonne Ladye": Samuel Ireland, ed., *Miscellaneous Papers . . . by William Shakespeare*, London: 1796, p. 120.

98   "her publisher put it": Catalogue of Sherwood, Jones & Co., dated London, Jan. 1824, p. 4.

99   "really meant 'Oh, Lord' ": R. B. Peake, *Memoirs of the Colman Family*, London: 1841, p. 431.

99   " 'great acquisition to the stage' ": *Alasco*, London: 1824, p. 114n.

99   "made Shee even madder": See J. F. Bagster-Collins, *George Colman the Younger*, Columbia U.P.: 1946, pp. 294–95.

100   "WE are sufficiently advanced": Frances Trollope, *op. cit.*, London: 1832, I, 123–25.

100   "expurgations back in": A. van R. Westfall, *American Shakespeare Criticism 1607–1865*, N.Y.: 1939, p. 147.

101   "only six plays": ed. Edward Slater, London: 1834. This was an attempt to undersell even Pitman.

105   "Kean": Charles Kean, ed., *Selections from the Plays of Shakespeare Especially Adapted for Schools, Private Families and Young People*, London: 1859.

105   "Kemble": R. J. Lane, ed., *Charles Kemble's Shakspere Readings*, London: 1870. Called "Shakspere for Schools" from the edition of 1879 on.

105   "Wordsworth's nephew": Charles Wordsworth, ed., *Shakespeare's Historical Plays*, Edinburgh: 1883.

105   "The Secretary": *Shakespeare for Schools and Families*, ed. Thomas Shorter, London: 1865.

105   "The novelist": Charlotte M. Yonge, ed., *Shakespeare's Plays for Schools*, London: 1883–85.

105   "Cundell": Henry Cundell, ed., *The Boudoir Shakespeare*, London: 1876–77.

105   "that he should have cut anything out!": Lewis Carroll, *Sylvie and Bruno*, London: 1890, p. xv.

105   " 'expurgated' or not": *ibid.*

108   " 'the son of Mary' ": C. and M. C. Clarke, eds., *Cassell's Illustrated Shakespeare*, London: [1864], fn. 31 to Act II of *Romeo and Juliet*.

108   "for whom I have laboured": Rosa Baughan, ed., *Shakespeare's Plays*, London: 1863–71, I, Preface.

108   "Girl's study": *ibid.*, publishers advertisement in the back of Vol. II.

108   "*thorough* weeding": *ibid.*

111   "overthrowing the whole delineation": Hudson, *op. cit.,* Boston: 1872, I, Preface.

111   "variation from the First Folio": Ebenezer C. Black, LL.D., and Andrew J. George, Litt.D., eds., The New Hudson *Hamlet,* Boston: 1909, p. iii.

112   "and controversial notes": Arthur Tillotson, ed., *Percy-Malone Letters,* L.S.U. Press: 1944, p. 9.

114   "Mathias in *Pursuits of Literature*": 3rd ed., 1797, Part I, p. 38n.

CHAPTER V

115   "Both read the Bible": William Blake, "The Everlasting Gospel," Section "a," ll. 13–14.

115   "The truth is": Albert B. Paine, ed., *Mark Twain's Letters,* N.Y.: 1917, II, 805.

118   "for the BIBLE": Sarah Trimmer, *An Essay on Christian Education,* London: 1812, p. 57.

118   "James Plumptre": *Letters to John Aikin,* Cambridge: 1811, p. 20.

118–19   "annals of a brothel": *The Monk,* London: 1906, II, 63.

120   "Puritan prayer book": *A Directory for the Public Worship of God, Throughout the Three Kingdomes . . . Together With an Ordinance of Parliament for the taking away of the Book of Common Prayer,* London: Printed for the good of the Common-Wealth, 1644.

120   "by the young and gay": Edward Harwood, *op. cit.,* p. v.

122   "or *practical* nature": *The Holy Bible, with the Porteusian Index,* London: 1822, "To the Reader."

127   "destitute of judgement": *Quarterly Review,* 1818, p. 253.

133   "benevolent design now on foot": Harry R. Warfel, ed., *Letters of Noah Webster,* N.Y.: 1953, p. 433.

134   "is to be executed": *The Holy Bible in the Common Version, With Amendments of the Language by Noah Webster, LL.D.,* New Haven: 1833, p. 5.

134   "Moses Stuart": E. E. F. Ford, *Notes on the Life of Noah Webster,* N.Y.: 1912, II, 186.

137   "I wish a few clergymen": Harry R. Warfel, *Noah Webster: Schoolmaster to America,* N.Y.: 1936, p. 412.

137   "withdrawn again in 1858": See T. H. Darlow and H. F. Moule, *Historical Catalogue of the Printed Editions of the Holy Scripture in the Library of the British and Foreign Bible Society,* London: 1903, I, 362–63.

138   "virgin bosoms handled": See the Revised Standard Version, 1952.

CHAPTER VI

139   "I commonly read with a pen": James Plumptre, *The English Drama Purified*, Cambridge: 1812, p. xiv.

140   "notion of my trifles": Unless otherwise identified, all letters to and from Plumptre are quoted from the originals in the University Library, Cambridge.

142   "Anson's *Voyages*": I haven't actually seen this book, and it is possible it was never published. There is an advertisement implying it was, however, in the back of Plumptre's *Robinson Crusoe*, London: Rivington, 1826.

142   "low buffoonery": James Plumptre, *Four Discourses . . . on the Stage*, Cambridge: 1809, p. 52.

143   "disgust, or aversion": James Plumptre, *An Inquiry into the Lawfulness of the Stage*, Cambridge: 1812, pp. 17f.

143   "of the degrees of vice": James Plumptre, *A Collection of Songs*, Cambridge: 1805, "Postscript to the Reader."

143   "cherisht woe": James Plumptre, *Letters to John Aikin, With a Collection of English Songs*, Cambridge: 1811, p. 251.

143   "deity to adore": *Collection of Songs*, "Postscript."

144   "act of suicide": *English Drama Purified*, vol. I, headnote to *The Gamester*

148   "revise all the old plays": *The Artist*, 1809, p. 315.

148   "in respect to Shakespeare": *English Drama Purified*, I, xx.

149   "permanent change": Letter to Mr. Fleetwood, Feb. 24, 1810.

150   "his biographer": James M. Rigg, "William Frederick," *Dictionary of National Biography*, XXI, 349.

151   "accustomed influence of the sun": *English Drama Purified*, I, xxvi.

152   "*King Lear* was done": Phyllis Hartnoll, ed., *Oxford Companion to the Theatre*, Oxford U.P.: 1951, p. 232.

154   "bad monarch, and a bad friend": John Hamilton, Lord Sumner, "George IV," *Dictionary of National Biography*, VII, 1083.

158   "John Clare": Plumptre's letters to him, dated April 26 and May 3, 1820, are in the British Museum.

159   "His Spanish dog": See the *Times* for July 28 and 30 and Aug. 6, 9, and 14, 1817.

CHAPTER VII

162   "The moment a woman": Noah Webster, *A Collection of Essays and Fugitiv Writings*, Boston: 1790, p. 408.

162   "Literature": Knapp, *op. cit.*, Middletown, N.J.: 1837, p. 10.

162   "A generation": Noah Porter, *Books and Reading*, N.Y.: 1871, p. 92.

163   "he allowed one to appear": [Arthur Stedman, ed.], *Selected Poems of Walt Whitman*, N.Y.: 1892.

164   "mastuprations": *Anatomy of Melancholy*, I, iii, II, iv (Everyman ed., II, 419).

164   "Swift and Dickens": Gulliver trained under the London surgeon Mr. James Bates, called by him "my good Master Bates"; Oliver Twist works in Fagin's gang along with Jack Dawkins, usually known as "the artful Dodger," and Charley Bates, usually known as Master Bates. (Other males in the book are called "Mr.")

165   "without a blush": Samuel Johnson, Jr., and John Elliott, *A Selected Dictionary*, Suffield, Conn.: 1800, Preface.

167   "essentially secular lessons": see Ervin C. Shoemaker, *Noah Webster*, N.Y.: 1936, p. 73.

167   "Augean stables": Harry R. Warfel, ed. *Letters of Noah Webster*, N.Y.: 1953, p. 330.

167   "the whole letter L": Joseph W. Reed, Jr., "Noah Webster's Debt to Samuel Johnson," *American Speech*, 1962, pp. 95–105. Reed compared the 1799 edition of Johnson, which Webster owned and worked from, with the 1828 Webster's Unabridged.

169   "Thoreau": George Whicher, *Walden Revisited*, Chicago: 1945, p. 41.

170   "tho' a much better one": E. E. F. Ford, *Notes on the Life of Noah Webster*, N.Y.: 1912, II, 187–89.

170   "Dr. Bowdler": Letter in the British Museum, dated Dec. 22, 1823.

171   "Pope's, but Webster's": Ford, *op. cit.*, II, 191.

172   "selected poems of the more obscure": Ezekiel Sanford, ed., *Works of the British Poets*, Philadelphia: 1819–23, I, ix.

173   "girl of bad character": Leonard W. Labaree et al., eds., *The Autobiography of Benjamin Franklin*, Yale U.P.: 1964, p. 33.

174   "Clarke": *The Riches of Chaucer*, London: 1835.

174   "Horne": *The Poems of Geoffrey Chaucer Modernized*, London: 1841.

174   "Bronson": *English Poems*, U. Chicago Press: 1908.

174   "Snyder": *A Book of English Literature*, N.Y.: 1926.

175   "Noyes": *The Golden Book of Catholic Poetry*, Phila.: 1946.

175   "Massinger": William Harness, ed., *The Plays of Philip Massinger adapted for Family Reading*, N.Y.: 1831.

179   "with forged names": Fields and Whipple, *op. cit.*, Boston: 1878, p. vii.

182   "Breach between us": Labaree, *op. cit.*, pp. 98–99.

182   "other circumstances": *The Autobiography of Benjamin Franklin*, Boston: Houghton Mifflin, 1902, p. 61.

182 "another matter": *ibid.*, N.Y.: Maynard, Merrill ("English Classic Series"), 1892, p. 49.

183 "Browne printed *eris*": *op. cit.*, Johns Hopkins Press: 1896, p. 126.

184 "out the line went": Neilson, *op. cit.*, p. 50.

CHAPTER VIII

185 "Prose and other": Matthew Prior, *Poems on Several Occasions*, London: 1718, p. [xxiii].

185 "I shall betake myself": J. De Lancey Ferguson, ed., *The Letters of Robert Burns*, Oxford U.P.: 1931, I, 378.

185 "It may be urged": William C. Macready, ed., *Poetical Works of Alexander Pope*, London: 1849, p. ii.

186 "blurred and blotted volume": *Quarterly Review*, 1834, p. 426.

186 "expurgated edition of Wordsworth": Kathleen Tillotson, *English Novels of the Eighteen Forties*, Oxford U.P.: 1956, p. 57.

186 "first major review": *Blackwood's*, Aug. 1819, pp. 512, 514.

186 "the most sensitive mind": Whitwell Elwin, ed., *Selections from the Writings of Lord Byron*, London: 1854, p. iii.

189 "doubt his eyes": R. H. Horne, ed., *The Poems of Geoffrey Chaucer Modernized*, London: 1841, p. viii.

189 "example of native genius": William Lipscomb, ed., *The Canterbury Tales of Chaucer; completed in a modern version*, Oxford: 1795, I, viii.

190 "quaint medieval jokes": see the preface to Southey's *Specimens of the Later English Poets*, London: 1807, I, xvii, and also his headnote to Aphra Behn in the same work.

191 "like a thunder-clap": John W. Warter, ed., *Selections from the Letters of Robert Southey*, London: 1856, IV, 213.

193 "stop our tales here": F. J. Harvey Darton, ed., *Tales of the Canterbury Pilgrims*, London: 1904, pp. 55–56.

194 "two in bawdy Italian": See Alec Craig, *Suppressed Books*, Cleveland: 1963, p. 199.

195 "He slipped his hand": Robert M. Lumiansky, trans., *The Canterbury Tales*, N.Y.: Wash. Sq. Press, 1960, p. 62. Lumiansky's translation was first published in 1948.

195 "amply explained in footnotes": James Paterson, ed., *The Life and Works of William Dunbar*, Edinburgh: 1860, p. vii.

197 "one or two of inferior worth": Charles Eliot Norton, ed., *The Love Poems of John Donne*, Boston: 1905, p. v. The edition was limited to 535 copies.

198 "view to education": *Selections from the Poetry of Dryden*, ed. "C.B.," London: 1852, preface.

199 "to the fame of the author": [Samuel W. Singer, ed.], *Hesperides*, Boston: 1856, p. 14. Singer is quoting Lord Dundrennon, who made the same defense for the unexpurgated edition of 1823.

200 "poisonous roots": W. Carew Hazlitt, ed., *Hesperides*, London: 1869, I, preface.

200 "lapsed into the indecorous": F. T. Palgrave, ed., *A Selection from the Lyrical Poems of Robert Herrick*, London: 1877, p. x.

201 "Herrick's tongue": Alice Meynell, ed., *Poems by Robert Herrick*, London: 1905, preface.

202 "a good deal that is licentious": Edward Everett Hale, Jr., ed., *Selections from Robert Herrick*, Boston: 1895, p. lxix.

203 "an admiring peer": Thomas Wentworth, 3rd Earl of Strafford. See Austin Dobson, ed., *Selected Poems of Matthew Prior*, London: 1889, p. lxi.

203 "unpretentious verse": *Edinburgh Review*, Oct. 1874, p. 190.

204 "earnest and tender": *Contemporary Review*, July 1872, p. 244.

204 "or dangerous to principles": W. L. Bowes, *op. cit.*, I, vi–vii.

205 "that it is a genuine production": A. Dyce, ed., *Poetical Works of Alexander Pope*, London: 1831–35, I, c.

205 "told a friend": Lord Bolingbroke. He reported Pope's concern for chaste ears in a letter to Swift, June 27, 1734. See the Twickenham Edition of Pope, ed. John Butt, VI, xxv.

205 "in Edinburgh in 1859": published by Gall & Inglis.

209 "low, tame, and loathesome ribaldry": J. G. Lockhart, *Life of Robert Burns*, Liverpool: 1914, II, 245–46.

209 "the old Scottish muse": *ibid.*, II, 37.

209 "into a 1792 Burns letter": See G. Legman, *The Merry Muses of Caledonia*, New Hyde Park, N.Y.: 1965, p. xxxi.

211 "unique and precious collection": Henley and Henderson, *The Poetry of Robert Burns*, London: 1896, IV, 296.

212 "under their own names": James Barke and Sydney Goodsir Smith, eds., *The Merry Muses of Caledonia*, Edinburgh: 1959.

212 "by Emerson": See Gay Wilson Allen, *The Solitary Singer*, N.Y.: 1955, pp. 237–38.

212 "largest poetic work of our period": Harold L. Blodgett, *Walt Whitman in England*, Cornell U.P.: 1934, p. 22.

213 "Bowdlerian honours": W. M. Rossetti, ed., *Poems by Walt Whitman*, London: 1868, p. 16.

213 "*parts* of poems": *ibid.*, p. 18.

214 "final, logical position": Blodgett, *op. cit.*, p. 29.

215 "an English young bride": Edward C. McAleer, ed., *Dearest Isa*, U. Texas Press: 1951, p. 106.

216 "was a *twat*": Edward Bulwer Lytton, *The Coming Race*,

London: Routledge, n.d. (Knebworth Edition), p. 120.

216 "the Aryan or Indo-Germanic": *ibid.*, p. 86.

217 "hinted at in reviews": *e.g., The Germ,* Jan. 1850.

CHAPTER IX

218 "I shall read Sterne's": Edward C. Mack and W. H. G. Armytage, *Thomas Hughes,* London: 1952, p. 46. First eight words supplied conjecturally by me.

218 "Mrs. Clemens received": Henry Nash Smith and William M. Gibson, eds., *Mark Twain-Howells Letters,* Harvard U.P.: 1960, I, 74.

219 "even to the word 'nasty' ": Edward C. Mack and W. H. G. Armytage, *Thomas Hughes,* London: 1952, p. 95.

220 "eternal anguish": William S. Ament, "Bowdler and the Whale," *American Literature,* March 1932, pp. 39–46.

220 "in a sweat": Arthur L. Scott, "The Century Magazine Edits *Huckleberry Finn,* 1884–1885," *American Literature,* Nov. 1955, p. 358.

220 "faint to hear of his breeches": p. 500.

220 "sent a telegram to Yeats": David H. Greene and Edward M. Stephens, *J. M. Synge,* N.Y.: 1959, p. 238.

220 "that ends in 'ift' ": *ibid.,* p. 247.

221 "frequently lost passages": Expurgated versions of *Religio Medici* include the Greenhill editions of 1881, 1885, 1889, 1892, 1898, 1901, 1904, etc., and the Everyman edition of 1909.

221 "Charles Lamb's letters": Percy Fitzgerald (1875) and W. Carew Hazlitt (1886) preceded Canon Ainger. See Henry Harper, ed., *The Letters of Charles Lamb, in which many mutilated words and passages have been restored to their original form,* Boston: privately printed, 1905.

221 "about the weather": R. W. Chapman discusses the cut (rather confusingly) in his edition of Jane Austen, and again in his bibliography of her (Oxford U.P., 1953, p. 1).

222 "violation of a virgin": Samuel Richardson, *Clarissa,* ed. E. S. Dallas, London: 1868, I, xxvii.

224 "a few supreme things": Jonathan Swift, *Gulliver's Travels,* N.Y.: Harper's, 1913, p. xvi.

224 "illegitimate of the mercenary": Leigh Hunt, ed., *The Dramatic Works of Wycherley, Congreve, Vanbrugh, and Farquhar,* London: 1840, p. xii.

229 "Irish Academy in 1862": John F. Waller, ed., *Gulliver's Travels,* London: Cassell, [1862].

229 "Stowe": Harriet Beecher Stowe, ed., *A Library of Famous*

Fiction, Embracing the Nine Standard Masterpieces of Imaginative Literature, N.Y.: 1873, introduction.

229 "an American critic": *Nation*, June 22, 1893, p. 457.

231 "not to decipher quite everything": "The Smith transcription was given to Magdalene by the Braybrookes in the 1890's; [it was not] complete on the erotic and scatological passages anyway." Letter from William Matthews, co-editor of the new Pepys, 2 Feb. 1968.

231 "Scott wrote": *Quarterly Review*, March 1826, pp. 287, 288.

232 "licentious days to which they relate": quoted from Braybrooke's 1848 preface in the *Edinburgh Review*, Oct. 1849, p. 292.

232–3 "*Edinburgh* complained": *ibid.*, p. 291.

233 "said *Blackwood's*": Oct., 1849, p. 501.

233 "omission of but a few passages": quoted from Bright's preface, *Edinburgh Review*, July 1880, p. 114.

233 "read it for the first time": *ibid.*

233 "cannot possibly be printed": Henry B. Wheatley, ed., *The Diary of Samuel Pepys*, Boston: [1893], p. vi.

235 "Globe Pepys": G. Gregory Smith, ed., *The Diary of Samuel Pepys*, 6th printing, London: 1925, p. v.

235 "he told his readers": Morshead, *op. cit.*, N.Y.: 1926, p. xvi.

236 "unprintable forty years ago": *TLS*, August 11, 1932, p. 569.

236 "Francis Turner . . . announced": *TLS*, August 18, 1932, p. 581; November 17, 1932, p. 859.

238 "the whole unexpurgated Pepys": W. H. Lewis, ed., *Letters of C. S. Lewis*, N.Y.: 1966, p. 294.

241 "racy paragraphs": *e.g.*, the one beginning "I cannot say but I had some reflections," which appears on p. 157 of the 1927 Knopf edition, and which should be on p. 140 of Saintsbury.

241 "line of dots": Saintsbury, p. 182 (and see p. 197).

241 "abide": *ibid.*, p. 149.

242 "genius conducted by art": *ibid.*, p. 135.

242 "conditioned the selection": *ibid.*, p. xvi.

CHAPTER X

244 "In 1911": Thurman Arnold, *Fair Fights and Foul*, N.Y.: 1965, p. 176.

244 "FUCK COMMUNISM": *The Atlantic Monthly*, March, 1968, p. 96.

244 "Quiller-Couch": *Studies in Literature, Second Series*, N.Y.: 1922, p. 283.

244 "Mencken": *Prejudices, Fourth Series*, N.Y.: 1924, p. 284.

246 "man may read": Frederick Wedmore in the *Academy*, Dec. 15, 1894, p. 504.

247 "Ernest Baker said": *The Novels of Mrs. Aphra Behn,* London: 1905, p. vii.

247 "*Athenaeum* answered": 1905, p. 263.

247 "*Saturday Review*": 1872, p. 109.

247 "*Athenaeum* did pick up": 1872, p. 302.

248 "very unjust to him": *ibid.,* 1905, p. 866.

248 "terrible excresences": C. B. Wheeler, ed., *The English Humourists of the Eighteenth Century,* Oxford U.P.: 1913, p. xvii.

249 "tainted": Summers is quoting Julia Kavanaugh's *English Women of Letters,* 1863, in his *The Works of Aphra Behn,* London: 1915, I, xxix.

249 "recoil should come": *ibid.,* I, lx.

249 "comparable desacralization": Douglas Bush, "Memoirs of a Virtuous Family," *Life and Letters,* Feb. 1929, pp. 114–21.

249 "most important of all": Richard Whiteing, "Bowdler Bowdlerized," *English Review,* August 1916, p. 110.

254 "expunged every adventure": quoted in Lewis M. Knapp, *Tobias Smollett,* Princeton U.P.: 1949, p. 211.

254 "current general edition": ed. James C. Clifford, Oxford U.P.: 1964. This is the dominant edition in America as well as England—the only one available here in paper, etc.

254 "connubial bliss she": Randall Stewart, ed., *The English Notebooks by Nathaniel Hawthorne,* N.Y.: 1941, p. 353.

255 "all eleven bowdlerize": Lynch and Evans, *op. cit.,* p. 103.

256 "Secretary wrote": in a letter to me, March 11, 1966.

256 "Oxford official": in a letter to me, May 10, 1966.

257 "first major review": *Times Literary Supplement,* Feb. 8, 1968, p. 129.

257 "Börje Knös": Letter from Mme. Kazantzakis to Prof. Peter Bien of Dartmouth, Feb. 8, 1969.

257 "Swinburne's": Cyril Pearl, *The Girl with the Swansdown Seat,* Indianapolis: 1955, p. 15.

258 "war is over": *The Enormous Room,* N.Y.: 1922, p. 219.

258 "*querre est fini*": *ibid.,* New York: Modern Library, [1934, 1949, etc.] p. 271.

258 "other current edition": N.Y.: Liveright, n.d. (copyright renewed, 1950).

258 "manifest from the sequel": Robert & Samuel Wilberforce, *The Life of William Wilberforce,* London: 1838, I, 67.

259 "sagacious reader": Henry Nash Smith and W. M. Gibson, eds., *Mark Twain-Howells Letters,* Cambridge, Mass.: 1960, I, 52.

259 "dash-*dashed*": *The Atlantic Monthly,* Jan. 1875, p. 73.

259 "my palm over the side": *ibid.,* May 1946, p. 50.

260 "gutter profanity": *ibid.,* Aug. 1946, p. 30.

260 "Oh, Philip": *ibid.,* Nov. 1957, p. 67.

260 "fucking course": *ibid.,* Aug. 1965, p. 95.

260　"to *** upon": *op. cit.*, June 11, 1967, p. 12.
261　"random issue": Dec. 29, 1968.
262　"expurgated new-style": Lynch and Evans, pp. 55–56.

CHAPTER XI

264　"When Thomas Bowdler": *Times* of London, February 15, 1988, p. 13.
264　"Redneck": C. Vann Woodward, *New York Times Book Review*, February 5, 1989, p. 7.
265　"Fucking long life": *The New Yorker*, August 15, 1988, p. 62.
265　"a commentator": Nancy Vasilakis, "Young Adult Books: An Eighties Perspective," *Horn Book*, Nov.-Dec., 1985, p. 768.
266　"Dorothy Weatherby": Lee Burress, *Battle of the Books: Literary Censorship in the Public Schools, 1950–85*, Scarecrow Press, 1989, pp. 93–94.
266　"320 lines": J. Kenneth Bradford, "To Be or Not to Be": Issues on Changes in Literature Anthologies, *English Journal*, Oct., 1986, p. 54.
267　"genuinely surprised": *ibid.*
267　"McGraw-Hill": *ibid.*, p. 55.
268　"girl loses": *New York Times*, July 8, 1983, p. C-17.
268　"Mr. Bonham said": *ibid.*
269　"Ballantine Books published": George Guffey, "*Fahrenheit 451* and the 'Cubby-Hole' Editors of Ballatine Books," in G.E. Slusser et al., *Coordinates*, Illinois University Press, 1983, p. 101.
270　"adult version vanished": ibid., p. 103. All other details of the story are from this same source.
270　"formal investigation": Gayle Keresey, "School Book Club Expurgation Practices," *Top of the News*, Winter, 1984, p. 131.
271　"sent a letter": ibid., p. 135.
271　"ceased to expurgate": direct information from Greg Holsch, editor of Scholastic's Teen Age Book Club, August 6, 1989.
272　"book club edition": This term also appears on the copyright page of Troll Book Clubs school editions. But it's there only "for inventory purposes," and does not indicate expurgation, says the president of Troll. (Letter to me, August 24, 1989.)
272　"Egypt": *New York Times*, May 20, 1985, p. A-6.

273   "stage expurgations": For example, the *Merchant* directed by Jonathan Miller in 1970, starring Lord Olivier.

273   "Thirteen hundred books": Deidre Johnson, *Stratemeyer Pseudonyms and Series Books*, Greenwood Press, 1982, p. xiii.

273   "personally wrote": ibid., p. 97, p. 170.

274   "no smooching": Carol Billman, *The Secret of the Stratemeyer Syndicate*, Ungar, 1986, p. 26.

277   "great operas": Album notes to *Porgy and Bess*, Columbia Records, August, 1951.

277   "seemed proper": ibid.

278   "young Patrick": *Walden*, Modern Library, 1937, p. 39.

278   "Emerson": *English Traits*, London, 1902, p. 165.

278   "Mark Twain": *Roughing It*, Penguin, 1988, p. 343.

282   "Walpole": In his introduction to *The Story of Doctor Dolittle*, Lippincott, n.d. (10th impression on), p. xii.

283   "*Trip to Coontown*": Frederick W. Bond, *The Negro and the Drama*, McGrath Pub. Co., 1940, p. 47.

283   "said coldly": quoted by Selma Lanes, "Doctor Doolittle, Innocent Again," *New York Times*, August 28, 1988, Sec. 7, p. 20.

285   "*Times* of London": February 15, 1988, pp. 1, 13.

285   "*New York Times*": Lanes, op. cit.

285   "*New Yorker*": December 12, 1988, p. 156.

286   "famous English schoolbook": Robert Trendel, "The Expurgation of Antislavery Materials by American Presses," *Journal of Negro History*, 1973, p. 285.

286   "farce and a lie": ibid., p. 277.

286   "voted to stop": ibid., p. 281.

287   "birthday cake": Bradford, op. cit., p. 54.

287   "five dictionaries: Burress, op. cit., p. 123.

287   "Tennessee": ibid., p. 92.

APPENDIX

292   "skill or labour can purify it" *The Christian Observer*, 1808, p. 390.

292   "£3,345 on paper": see Marjorie Plant, *The English Book Trade*, London: 1939, p. 339.

INDEX

Index

Index

Index

Index

Noel Perrin

NOEL PERRIN, teacher, writer, and farmer (in that order) is a professor of Environmental Studies at Dartmouth College. He and his wife, the novelist Anne Lindbergh, live partly on his farm in Thetford, Vermont, and partly on hers in Barnet. His articles and reviews have appeared in *Country Journal, Vermont Life, The New Yorker, New England Monthly*, and many other publications. His books include *Giving Up the Gun: Japan's Reversion to the Sword, 1543-1879*; *Dr. Bowdler's Legacy: A History of Expurgated Books*; and *First, Second, Third, and Last Person(s) Rural*, all published by Godine.